THE AMERICAN FAMILY

Previous Publications

What Trouble I Have Seen: A History of Violence against Wives

Beaten Down: A History of Interpersonal Violence in the West

Oregon's Promise: An Interpretive History

Through the Eyes of a Child: The First 120 Years of the Boys and Girls Aid Society of Oregon

Environmentalism

The American Family

From Obligation to Freedom

David Peterson del Mar

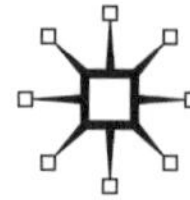

THE AMERICAN FAMILY

First published in 2011 by
PALGRAVE MACMILLAN®
in the United States—a division of St. Martin's Press LLC,
175 Fifth Avenue, New York, NY 10010.

Where this book is distributed in the UK, Europe and the rest of the world, this is by Palgrave Macmillan, a division of Macmillan Publishers Limited, registered in England, company number 785998, of Houndmills, Basingstoke, Hampshire RG21 6XS.

Palgrave Macmillan is the global academic imprint of the above companies and has companies and representatives throughout the world.

Palgrave® and Macmillan® are registered trademarks in the United States, the United Kingdom, Europe and other countries.

ISBN: 978–0–230–33745–9 (paperback)
ISBN: 978–0–230–33744–2 (hardcover)

Library of Congress Cataloging-in-Publication Data

Peterson del Mar, David, 1957–
The American family : from obligation to freedom / David Peterson del Mar.
p. cm.
ISBN 978–0–230–33744–2 (hardback)
1. Families—United States—History. 2. Families—United States. I. Title.

HQ535.P48 2011
306.850973—dc23 2011026994

A catalogue record of the book is available from the British Library.

Design by Newgen Imaging Systems (P) Ltd., Chennai, India.

First edition: November 2011

10 9 8 7 6 5 4 3 2 1

Printed in the United States of America.

For Wendy

Contents

Acknowledgments

This book is the child of my engagement with two dissimilar communities: countless scholars whose work I have read and profited from for more than thirty years (many of whom are identified in this book's Notes and Additional Reading); countless family members and friends who have shown me kindnesses, large and small, for more than fifty years, from my birth family to the families of SK BRANN.

I am particularly indebted to Wendy and Peter del Mar. Peter is my delightful, grounded son, who tolerates my shortcomings with good grace and humor. Wendy, my life partner and best friend, has taught me most of what I know about family. She also, along with Jeffrey Ostler, improved the manuscript in more direct ways. Its many imperfections notwithstanding, this book is for her.

Introduction

This book began nearly thirty years ago, when I made the mistake of asking Professor Robert Wiebe of Northwestern University what I thought was a simple question. I had just visited the Mormon Tabernacle in Salt Lake City during a long bus ride to Chicago, and the museum's sanitized dioramas and fantastical accounts of the past had left me befuddled and indignant. What better way to burnish my thin intellectual credentials than to invite my new teachers to confirm what, to me, was the only point about Mormons worth making, namely, that they were a pack of idiots?

But Mr. Wiebe was not in the business of telling people what they expected to hear. His rejoinder went something like this: "Mormonism is one of modernity's few refuges from hyper-individualism." In other words, the Church of Latter Day Saints was countercultural.

I had always assumed the reverse. Mormons conjured up images of Donnie and Marie Osmond: wholesome and boring—like my parents, only better looking. My counterculture belonged to people like Ozzy Osbourne of Black Sabbath or Cheech and Chong, guys who said and did outrageous things. But here was this slightly built, intensely brilliant man suggesting that drug overdoses and four-letter words were passé.

A few years later, another epiphany arrived as I labored to construct what Micki McGee would later term a "belabored self."[1] I had dropped out of graduate school, divorced, moved to Alaska, worked in a daycare, and now worked for a small historical society while trying to figure out—sometimes on an hourly basis—what to be when I grew up. Becoming a foster parent seemed like a good idea. I enjoyed children, and providing a home for a vulnerable orphan would establish beyond doubt my bonafides as a sensitive and heroic guy. A few months later, the local child-welfare agency became desperate enough to entrust me with a child who did not seem too damaged.

That appraisal was wrong. Lonnie (not his real name) had suffered acute sexual and physical abuse, and as his rage and pain erupted, I found myself completely out of my depth. I came to find out I was not especially patient, or understanding, or empathetic. I was not able to be the sort of parent that Lonnie deserved even after I had learned what he had gone through. Most days were anything but sublime and were just about putting one foot in front of the other, if not dodging or surviving crises.

Yet from these frustrations and humiliations grew a sense of clarity and peace. He was a sweet, vulnerable boy whom I could not help but cherish even when I wanted to wring his neck. There was a great comfort in knowing that I really had no choice but to be his dad for as long as he needed me to be his dad. His frantic needs put my own in perspective—or shouted them down. The restlessness that had dominated my life ebbed away. Our stubborn devotion to each other taught me something very new and precious about what I was—and was not—capable of. Years later, I was not surprised when a mental-health therapist told me that most of her clients became more depressed as they shed social commitments in their search for an ideal self.

These personal insights have been accompanied by academic ones. I started my first book, a history of violence against wives, in an activist state of mind. I had volunteered in the battered-women's movement, and I was going to serve that cause by establishing that there was a long tradition of wife beating. But while doing the research for *What Trouble I Have Seen: A History of Violence against Wives*, I was confronted with the discomfiting fact that my subject had a complicated history. Male violence and other forms of abuse were not static or stable facts of life; they were conditioned by dynamic social and cultural contexts. I was particularly surprised to find that husbands' violence tended to become less common and extreme as the nineteenth century progressed, a characteristic that historians of homicide had already linked to a spreading ethos of self-restraint. People's capacity for self-control receded in the twentieth century, coming apart in the same solvent of self-actualization that had done so much to shape my own problematic search for happiness.

Yet the title of this book did not occur to me until I was well into the project. I had always focused on gender inequality as the organizing principle of my courses on the history of the family. But it was difficult to ignore the fact that most of my historical subjects—wives and children, as well as husbands—would have found that emphasis nonsensical. The fixation with individual choice that suffused my life was a relatively recent development even in the Western world. People across the globe had, until recently, assumed that people existed not to fulfill some sort of personal destiny but rather to care for one another, to meet intensive and extensive social obligations. "Traditional societies," observes Louis Dumont, "have basically a collective view of man" and "know nothing, . . . of the individual."[2] A consuming search for self-fulfillment became common only over the past century, and largely in the Western world. People from other places and times have considered this obsession, if they happened to encounter it, bizarre and dangerous.

Social conservatism was deeply ingrained in North America, West Africa, and England in the fifteenth and sixteenth centuries, and it survived the voluntary and involuntary immigrations to the New World and the founding of diverse colonies. The eighteenth century brought economic maturity and cultural complexity without much disturbing the nature of familial relations, and the culture of obligation also survived the growing prosperity and industrial upheavals of the nineteenth century.

Not until the early and especially mid-twentieth century did freedom threaten obligation as the nation's most fundamental social organizing principle. Freedom owed its ascendancy to interlocking economic and cultural shifts—a massive transformation from an economy and culture centered on self-restrained production to one centered on self-actualized consumption. Modern prosperity has both freed us from relying on each other for survival and redefined the purpose of life.

The nine chapters detailing this transformation from obligation to freedom are generally chronological. There are two exceptions. Chapters 4 and 5 cover middle-class and more marginal or poorer families, respectively, during the nineteenth century, as their circumstances and cultures were so different from each other. Likewise, chapters 8 and 9 consider different aspects of the past half century. Chapter 8 treats the florescence of individualism that has washed over virtually all of us, and chapter 9 addresses how effective various countercultural groups have been in carving out alternatives to it.

The shift *From Obligation to Freedom* is worthy of close study for three reasons. First, this transformation goes a long way toward explaining a central and peculiar feature of modern Western life. Arrivals from more traditional societies are uniformly stunned by how lightly we take social commitments. Second, this embrace of freedom is not simply a matter of individual personality or choice, but is rooted in widely shared economic and cultural shifts. Individualism has become the oxygen that the great majority of Americans breathe. To move toward an ethos of obligation therefore requires swimming against deeply ingrained elements of modern life. Third, the shift from obligation to freedom is largely unacknowledged. Our immersion in a fast-paced world in which we are constantly urged to develop and indulge ourselves makes it difficult for us to fathom an alternative universe. Hence it required decades of historical research and reflection for me to arrive at the conclusion stated in this book's title, an observation that in retrospect seems self-evident. It is difficult for us to come to terms with the fact that the self, as we understand it, scarcely existed until recently, that such a deeply rooted part of our collective consciousness is a radical departure from how our ancestors across the globe understood the human condition and prospect.

Radical change is not necessarily bad. Consider the revolutions in health and comfort and human rights that have accompanied, and are in fact bound up with, our growing desire for freedom and individuality. Freedom's florescence has also multiplied the types of families that Americans have been able to create. It is neither possible nor desirable to reinstate "the good old days" of social solidarity that are rooted in social inequality. But neither should we ignore nor dismiss the social fragmentation and other cruelties that have been bequeathed by individualism's ascendance.

Family and freedom are as American as apple pie. Most of us would like to believe that both can be pursued absolutely and fully. History suggests otherwise. Family and freedom have always existed in a state of tension, and until recently the claims of the former usually trumped the possibilities of the latter. I cannot claim to have answered the question of what the proper mixture of obligation and freedom should be, and thoughtful people will disagree over whether or not sustainable families can survive, let alone flourish, in a society based largely on the individual pursuit of happiness. Certainly, an account of how these two great American ideals have interacted is a necessary beginning.

Chapter 1

Societies of Obligation

Historians trade in differences, and the differences between North America, West Africa, and Western Europe were indeed profound by the fifteenth century. Their residents ate, dressed, danced, and of course spoke differently from one another. They had recourse to different gods, used different sorts of tools, and organized their communities in varied ways. Western Europe, moreover, stood poised on the edge of a great transformation. Capitalism had begun to offer advantages that would bring demographic, technological, political, and military dominance across the globe.

Yet these three diverse sets of people shared a strong sense of social solidarity. Yes, they formed families in varying ways. Some allowed or encouraged polygyny, or multiple wives, for example, and some reckoned lineage through their fathers, whereas others reckoned it through their mothers. But all of them made a fundamental assumption that most of the readers of this sentence do not make: that social obligations, particularly obligations to people considered kin, were the bedrock of life. They accommodated varying degrees of personal ambition. But one's life was not one's own. People lived and sought meaning within an extensive web of relationships. This way of life prevailed among the merchants of Timbuktu, the nomads of the Great Plains, and the farmers of England.

* * *

Interdependence characterized life in North America from its inception. Most anthropologists believe that indigenous peoples arrived in what we know as the Americas between 12,000 and 30,000 years ago by walking across "Beringea," a land bridge then connecting North America with Siberia, as they followed wooly mammoths, mastodons, musk oxen, long-horned bison, and other massive mammals.

This journey required substantial interpersonal skills, not just physical fortitude. "As people dispersed into new territories and as relatives maintained contact with one another, the social networks that linked individual groups probably strengthened."[1] Humanoid brains evolved and improved in large part to communicate and cooperate in ever-more sophisticated ways—"to deal with social matters," as Michael Gazzaniga puts it.[2] These skills enabled parents to devote more time to nurturing infants and enabled groups that were adept at cooperation and communication to surpass those with less advanced social skills. "The selfish gene had given rise to," had been supplanted by, "a social brain and a different kind of social animal." Evolution is commonly understood as entailing the survival of the fittest, most ruthless individuals. But success was a collective achievement. Human beings have been shaped "by nature to function in a social setting."[3] This capacity for cooperation played a crucial role in the ability to create tools, clothing, language, reasoning, and other innovations that launched a new, much more powerful and adaptable mammal out of East Africa and across the globe, into the Americas.

The warming of North America prompted mobile bands to create more stable societies. Survival depended on learning the particular characteristics of a given area: which plants and animals were edible, or could be made edible; when and how they could be gathered, captured, hunted, preserved, and stored; the medicinal uses of plants; which streambeds or hillsides yielded flint, obsidian, or other sharp, durable stones that could be worked into tools. This knowledge became part of the socialization process for each generation, as groups became at home in their particular ecosystems and developed seasonal subsistence rounds.

Thousands of years later, some peoples in the Mississippi River Valley and pockets of the Southwest created more complex social structures and relations. About 3,000 years ago, peoples in the Southwest were planting maize (corn) in fields that had been cleared of other plants. They soon added squash, beans, and dozens of other, less important plants, along with pottery for the cooking and the storing of grains. The Hohokam people, in what is now southern Arizona, had irrigation canals up to thirty feet wide and ten miles long. Just a few acres of maize could provide the great majority of calories for a large family. Cahokia, located near what is now St. Louis, housed about 30,000 people at its peak, around 1200 A.D. Elaborate structures and ritual centers, some of which are still standing, appeared in the Southwest. Ceremonial life became more intricate as agriculture freed an expanding elite class from labor. Burials in highly agricultural societies were therefore diverse, with a few leaders interred in large mounds along with expensive luxury items. A heavy reliance on agriculture fostered a socioeconomic hierarchy while maintaining a strong sense of solidarity. Scholars posit that commoners tolerated inequality because they believed that priestly leaders had the ritual knowledge required to keep the world balanced, to sustain life.

Yet highly agricultural societies were brittle. A diet dominated by a few cultivated foods was not as healthy as one comprising diverse plants, animals, and insects that had been consumed by hunter-gatherers. In addition, climatic changes or other disasters could destroy crops—calamities that probably discredited leaders whose legitimacy had rested on their ability to coax sufficient rain from supernatural forces. Political fragmentation therefore followed crop failures. By 1200 A.D., three centuries before Columbus set sail, most of the largest cities in what would become the United States had been abandoned.

The agricultural societies of the Mississippi River Valley and the Southwest became fragmented. Survivors joined or reconstituted themselves as groups that were less reliant on agriculture and were less hierarchical. The disintegration of the most intensively agricultural societies at Cahokia and Snaketown probably helped to restore more egalitarian social relations, including the one between women and men. Indeed, horticultural societies (which practiced less intensive farming methods than agricultural societies and also hunted and gathered) tended to be matrifocal, with women controlling the production and distribution of most of the food and men leaving home to marry as their sisters stayed put.

The abandonment of agriculture for horticulture, hunting, and gathering expressed indigenous people's bias toward sustainability and continuity. Most groups had little interest in increasing their populations; more people invited famine. Some practiced geronticide and infanticide. Twins or babies deemed physically defective might be killed. Prolonged breast feeding and restrictions on intercourse served the same purpose. Rapid growth, like any abrupt change, could be dangerous.

This commitment to sustainable communities fostered a profound sense of interdependence. Individuals conceived of and located themselves in a web of relationships that literally defined them.

Relationships operated at several levels. Language and other elements of culture differentiated groups from one another, of course, but more particular identities shaped most interactions. Multigenerational house groups commonly worked together and formed the most basic economic component. One or more villages usually shared political decisions. Clans tended to be the most critical part of one's identity. Established by a common, often mythic, ancestor, clan membership could be inherited through one's mother (matrilineal), father (patrilineal), or through both. Outsiders who were not related by blood could be adopted into clans. Clans might be divided into two moieties or phratries. Moieties were ceremonial: people from one's opposite moiety presided at key rituals; to marry someone of the same moiety was to commit incest.

Groups organized kinship in diverse ways. Larger, more sedentary nations usually had more intricate and elaborate kinship structures and stressed vertical, cross-generational relationships. The Tlingit, who lived in what is now southeast Alaska, were relatively wealthy and numerous. They were organized into two moieties (exogamic, ritual halves), scores of villages (people who lived in the same place) and clans (the most basic social units and the repository of political authority, though members of clans could be distributed across the landscape), and many more lineages or house groups, that were subsets of clans that resided in a particular locale and shared economic production with one another. The result was an extensive and complex network of overlapping ritualistic, social, political, and economic relationships. Smaller nations, in which male peers continually worked together in hunting and war, emphasized horizontal kinship relations: brotherhood and sisterhood, very broadly defined. The highly mobile Chiricahua Apache, for example, had extended but relatively small matrilocal families that performed social, political, and ritual functions.

In all instances, kinship established an extensive set of reciprocal social relationships. Kinship was a verb, not a noun, a relentlessly inclusive action, not a static genealogy. Kinship "embraced all significant social interaction" among the Sioux.[4] The word "mother" or "father" might be used toward several people in the clan group, and "sister" or "brother" might refer to all of one's peers. Cherokee children had many "mothers," women who belonged to their clan. Native peoples of the Columbia Plateau had distinct terms for different types of nieces and nephews. People who shared no biological ties might also be kin. "Friends are like brothers," remarked a Kiowa-Apache man.[5]

To be without kin was to have no responsibility to, nor claim on, another, to have no basis for life. To be without kin was to be vulnerable. Such unfortunates among the Cherokee might "be killed almost at whim," notes Theda Purdue.[6]

Knowing the particulars of kinship was extremely important. A Cherokee could, as one observer put it, "tell you without hesitating what degree of relationship exists between himself and any other individual of the same clan you may see proper to point out."[7] These names, these relations, were at the foundation of each social interaction and were commonly included whenever one person addressed another. "One must obey kinship rules," explained Dakota Ella Deloria, "one must be a good relative."[8]

Kinship entailed a succession of gifts. Elders bequeathed care and specific skills to children, from how to acquire particular foods to how to propitiate particular spirits. Children reciprocated with respect and then, when able to, with food. Even the dead required gifts. Such generosity elicited the gift of status. Tangible service to the group through gathering, hunting, warfare, or the distribution of property brought recognition and leadership. Marriage, the gift of a wife or a husband, prompted elaborate exchanges between the two groups joined by the relationship. Kinship and mutuality were indivisible.

Kinship promoted harmony. To attack a kinsman was akin to committing fratricide; intragroup conflict was rare. "Adults who received insults without retaliating were given the highest praise," reported an ethnologist among the Skagit of Puget Sound.[9] Cherokee women cemented a peace treaty with the Seneca by choosing brothers and uncles from among them. Intermarriage and adoption transformed strangers—potential enemies—into allies.

Politics and kinship could not be separated. When the Cherokee made peace with the Delaware, the Delaware became their "grandfathers," because the latter were the dominant partners. By the same token, the Cherokee explained that the Chickasaws were their "youngest brothers and nephews" because "they are few in number" and had been driven from their former homeland by the Cherokee.[10] Warfare, or raiding, often involved both the killing and the adopting of captives to cover or avenge the death of kin. The Mohawk were at first ruthless toward the Algonquin captives they took in the mid-1600s, killing those who could not keep up with them, even severing the fingers of some survivors and torturing others to death. But those who were spared, often young women, were soon treated with great care and tenderness and became Mohawk. Some would eventually become Mohawk leaders. But even those who were killed were, in some sense, adopted. "The tortured body always belonged to an outsider in the process of being turned into an insider," explains Allan Greer, "an alien enemy who was ritually incorporated into an Iroquois lineage to replenish its spiritual strength before he or she was physically destroyed." Hence women and children commonly addressed the tortured as "uncle" or "sister" as they burned their living flesh.[11] On the Great Plains, also, raiding and warfare were bound up with kinship and adoption. The Hidatsa distributed captured children to households that had recently lost children, and captive women married Hidatsa men. To be sure, abducting one's enemies invited retaliation, not least because it created rents in the enemies' social fabric that had to be avenged or covered. But abduction also created new kin relations. Powhatan, the leader of the Chesapeake group whose name he bore, expanded his political power in the late sixteenth and early seventeenth centuries by marrying members of the royal families he conquered. The sons of such marriages remained—thanks to matrilineal descent—part of their mother's royal line, even if they went to live among, and became loyal to, the Powhatan. Marriage integrated newcomers into the Powhatan Confederacy.

Gender constituted a key divider within kin groups. As historian Mary Ryan neatly puts it, "Men and women developed their own separate scales of honor and reward."[12] In general, women focused on internal work, men on external. Women cared for the children; gathered, cultivated, and processed most of the food; and, in addition, did most of the work associated with the home. Men hunted, fished, warred, and conducted diplomacy. This division was particularly stark in matrilocal and matrilineal societies, for women owned homes in which men were perpetual visitors. Hence the Cherokee identified the moon as male since it "travels by night."[13]

Gender roles could blur. The most obvious examples were *berdaché* (two spirits)—men and, less commonly, women—who adopted the clothing and roles of the opposite gender. Women occasionally participated in warfare, and, more commonly, men cleared fields or built homes. California men dug holes for and cut timbers, as women gathered the lighter materials that would cover the structure.

In general, however, the line between male and female activities was thickly drawn. The Pueblo posited women as seed and corn (passive and generative) to men's rain and flint (active and germative). They held a gourd (from the earth) over a newborn girl's vagina and sprinkled water (from the sky) on a newborn boy's penis. Male and female constituted opposite and impermeable halves. The Oglala required even male and female siblings to avoid each other. Family members resided in separate sections of the tipi, and the men ate before the women did. Women were not to touch men's tools and, on the Columbia Plateau, men were to keep their distance from women's root ovens. The essences of the two sexes could easily disable each other. These two solitudes could, to be sure, mingle productively under certain conditions, just as rain could water seeds. Southwestern places bore names like "Clitoris Spring" and "Shove Penis."[14] Sex was pleasurable and, of course, productive; life depended on it. But sexual intercourse was hedged about with restrictions. Copulating at an inappropriate time, or with the wrong person, could throw the cosmic balance out of kilter and bring disaster to the entire group. Two spirits were so potent precisely because they constituted, in their very person, a harmony of opposites. Indeed, some of the most powerful Southwestern deities were bisexual.

Sex-role specialization served the larger group's needs. Indigenous peoples strongly associated women with fertility. They emphasized their capacity to give birth, of course, but women tended also to gather, process, and grow most of the food, particularly in horticultural societies. Hence the Cherokee spoke of how corn grew from ground soaked by the blood of Selu, the first woman. Pueblo women's provision of food and sex marked them as powerful life givers who nurtured and domesticated all manner of outsiders. Women sustained a group's life.

If women created life, men defended and took it. Warfare and hunting, much more so than the communal and feminine activities of gathering and horticulture, created opportunities for individual achievement. But status came with a price: the risking of one's life. Men were, after all, more expendable than women. Only women could reproduce, and, as a husband, one prominent man could meet the economic and sexual requirements of several wives.

This emphasis on manly courage was particularly strong on the Great Plains. Crow leaders each year selected young men deemed to be "Crazy-Dogs-Wishing-to-Die," warriors whose bravery won them great respect. Distinguished warriors received: a public accounting of their deeds; the right to wear special feathers; the right to marry; and the right to ride first with their wives in ceremonial processions. Assiniboine fathers advised their sons to "join at least one war party" before marrying, "so that you can tell of it whenever the occasion arises." Death in battle brought a sort of immortality. "Even though you may lie dead in the enemy country and make green grass, your name will always be mentioned when that part of the country is talked about." There were, of course, very practical reasons for encouraging and rewarding such bravery. As Jonathan Lear explains, the Crow fought "to prevent *utter devastation* at the hands of the Sioux," an eventuality in which "men, women, and children would be slaughtered—the tribe would be exterminated—with perhaps a few survivors taken into captivity as slaves. This was a very real possibility."[15] Convincing men to risk their lives for the group's benefit had obvious, utilitarian applications.

It is therefore largely beside the point to rank Indian societies on a sort of matriarchy-to-patriarchy scale that reflects modern, Western emphases on freedom and individualism. True, men usually filled positions of political leadership. But political position counted for little when people shared power so broadly. "It is no rare occurrence to see a woman step in during council and severely upbraid the chief," remarked a Jesuit priest on the Columbia Plateau.[16] Iroquois women nominated and deposed male leaders. They also used their control over food distribution and the covering or the avenging of deaths to both preclude and demand warfare.

The welfare of the group shaped sexual practices. Most societies expressed little concern over premarital intercourse (as long as it occurred outside one's lineage) or divorce. Serial monogamy tended to be the norm in matrilocal societies, with women and men being allowed to leave unsatisfactory marriages, particularly before children appeared. Cherokee women were especially independent; even their adulteries generally went unpunished. In most parts of what would become the United States, however, wives' infidelities were taken very seriously. Wives who were suspected of adultery were commonly beaten or tortured to extract confessions and were occasionally killed. By the time of contact, at least, women on the Great Plains who were accused of having sex with men other than their husbands might be disfigured by having their noses cut off. But women's infidelity provoked such intense punishment not so much out of male jealousy as out of concern over descent, the very glue that bound people together. "Unlike the 'privatized West,'" observes anthropologist Rebecca Morley, "wife beating in traditional societies may be inextricably linked to the political context of kinship."[17] Being able to trace the ancestry of each person was critical to the well-being of everyone: the dead, the living, and the unborn.

This is not to say that women's status never varied. Societies that depended heavily on men's activities, such as the buffalo hunters of the Great Plains, tended to elevate men's roles. Women's control over food was much more pronounced in the horticultural Southeast and Southwest. These peoples were matrilineal and matrilocal, meaning that descent was reckoned through one's mother, and that men lived with their brides upon marriage. In much of the Great Lakes and California, by way of contrast, children inherited privileges through their fathers, and women lived with their grooms' kin. Patterns of descent and residence could vary within regions, and descent could be reckoned bilaterally, through both parents. These variations had significant ramifications for how much influence males and females wielded. But women in all groups enjoyed at least a modicum of power and status despite, or because of, their distinct sex roles, and women and men alike shared a collectivist mentality.

Girls and boys prepared for complementary roles in childhood. The Pueblo buried the umbilical cords of girls within the house, beneath a grinding stone. Those of boys were buried outside. Four days after birth, girls received a perfect ear of corn, boys a flint arrow. The Seneca separated boys and girls at around age eight. Girls learned the work of their mothers, aunts, grandmothers, and other female kin, boys the work of their fathers, uncles, grandfathers, and other male kin. For girls, this meant mastering domestic skills and demonstrating the capacity for hard, sustained work. An Apache woman recalled adults making children swim in icy water and then making them run around to get warm. They ordered young girls to "Grind corn! Grind! Grind lots of corn and that will make you strong!"[18] Tolowa men in California examined the hands of prospective wives to see if they were sufficiently hardened by physical labor. Boys had less onerous workloads and learned the skills of hunting and then warfare, activities that required discipline and an indifference to discomfort and pain. Elderly men of the Coast Salish of Puget Sound ordered their young charges to squat in frigid water and to undertake solitary, five-day expeditions into the woods. Likewise, the Chiricahua Apache required boys in their mid-teens to arise before dawn, submerge themselves in cold water, and then run long distances over difficult terrain, while breathing only through their noses. The capacity of men to endure the privations of hunting, warring, and perhaps torture at the hands of enemies would bear and reflect on their people's character and well-being.

Rituals marked benchmarks in children's capacity to serve the group. Females' seclusion at the onset of menarche often entailed focusing on domestic skills. Researchers among the Halapai noted that the community expected such young women to "be busy all the time, rising early in the morning to bring wood and water, and cooking meals whether she previously knew how or not," skills that "would make her a diligent and good wife."[19] Ceremonies celebrated girls' first successes at gathering food and boys' first hunting kills. It is very significant that those honored by these ceremonies were not allowed to eat the long-anticipated fruits of their labors. The Sanpoil and Nespelem of the Columbia Plateau believed that a boy who ate of the first deer he had killed would never be able to kill another one. Gathering and hunting, like the rest of life, transpired within webs of obligation.

Childhood consisted of one lesson after another on the importance of always considering the group's welfare. Children could see that adults won status through serving their kin: women through working hard, men through giving away meat or risking their lives to defeat enemies. Story after story drove this point home. Wasco children, on the Columbia River, heard the story of "Little Raccoon and His Grandmother," in which a selfish young boy first refused his grandmother's food and then ate the prized acorns she had stored for the winter. Matters soon went from bad to worse, and little raccoon's selfishness caused the death of his grandmother and left him alone, for who would tolerate such a child? A Winnebago woman born in the 1870s recalled that as a child "I never received a cross word from anyone, but nevertheless my training was incessant," for her early memories were of being "lulled to sleep night after night by my father's or my grandparent's recital of laws and customs that had regulated the daily life of my grandsires for generations and generations, and in the morning I was awakened by the same counselling."[20]

Indigenous families taught children by example and admonition much more often than by violence. Peer pressure was, of course, a potent weapon in societies where anonymity was impossible. The Blackfeet talked up youthful missteps to such an extent that offenders commonly hid until they could accomplish a praiseworthy feat that would erase their shame. Particularly egregious acts, such as theft from kin or cowardice, might saddle one with a name that was carried to the grave, a constant reminder of the costs of betraying the group's trust. Adults invoked supernatural spirits, such as owls, to threaten recalcitrant children. The Chiricahua Apache chastened insubordinate children by enlisting the services of fierce-looking old men who stuffed offenders into a bag and sat on them while parents ignored their cries.

When elders employed violence, it was not necessarily punitive. Being ducked into frigid water or whipped was part of many toughening exercises. Some peoples on the Columbia Plateau featured a ritual in which children who maintained their poise when confronted by a whip-bearing elder escaped unscathed. Or a bold child might choose to absorb all the blows for the household, thus sparing the others. In either instance, violence, or the threat of violence, offered children the opportunity to prove themselves, to make choices that could bring credit to themselves and to their kin.

This whipping ritual neatly illustrates how indigenous peoples paired autonomy with interdependence. The children who were confronting the whip wielder were not compelled to react in a particular way. They could choose to cower, to accept the blows stoically, or to sing, dance, or speechify with sufficient aplomb to escape being hit. Caucasians who were captured and adopted by northeastern Native Americans commonly reported that children and adults enjoyed a great deal of freedom in how they chose to spend a given day. Modoc parents, according to anthropologist Verne Ray, respected their children's "individuality and prerogatives" by allowing them to eat whenever they pleased rather than requiring them to be present at mealtime.[21] But powerful social and cultural forces conspired to ensure that individual behavior served the group's welfare. Hence children who overcame their fear of being whipped were honored and feasted, as were youth who brought food to their elders and adults who served their kin.

Indigenous peoples thus linked personal freedom with a strong sense of interpersonal obligation and self-reliance with social responsibility. The Hopi, for example, made self-reliance one of their five principal virtues, but it was accompanied by four more social ideals: peacefulness; responsibility, cooperation, and humility.[22] Indigenous peoples enjoyed a great deal of autonomy but seldom chose to act in a way that would harm the group.

The Iroquois developed intricate mechanisms for allaying the psychological pressures that were generated by the group's daunting demands. They took dreams seriously and did their best to satisfy the desires expressed in them. They believed, as a French priest explained, that not all thoughts were rational or voluntary, "that our souls have other desires, which are, as it were, inborn and concealed" impulses that "come from the depths of the soul, not through any knowledge." These desires needed to be attended to.

In 1656, for example, an emaciated warrior who had been absent for a year reported that a powerful, supernatural figure had ordered that dogs, food, and valuable goods be sacrificed to him, the spirit, and that the warrior enjoy the sexual favors of two married women for five days. The community complied.[23]

But dreams describing aggression toward fellow community members were assuaged symbolically rather than literally. When someone dreamed that a particular young woman was adrift in a dangerous stream without a paddle, for example, the dream was propitiated by the presentation of a miniature canoe, not by putting the young woman in danger.[24] The bonds of kinship required that aggression be repressed or sublimated into nonviolent forms.

As for North America, it is difficult to generalize about West Africa, a region that was (and is) diverse in its physical and human geography. West Africa was roughly divided between the northern savanna, south of the Sahara Desert, and the southern forest, nearer the coast. The savanna, particularly along the Niger River Valley, had extensive agriculture that was aided by iron implements and therefore had a relatively dense population and a series of large, powerful states or kingdoms (Ghana, Mali, and Songhay). Southern polities tended to be much smaller, sometimes a single forest village. The balance of power and population shifted in the sixteenth century, as Songhay fragmented under pressure from Morocco, and some southern states, such as the Asante, grew more powerful and centralized from growing trade with the Europeans—as did the Kongo, on and near the central, southern African coast.

The tenuous nature of life in West Africa shaped its societies and cultures. Famines and epidemics struck down a third or more of a region's population every two or three generations. Infant mortality rates were high, and few lived more than half a century. Religion focused on the pragmatic: health and security—though Islam had made inroads among savanna leaders, especially. Control of labor counted for more than control of land; children were a form of wealth and security. West Africans celebrated women's fecundity and men's potency; childlessness was a calamity. "Without children you are naked," remarked the Yoruba.[25] Precarious health prompted West Africans to space births so as to encourage the survival both of infants and their mothers.

The labor-intensive nature of West Africa's economy meant that being a "big man," a powerful leader, depended on having many dependents: wives, children, and slaves. These people, and other kin, farmed, traded, or raided on the leader's behalf. An ethnologist who lived among the Gonja of Northern Ghana in the 1960s found that compound heads called upon subordinate men to clear farms and "that his fields are cleared first." Adults greeted this man in the early morning and in the evening "in the same way as his children."[26] Indeed, each day began and ended with children (of all ages) going to the doorways of their parent's and grandparent's rooms, where they crouched, greeted, and received instructions from their superiors. Wives did the same with their husbands and with close members of his family.

As in North America, kinship trumped marriage, for Western Africans "living and dead, had foremost obligations to the patrilineage. They literally received life and livelihood through its good offices..."[27] Historian James Sweet recounts the struggle of Manuel da Costa Perico of Angola to buy the freedom of a sister who had been enslaved for more than twenty years in Brazil during the mid-eighteenth century, an act that "rescued her from the oblivion of kinlessness."[28] Meyer Fortes, who lived among the Tallensi of the Ivory and Gold coasts in the first half of the twentieth century, described "kinship as the rock-bottom category of social relations." Told that some Europeans chose not to have children, "they were either sceptical or appalled."[29] (Childless Ghanaian women and men are still commonly suspected of trading their fertility for riches to the devil.[30]) Kinship, moreover, was construed and understood very broadly. In matrilineal societies, for example, a young man might owe as much or more respect to his maternal uncles as to his father.

West African society tended to be more hierarchical than in North America. The Dahomey, who lived along the coast, assigned different levels of status even to twins. Among the Gonja, "an older brother or sister may correct, chide, or even abuse a younger sibling of either sex and the latter ought to accept this in good grace."[31] "No two individuals ever occupied the same rank," notes historian Edna Bay.[32] West Africans expected children to respect their parents, particularly once the latter were dead. The eldest surviving sons and daughters of deceased Gonja carried small replicas of handcuffs, once used to control slaves, to symbolize their continued obedience to their parents. Indeed, not until everyone who had remembered a living person had died did that person truly die. For several generations, then, the deceased were members of the "living dead," spirits who remained interested in, and engaged with, their families.[33] These spirits advised and reproved their living family members and were deeply concerned that their descendants showed proper respect to their elders, dead and living. A Gonja man remarked: "You must give plenty of food to a sister living with you or else she will be talking [and the dead ancestors will hear her] and you will die."[34]

This respect for deceased ancestors reflected a reverence for elderly people in general. "A child does not look at an old man's face," remarked the Ewe of Ghana.[35] In the 1960s, Anlo Ewe sons were not permitted to call their fathers by name, to stand or sit in their presence (squatting was the proper attitude), or to begin eating before their fathers did. Elders expected the younger generation to render them material aid and comfort, along with obedience. Among the Mende of Sierra Leone, sons or nephews who left home to pursue their own interests without permission risked suffering this curse from their fathers: "(O God), you know this is my son; I begat him and trained him and laboured for him, and now that he should do some work for me he refuses. In anything he does now in the world may he not prosper until he comes back to me and begs pardon."[36] When the wayward son did return, he went first to his mother, then, with gifts of money and food, to his father. He knelt at his father's feet. He took his father's right foot in his right hand. He asked his father's forgiveness and hoped that he would withdraw the curse that had blighted his, the son's, prospects.

Men were much more apt to hold positions of formal authority and power than were women. G. K. Nakunya, a scholar who lived among the Anlo Ewe of Togo and Ghana in the 1960s, found: "A wife addresses her husband as *efo*, which means 'elder brother.' "[37] Men tended to be especially dominant in areas where Islam had displaced more traditional religions and in the Kongo of west-central Africa, where the elite adopted Christianity in the late sixteenth century. Islam and Christianity fostered movements from matrilineal to patrilineal kinship.

But women were important across West Africa. Powerful men gained wealth through the work of wives and the children birthed by those wives. Wives could be had by paying a bride price to her family or through capture. Indeed, West Africans considered women slaves to be much more valuable than male ones, as women could literally multiply a man's family. Mistreated wives could return to their families (if they were not slaves) and often owned their own property and businesses. As in other hierarchical relationships, furthermore, power brought responsibility. "If you marry a woman she must eat," sang Anlo Ewe women.[38] The practice of polygyny and the skewed sex ratios engendered by the trans-Atlantic slave trade fostered households that were matrifocal in their everyday functioning. Coniagui adults remained particularly close to their mothers, and sons and mothers were expected to look out for and care for each other. Women, moreover, had their own lines of organization and authority and enjoyed considerable autonomy from men in their economic, ritual, and social affairs. Husbands commonly commanded the deference of their wives, but they did not have the right to tell them how to go about their work. As among Native Americans, West African society tended to be sex segregated. Among the Asante and Fante of Ghana, for example, women commonly left their husbands' homes once they became pregnant. After several years, they returned, but their children remained at her parents' home, to be raised by her lineage. After menopause, these women returned home for good.

As with indigenous North Americans, to focus simply on the role of power and on the extent of autonomy would be to miss what made West African society tick. *Sundiata*, the epic oral account of the founding of the Mali Empire early in the thirteenth century, describes the attributes of the ideal ruler. Sundiata is great because he is strong and defends those who are not. His rule began with a military triumph but ushered in an era of prosperity and peace. "Under his sun the upright man was rewarded and the wicked one punished." The depravity of Sundiata's opposite number, the evil Soumaoro, manifested itself in social transgressions, such as the public floggings of old men and the forcible abductions of girls whom he refused to marry: "He had defiled every family . . . " The ideal kings "are feared because they have power, but they know how to use it and they are loved because they love justice."[39] Powerful men had heavy responsibilities. Poorer families commonly sent their children to serve and to be cared for by wealthier kin.

As Bay notes, "Dahomeans could look to their patrilineage for basic shelter, protection, and nurturance, along with access to land and training in artisan or other economic skills." In sum, one lived within a web of relationships that were both hierarchical and reciprocal.

Slavery is a particularly striking example of this unequal interdependence. West Africans might choose slavery as an alternative to being without kin. "In most African societies," explain Igor Kopytoff and Suzanne Miers, "'freedom' lay not in withdrawal into a meaningless and dangerous autonomy but in attachment to a kin group, to a patron, to power—an attachment that occurred within a well-defined hierarchical framework."[40] Among the Akan of West Africa, "the severance of lineage ties constituted an isolation that was tantamount to a death sentence."[41] As an Akan proverb put it, "Because the tortoise has no clan, he has already made his casket."[42] This is not to say that slavery did not matter, let alone that slaves were equal to their masters. If a free man "is ten, a slave is never more than nine," the Soninke liked to say, for "just as the fingers of the hand were created of unequal lengths, so people are of unequal value."[43] Mutual rights and obligations did not imply equality, and not all slaves were treated well. Slaves constituted about one-third of the population of the great interior states of Ghana and Mali, even more in Songhay. These powerful empires of the savanna and the states of the southern forests that grew with European contact often treated their slaves brutally, and recently acquired slaves had fewer rights than those who had lived with their owners for a long time. But slavery often entailed reciprocity. After all, a slave's master was obligated to care for the slave, even in old age, and a slave's children might be fully integrated into the community. "No one reveals the origins of another," was a maxim that the Asante made into a law in the eighteenth century.[44] Slaves among the Efik of the Bight of Biafra called their owners "father" and "mother."[45]

John Mbiti asserts that African social relationships must be understood in a religious context. Africans expect everyone to marry and to bear children, because marriage "forms the focal point where departed, present and coming members of society meet." Familial terms include everyone one knows; "a person has literally hundreds of 'fathers,' hundreds of 'mothers,' hundreds of 'uncles,' hundreds of 'wives,' and hundreds of 'sons and daughters.'" Each of these relationships entails—requires—the performance of specific duties. The family also extends vertically, across time. Hence the African emphasis on genealogy, a knowledge of ancestors that bequeaths a "sense of depth, historical belongingness, a feeling of deep rootedness and a sense of sacred obligation to extend the genealogical line." To not marry, to not have and bear and cherish children, is to commit an act of corporate suicide, to kill an immense lineage that stretches outward in the present and backward and forward in time. A less cosmic choice, such as stealing a villager's animal, also has severe consequences. In a community in which "everybody is related to everybody else," an act of theft is also an act of aggression against a family member, a violation that obligates the victim's parents, siblings, and cousins to involve themselves in the dispute. No misfortune, large or small, moreover, is accidental; each is the responsibility of someone. The family, very broadly understood, is "the centre of love and hatred, of friendship and enmity, of trust and suspicion, of joy and sorrow, of generous tenderness and bitter jealousies." In such a world, "a person cannot be individualistic, but only corporate," for "the human being is claimed as a communal subject."[46] Everyone is implicated in a web of reciprocal, often hierarchical relationships.

Philosopher Kwame Gyekye, drawing heavily on the proverbs of the powerful and expansionistic Akan, suggests that Africans were not simply communal. The Akan celebrated the accumulation of wealth. Individuals had to take care of themselves. "The lizard does not eat pepper for the frog to sweat." But individual initiative could only take one so far. A man "is not a palm-tree that he should be self-complete." "The individual cannot develop outside the community," summarizes Gyekye, "but the welfare of the community as a whole cannot dispense with the talents and initiative of its individual members."[47] The Akan integrated "individual desires and social ideals and demands."[48]

Western Europe in general, and England in particular, would seem to have very little in common with West Africa and North America at the dawn of the sixteenth century, as it entered a period of great population and economic growth. England's population doubled between the 1520s and 1680, when it stood at 5 million. A process often referred to as proto-industrialism fueled this expansion. Manufacturing, dominated by cloth, remained small-scale, but engaged more and more labor. Agriculture was still the most important segment of the economy. Farmers increased their yields through efficiency (using fertilizers more extensively, for example) and by bringing more and more land under intense cultivation.

Growth brought instability. The cost of food multiplied, as did the number of people who were landless, poor, and starving. But others, particularly farmers who managed to gain a foothold in the new economy, saw their standard of living soar. London and smaller cities and towns expanded dramatically, as rising farm rents and enclosure combined with the possibilities of manufacturing and other urban opportunities to pull and push many away from their homes—though many migrants were simply moving from farm to farm, as former renters became farm laborers. More than half of the residents of a community in Northamptonshire disappeared between 1618 and 1628, for example.[49]

This disruption affected families and communities a great deal. Kinship ties became less entrenched in everyday life, as individuals and nuclear families sought opportunities that took them away from grandparents, aunts and uncles, and cousins. Of the 122 householders living in an Essex village in 1671, less than one half were related to another householder.[50]

This economic and social dynamism, this emphasis on geographically mobile nuclear families, set England apart from North America and West Africa, as these three parts of the globe prepared to meet each other in what would become the United States.

But England's geographic mobility and the isolation from kin that it entailed still left people highly dependent on their neighbors. Farmers relied heavily on each other for agricultural and household labor. Villages—if not cities—afforded little privacy. Everyone knew everyone else, and those who failed to conform to village norms courted excommunication from the church and the community, perhaps even accusations of witchcraft. A good man or a good woman was a good neighbor who avoided gossip and slander and readily helped those in need.

England, like the rest of Europe, emphasized order. Sir John Fortescue, a fifteenth-century attorney, described a Great Chain of Being in which every object of creation occupied a precise niche: "In this order angel is set over angel, rank upon rank in the kingdom of heaven; man is set over man, beast over beast, bird over bird, and fish over fish, on the earth in the air and in the sea: so that there is no worm that crawls upon the ground, no bird that flies on high, no fish that swims in the depths, which the chain of this order does not bind in most harmonious concord."[51] Everyone, no matter how high or how low, had extensive social obligations. A wealthy merchant could wear clothes that a peasant could not. But he could not charge whatever price for bread that the market would bear; status brought obligation. "Mutuality, subordination, and public service constituted a kind of sacred trinity of all respectable societies," notes Stephen Foster.[52]

The economic dynamism of the Early Modern Period of course threatened the Great Chain of Being. A younger son, purportedly inferior to his older brothers, might utilize the era's unprecedented opportunities to outstrip them. For that matter, what if the ruler of England was a woman rather than a man?

The Great Chain of Being accommodated growing exceptions to its dictates even as it continued to provide a widely accepted template for ordering society. The English of the sixteenth and seventeenth centuries believed that the family was a miniature version of God's creation inasmuch as everyone occupied a precise place in a decidedly hierarchical system. Patriarchs headed families. One authority on family life defined a husband as "he that hath authority over the wife." Wives were "wholly to depend upon him, both in judgement and will."[53] Patriarchy was necessary, men asserted, to safeguard women from their weak natures. "Females are more wanton and petulant than males," remarked a writer in 1615, "because of the impotency of their minds…for the imaginations of lustful women are like the imaginations of brute beasts which have no repugnancy or contradiction of reason to restrain them."[54] This reflexive misogyny, this widespread belief that women were closer to nature and therefore inferior to men, was undercut by the acknowledgment that individual women could overcome these proclivities to achieve wisdom and restraint. But Englishmen expected husbands to rule wives.

They also expected parents to rule children. No one of this place and time, observes Anthony Fletcher, doubted "[t]he necessity of children obeying their parents." Obdurate children were abnormal. A daughter who would "not do anything that her parents bid her but at her own mind" was judged to be "apish, foolish, untoward."[55] The gentry required their children to stand before them bareheaded and to kneel to receive their blessing. Society tolerated, or even encouraged, at least moderate violence toward children and wives who were deemed rebellious.

Yet strong bonds of mutual obligation and love flowed between these family members. Clerics urged husbands to abjure violence and other forms of naked authoritarianism. A husband should instead view a wife as a "yokefellow and companion," even as he ruled her. A good husband exercised "justice, wisdom, and mildness."[56]

It is, of course, much easier to discern what the dispensers of marital advice said, rather than how they acted. But many couples claimed to have loved each other deeply. "Whatever was real happiness," said Lady Fanshawe of her deceased husband, "God gave it me in him."[57] Contrary to what historians of a generation ago commonly asserted, parents and children routinely expressed affection for one another. An English aristocrat, late in the seventeenth century, wrote his wife: "You cannot imagine how pleased I am with the children, for they . . . are so fond of me that when I am at home they will be always with me, kissing and hugging me."[58] Adult children visited their parents frequently, described them as loving, and grieved their deaths.

Husbands and parents clearly had authority over wives and children. But authority brought responsibility—a responsibility to cherish as well as to guide. The Great Chain of Being was a hierarchy, but a hierarchy that was characterized by relations of obligation that flowed downward as well as upward. Paternalism, observes Steven Ozment, required "a mutual willingness to make sacrifices for one other."[59] Nor did dominance preclude love.

* * *

Paul Riesman, an ethnologist who studied the Fulani of West Africa in the 1960s, was often exhausted by their intense social obligations. "The presence of people demanded of us a sort of state of constant alert," particularly as time passed, and the Fulani began to treat him and his wife as part of the community. Every person one met had to be greeted in a prescribed, often lengthy manner. Only prayer was an acceptable reason not to set aside whatever one was doing to exchange greetings to passersby. The Fulani loved to travel and to visit, so these stylized conversations filled a large portion of each day. The Fulani also expected one another to bear their many sorrows as their own and to demonstrate great sadness whenever misfortune struck. They counted on others to intervene when their anger or other emotions got the better of them, to stop them from acting rashly. Self-restraint, internalized in the West, was "maintained by the actual presence of others." In sum, "the personality is not entirely localized in the body and mind of a person, but . . . also includes the people with whom he has relations. Without the others, a man lacks a part of himself; this is not simply a poetic way of seeing things but an objective statement of fact." The individual, as understood by modern Westerners, did not exist. The expectation that Riesman would, for example, "stop everything and reply immediately" to a greeting constituted "a heavy obligation and an imposition on my freedom," specifically the freedom "of being left alone."[60]

The freedom to be "left alone" was hard to come by across the globe during the sixteenth and seventeenth centuries. The land that would eventually become the United States was populated by indigenous nations that defined one's very identify in the context of kinship. West African communities were more hierarchical, but extremely interdependent. England afforded a growing sliver of its population a chance at uninherited wealth, and broad portions of the populace enjoyed increased material comfort. But these developments transpired within a system of mutuality and obligation.

These three divergent societies would soon intermingle under very different circumstances in North America—and in ways that often stretched, or even transformed, their patterns of kinship and family.

Chapter 2

The Search for Order in North America

The restless ambition that drove a small minority of Western Europeans across the Atlantic Ocean profoundly affected millions of Native Americans and West Africans. Native American groups suffered widespread death, dependency, or even extinction from disease and, often, warfare. European demands for cheap labor in the Americas wrenched West Africans from their villages and left them with the work of creating new societies essentially from scratch. The great majority of European colonists went voluntarily to North America, but most of them at first came as individuals rather than in families and went to places where white women were few and death was common. In sum, European colonization of the Americas mingled and disrupted the lives of people from three continents.

Despite this geographic and ethnic diversity and all the variations of place, race, status, and circumstance, North Americans shared a common endeavor: restoring social equilibrium through the use of family, kin, and neighbors.

* * *

The arrival of Europeans in the Americas provoked the greatest demographic disaster in recorded history. The rate of population decline averaged about 90 percent per century. Many died well before they met European people. Smallpox swept down the Columbia River and northward through the Puget Sound in the 1780s, killing in a few years roughly one-third of the populace. Losses were heaviest among densely populated peoples, such as the Pueblo, and lighter on the Great Plains, where settlements were more dispersed. But no nation escaped death. Disease inflicted a horrible toll on societies where each individual was linked intimately to scores of others; depopulated clans lost their capacity to function. The proliferation of corpses and pockmarked faces also constituted a psychological and spiritual reproach. Calamity always happened for a reason; death and suffering on such an epic scale could only mean that the world was out of balance. Disease inflicted tremendous tangible and intangible costs upon Indians, including a much weakened capacity to resist Europeans.

Conquest brought still more death. Some Europeans wanted only to trade. But many wanted land, and they were willing to take it by force. Puritans killed the great majority of the Pequot in their 1637 war, through summary executions. Most of the surviving women and children were captured and enslaved, even if this meant separating mothers from their children, with many being shipped to the Caribbean. The dwindling remnant of New England Indians struggled to find a niche for themselves and their kin. The Wampanoag or Pokanoket at Martha's Vineyard succeeded for several generations at creating a reasonably stable and independent community in which residents blended Christianity with traditional kinship ties. But these communities fragmented in the eighteenth century. The indigenous people of Natick lost about one-third of their land in just twenty years. Dispossessed Indians wandered from place to place, selling crafts or their labor. One Hannah Cousett noted in the 1750s "that for 30 years past she has been [strolling] about from Town to Town geting her living where she could but never lived During that time the space of one year at any Town at any time."[1]

Less lethal forms of contact also harmed Native Americans. The Spanish completed a brutal conquest of the Pueblo in 1598 and then hoped to live off the labor of the latter while transforming their culture. Franciscan priests had no use for premarital sex, polygyny, nudity, or two spirits. They punished the Pueblo, who persisted in such practices, by putting them in stocks, by whipping them, or worse. They required men to give up hunting and warring and occupy themselves with tasks that had been women's work. The priests focused their religious instruction on the young and rewarded converts with livestock, seeds, and tools. The groups that were most receptive to their teachings became patrilineal or bilateral, rather than matrilineal and matrilocal.

Simply avoiding white newcomers was not a viable option. As in West Africa, trading with Europeans brought telling military advantages. The Nez Perce welcomed the exhausted members of the Lewis and Clark Expedition in 1805, in large part because they hoped that the newcomers could provide the guns or perhaps even the diplomacy to counter the growing power of the Blackfeet and the Shoshone, who already enjoyed access to firearms.

Europeans brought opportunities as well as calamities. Horses dispersed northward after the Pueblo Revolt of 1680 across the Great Plains and the Columbia Plateau. Horses propelled the Teton and Yankton westward, onto the Great Plains, in the 1700s. They had by then acquired firearms from French traders, and the opportunity to trap more beaver and acquire buffalo hides figured into their decision to wrest territory from the Omaha, Pawnee, Crow, and others. Leaders like Comcomly of the Chinooks used the fur trade to achieve unprecedented wealth and influence.

But for every group and person who profited from the arrival of horses and trade, others suffered. This was particularly true in the Southeast, where the Spanish, the French, the British, and then the Americans struggled to establish supremacy over indigenous nations and over one another. The contest between Europeans gave some, like the Choctaw, temporary leverage. But it also made them vulnerable to attack from indigenous nations that were allied with the Europeans. These conflicts prompted a much-expanded slave trade in which Indians captured and sold each other across the Southeast in the seventeenth and early eighteenth centuries. The Yamasee traded both indigenous and escaped African- American slaves to the English and Spanish, and they helped the English defeat the Tuscarora in 1713. They then began to suffer from slave raids themselves, revolted against the English, and were ruthlessly punished for it. Indians made up much of the plantation workforce in South Carolina and elsewhere, well into the eighteenth century. More indigenous slaves ended up in the Caribbean, where they had no chance of returning home. Disease, paired with the brutality of warfare and raiding, destroyed some nations altogether. Remnants joined stronger groups, such as the Cherokee, or coalesced to create new ones, such as the Catawba and Seminole. Indigenous peoples' capacity for creating new social and political relations proved to be essential to survival.

Contact encouraged hierarchy. Increased trade and warfare enhanced men's status and power. Southeastern women had controlled the extent of raiding by demanding captives to cover the deaths of kin and supplying—or denying—provisions. But the bloody wars of the seventeenth and eighteenth centuries were fought at the behest of Europeans who paid indigenous men for captives. The slave and deerskin trades tilted aboriginal economies in favor of male activities and brought European blankets, utensils, and other goods that were once fabricated by women. Men on the Great Plains were much more likely to own horses than women were, and their status increased at women's expense. Women spent more and more time at the tedious work of processing the thick hides procured and traded by men. This infusion of male wealth led to greater stratification. Polygyny grew, particularly when so many captives were young women. Status was increasingly measured not by service to the group, but by the accumulation of livestock and other forms of wealth.

Most Indian nations of the Southwest retained their political autonomy for centuries. This owed something to low numbers of Spanish and the military prowess of highly mobile nations such as the Apache and Comanche. But such groups also survived by incorporating the newcomers' weapons, animals, and people. Slave raiding and trading in the Southwest constituted what historian James Brooks in his aptly entitled *Captives & Cousins* calls a "pragmatic and often violent business of mingling families and producing hybrid cultures."[2] Slavery both destroyed and created kinship. As late as the mid-nineteenth century, starving Indians essentially pawned themselves into slavery to the Comanche for the food and other benefits of fictive kinship. Membership, even at the bottom rungs of Comanche society, brought a modicum of security, and their children might become important family members of the people who had enslaved their parents.

Natives tried to make Europeans kin. The Dutch reported in 1655 that the Mohawks could not understand why the Europeans "did not entertain them in such a manner as they entertained us when visiting their land," a slight that "was not altogether brotherly."[3] Indigenous peoples commonly chose prominent traders as both husbands and godparents. The Caddos—of what would become Texas—expected that intermarriage would be accompanied by a willingness to fight alongside them in their battles, and the Apache sought marriage with Spaniards in the mid-eighteenth century to secure peace with them. Groups such as the Apache, the Comanche, and the Navajo also took hundreds of Spanish and, later, American captives, whom they integrated into their villages.

But intermarriage often led to sociocultural fragmentation elsewhere. New England Indians worried that women's marriages to African Americans threatened the group's solidarity. Indeed, African American men chafed at indigenous communal traditions, particularly when their wife's death stripped them of the land on which they had worked so hard. It is difficult to discern the precise motives that prompted Pocahontas to marry John Rolfe in 1614 on the Chesapeake, but it certainly served to raise her status, even as it removed her from the Powhatan. Intermarriage remained common in the Southeast well into the nineteenth century, as women of powerful families attracted white traders as suitors. The children of such unions seldom joined white society and instead became liberal forces within indigenous communities. They were much more apt than their counterparts to read and write, to become Christians, to own livestock, to practice European forms of agriculture, and to establish trading posts. They also moved their societies closer to European cultural ideals—by switching to patrilineal forms of inheritance, for example. These innovations led to considerable hard feelings and, in the case of the Muskogee or Creek, to widespread violence when traditionalists attacked the mixed bloods.

English colonies largely succeeded in both changing and maintaining a thick line between themselves and Native Americans. Spanish colonists were more adaptable, their communities more diverse. Many Indian servants and slaves eventually became part of New Mexico's Spanish community. Some, to be sure, were transported south, to the heart of New Spain. But those who stayed might become a Spaniard's wife or otherwise gain their freedom and become Spanish-speaking members of the community. The children of women who married Spaniards became Spanish, as New Mexicans applied the appellations "Spaniard" and "white" more culturally than racially. A person of high status was white, regardless of skin pigmentation—in part because just about everyone in New Mexico had some Indian or African ancestry. Indian men and their progeny found it more difficult to become white. They constituted most of the *genizaro* (rough people) community, which formed the bottom rung of the Spanish social ladder. In 1733, a group of more than one hundred *genizaro* family heads included men from at least seven different Indian nations. By 1800, New Mexico's "Spanish" population outnumbered its Indian population by a ratio of roughly 2:1. But most members of the Spanish colony had some Indian ancestry.

New Mexico was racist, hierarchical, and often brutal. In 1638, Isabel Yantula charged Fray Nicolas with the killing of her husband and then with using her as his concubine. Even after the reconquest, Pueblo leaders complained that Spanish men commonly raped the women who "enter Santa Fe to mill wheat and spin wool." *Genizaros* were supposed to remove their hats and bow their heads in the presence of their superiors. Eusebio Chávez beat Andrés Martín, his father-in-law, in 1765, when Martín called him a "mixed-blood dog son of a whore." Part of Chávez's restitution was to kneel publicly at Martín's feet and ask for forgiveness "for having lacked in the respect" owed him "due to his age and the dignity of being his father-in-law."[4]

But even those who were at the bottom of New Mexico's social ladder were still on the ladder. Freed *genizaros* commonly formed their own communities and could receive property through military service to the colony. *Compadrazgo* (godparenthood) constituted a system of fictive kinship in which *genizaro* or other marginal youth acquired powerful godparents, sponsors from the Spanish community.

Reciprocity also modulated hierarchy inside Northern New Spain's families. Well-to-do families guarded the honor, the virginity of their daughters, closely, but New Mexico did not have a lot of wealthy families. Its social fluidity and lack of compact settlements abetted the freedom of women and youth, many of whom had to work outside the home to help their families to survive. Subordination, furthermore, did not entail helplessness. Spanish tradition encouraged young people to choose their own spouses. Steve Stern's brilliant *The Secret History of Gender: Women, Men, and Power in Late Colonial Mexico* notes that women perceived marriage as a "relationship of unequal mutuality that imposed permanent moral responsibilities on men." Men's greater status entailed responsibility to their wives and children, and women complained to neighbors and civic and religious authorities when their husbands fell short of that ideal. They "contested not patriarchal first principles as such but their operational meaning in the practical workings of everyday life."[5]

The same could be said of subordinates more generally who were on New Spain's northern fringe. Colonists and indigenous people became deeply implicated in each others' families and communities. New Mexico was hierarchical, violent, and race conscious. But it was also a place of great racial and cultural diversity and social interdependence.

The Chesapeake (coastal Virginia and Maryland) colonies both resembled and differed from New Mexico.

Like the Spanish, early arrivals on the Chesapeake sought immediate wealth, and few women accompanied the treasure seekers. An early Virginia Company pamphlet boasted of their male settlers that "neither the imbracements of their wives, nor indulgences to their babes, nor the neglect of their domesticke fortunes, nor banishment from their native soile,...have broken their noble resolution" to the colony.[6] Most of these colonists died within a couple of years. Children were, of course, rare. The discovery in the 1610s that tobacco was a valuable cash crop fostered economic success but continued social instability. Tobacco required a great deal of land and labor, mostly in the form of indentured servants, who traded transportation from England and a chance to some day become planters themselves upon completing about seven years of labor. About three-quarters of the British immigrants to the Chesapeake at that time came as indentured servants. A significant minority would become prosperous farmers in their own right, for the Chesapeake offered, perhaps, the best chance for socioeconomic mobility in the English-speaking world. But indentured servitude exacerbated the region's unstable social structure. About six out of seven of these servants were men for much of the seventeenth century, and most of them, like their more well-to-do counterparts, proved reluctant to marry Native American or African American women. Women servants were supposed to remain childless. About half the number of servants died before they became free; planters had little incentive to treat them with much consideration. All of this skewed the Chesapeake's sex ratios and retarded family formation throughout the seventeenth century.

Families that did form struggled with the consequences of death throughout the seventeenth century. Even by the turn of the eighteenth century, most children who were born in Middlesex County, Virginia, had lost one or both parents by the age of thirteen. A hypothetical but representative couple of this time and place married when the husband was twenty-four and the wife twenty. They had five children before the wife died at age thirty-nine. The husband would quickly remarry, have two or three more children by this second wife, and die at forty-eight.[7] Death repeatedly reshuffled families. Successful households required the services of skilled housekeepers, women who produced, processed, and prepared food, made and mended clothing, and of course birthed and raised children. Children usually grew up with two parents, though one (or even both of those parents) was apt to be a stepparent. Those with no biological parents or inheritances were commonly bound out as servants, trading their labor for room and board, until they reached their majority.

As in England—also a very volatile place—bonds of neighborliness often substituted for a lack of blood kin. Friendships were especially important, for a man often had to count on male friends rather than on male kin to oversee their estates and to ensure that fatherless children were not abused or their inheritances squandered. Just 17 percent of identifiable friendships among household heads entailed relations of kinship (blood or marriage) in 1687. In Middlesex County around 1700, 36 percent of marriages were between people who had lived within a half- mile radius of each other, 95 percent within five miles. "The great majority of planters were embedded in an intricate network of friends and neighbors," concludes James Horn.[8]

New England families were stable from the outset. Most immigrants came for largely religious reasons; they therefore came to stay, and about seven out of every eight arrived with one or more relatives. They also settled where epidemics had killed most of the indigenous inhabitants, a circumstance that spared them from much of the armed conflict that beset the early Chesapeake. Rapidly moving rivers bequeathed healthful conditions, an advantage they improved upon by focusing on disciplined subsistence agriculture rather than get-rich-quick schemes. If the Chesapeake was like England, only more so, early New England constituted something of a refuge from the mother country's dynamic economic and social changes. Most people who lived to see their twentieth birthday could expect to survive into their sixties and to know their grandchildren. The great majority of children grew up with both parents. Parents commonly compelled their sons to serve for many years before releasing their inheritances. Women were less apt to be widowed or to be independent than in the Chesapeake.

Puritan society was close-knit by design. The Puritans were dissenters, religious idealists who were attempting to live out their understanding of what constituted a biblical, Godly community far from the powerful heads of England or the Church of England. As Calvinists, they knew that humans were bound to sin. Hierarchical, orderly, and harmonious communities and families would both foster happiness and please God. Everyone had to live near a church or a town. A Connecticut law from the 1630s stipulated "that noe yonge man that is neither maried nor hath any servaunte, and be noe publicke officer, shall keepe howse by himself, without consent of the Towne where he lives." In 1675, Massachusetts provided for a cadre of tithingmen, "sober and discreet" people, to inspect ten to a dozen families apiece and to report those guilty of disorder.[9]

Hierarchical families constituted the building blocks of the community and of the holy commonwealth. Men governed women, and the young were to defer to and respect their elders. Parents could be fined for not restraining their children's behavior or for punishing them too harshly. The Puritans were the first in the Western world to pass laws against wife beating—though here, as elsewhere, men were allowed, or even encouraged, to use moderate violence to "correct" wayward or disobedient wives. Divorce, though easier to come by than just about anywhere else in the Western world, was rare, and New England courts ordered separated couples "to live quietly and peaceably together as man and wife" or face imprisonment or expulsion.[10] Scholars have found that women who were accused of witchcraft tended to be independent—to have their own livelihood—or to be single, for example. Puritan authorities ran Anne Hutchinson out of Massachusetts for heresy. She acted as "a Husband" rather than as "a wife, and a preacher than a Hearer; and a Magistrate than a Subject." Governor John Winthrop impugned her husband as "a man of a very mild temper and weak parts, and wholly guided by his wife," of not being, in sum, a man.[11] Puritans constructed gender and familial relations within a tightly organized and hierarchical social structure.

But in New England, as in Old England, domination entailed affection and obligation. Samuel Sewall was distressed when Betty, his fourteen-year-old daughter, revealed her fears of going to hell. "I answer'd her Tears as well as I could, and pray'd with many Tears on either part; hope God heard us."[12] Married couples grieved at the loss of their children and at the loss of their spouses, too. Sarah Goodhue wrote in around 1681 to her husband, as she sensed that death would soon take her:

> In all my burthens thou hast willingly with me sympathized, and cheerfully thou hast helped me bear them:...This twenty years experience of thy love to me in this kind, hath so instamped it upon my mind, that I do think that there never was man more truly kind to a woman: I desire forever to bless and praise the Lord, that in mercy to my soul, he by his providence ordered that I should live with thee...[13]

Winthrop, in his oft-cited 1630 sermon on the Arbella, proclaimed that good Christians must treat each other with "meekness, gentleness, patience and liberality, we must delight in each other, make others' Conditions our own, rejoice together, mourn together, labour, and suffer together,..."[14] He believed that social inequality reflected God's way of making people depend on one another for love and care. Wives and children should be as eager to obey their husbands and parents, respectively, as humans were to obey God. "It should be the very Joy of your Life, to yield *Obedience* unto the commands of your *Parents*," remarked Cotton Mather.[15] Salvation by grace freed people to choose subordination to one's heavenly and earthly superiors. Affection and service worked both ways, moreover. "Everyone was not equal, but neither was anyone autonomous," sums up Lisa Wilson. "Fathers asserted their authority in early New England within a context of mutual obligation and love."[16] Puritans expected fathers to support their families materially, to work hard, and to make a good living. They were also responsible for their family's religious well-being, the spiritual, moral, and practical education of their children, so that they could make their own living and way in the world. The Puritans' "patriarchal ideal of manliness," notes Anne Lombard, "expressed what they saw as a desirable arrangement of interdependencies between human beings, one that ensured that the strong cared for the weak, that children grew to be healthy adults, and that human society was as peaceful and stable as possible."[17] No one was free to do as he or she wished. "In the hierarchy of the church (as in the state) man could be subordinate as well as dominant," Margaret Mason observes.[18] All men had to answer to God, of course, but virtually every husband had to answer, to pay his respects, to earthly superiors, even as he governed his own household. The Puritans had an abiding belief in sin, in the reality and potency of evil, and they believed that subordinates should both love and fear superiors, just as even the most powerful minister both loved and feared God. Love was not enough. Love without fear of God and other superiors, love without discipline, would ruin a child's material and spiritual future. A successful life, even the making of a bare living, required cultivating a spirit of obedience and industriousness.

This industriousness eventually undermined New England communities. During the second half of the seventeenth century, merchants became more wealthy and gravitated to Boston and other cities. Tradition-minded ministers criticized them in particular, and other people more generally, for losing the fire of the first generation. The last spasm of witch-hunting, in 1692, arose in part because of intertwined economic, cultural, social, and religious differences between subsistence-oriented Salem Village and their more cosmopolitan, market-oriented neighbors.

New England remained much more coherent and stable than did the Chesapeake at the turn of the eighteenth century. But the two areas were becoming much more alike than they had been during the first half of the seventeenth century.

Puritans had the easiest time creating families on the North American continent, Africans the most difficult. Slavery was well-established in West Africa by the fifteenth century. Slaves were people who had committed serious crimes, had been captured in warfare, or had sold themselves to avoid hunger or other dire consequences. But as the European demand for slaves grew, West African leaders carried out slave raids along the coast and then penetrated more and more deeply into the interior, enslaving millions, who would then be transported across the Atlantic Ocean.

Historians still debate the moral, political, demographic, and economic consequences of the slave trade for West African states. But there is no doubt that the practice constituted a horrible tragedy for those who were victimized by it. Roughly half the number of West Africans who were captured for the trade never boarded a ship; they died on the long march to the ocean or in the dismal holding pens that awaited them there. Those who survived were herded into holds and packed into spaces too small to even turn over in. Roughly 15 percent of those who began the trans-Atlantic journey died on the way, and many others would have died had the crews not force-fed them or surrounded the ships with nets to ensnare those who attempted suicide by jumping off their decks. Slave trading was a brutal business in which the dual prospects of huge profits and shipboard revolts caused slave traders to treat their captives with extreme cruelty.

But the physical cruelties of the slave trade were arguably dwarfed by its social consequences. West Africans defined and located themselves in relation to others in their village, clan, or nation. One was a daughter, son, mother, father, aunt, uncle, or cousin to hundreds of others. As slaves were ordinarily captured in small groups, or even singly, enslavement meant being torn from the great majority of one's family and kin and then subsequent renderings as fellow villagers died or were purchased by a succession of slave traders on both sides of the Atlantic. West Africans had sometimes chosen slavery to become implicated in kinship relations. But this new form of slavery meant being ripped involuntarily from that life-giving context. In the words of James Sweet,

> To be removed from the kinship network was to alter the life cycle in ways that are unimaginable for most Westerners. The meanings of the markers that define the human life span—birth, childhood, adolescence, marriage, child-rearing, old age, and dying—were all radically transformed. To face these challenges alone, without the collective support and shared understanding of the natal network of kin, was tantamount to social death.[19]

Stephanie Smallwood's *Saltwater Slavery* points out that re-creating kinship was not the work of a week or even of many years. Slave ships contained "not a functioning whole but rather an arbitrary collective of isolated and alienated persons." The enslaved could hardly hope to be reunited with kin, even in death. To die without a funeral, to expire without food and drink, to be buried away from the West African earth of one's ancestors, was to die in a completely new and horrifying way. Hence in South Carolina, an African-born slave "decorated the grave of his departed son with 'a miniature canoe, about a foot long, and a little paddle, with which he said it would cross the ocean to his own country.' "[20]

Those who survived the slave coffles, pens, and dungeons of Africa and the middle passage across the Atlantic Ocean faced the daunting task of re-creating, from scratch, with highly diverse and traumatized parts, a new society. The great majority of enslaved Africans went to the Caribbean or to Brazil, where they typically worked on large plantations and died young. These societies were characterized by: a continual influx of Africans purchased to replace those who died; highly skewed sex ratios; few children; and social and cultural separation from the white minority.

Those who came to the North American continent found conditions that were much different and, in some respects, better, during most of the seventeenth century. These early African Americans enjoyed more rights and autonomy than their descendants would. The English enslaved defeated white opponents for much of the seventeenth century. Slavery was not yet understood and practiced as a purely race-based, permanent institution. Early slave owners often purchased so-called "Creoles," slaves who had already lived for some years in the Caribbean, for example, rather than slaves who had freshly arrived from Africa. Many early slaves were from the Caribbean or West Central Africa, the Kongo or Angola, where the Portuguese had spread Christianity. These slaves were apt to have learned English and to possess other marketable skills before arriving on the continent, advantages which might help them to buy their freedom. In Northern cities, especially, slaves more often served in the house than in the fields. Whites greatly outnumbered them and did not worry as much about slave rebellion. Racism existed, to be sure. But significant numbers of African Americans paid taxes or even owned land on the Chesapeake by the 1660s, and a few were married to whites.

All this changed in the South during the last third of the seventeenth century, when black slaves replaced white indentured servants as the primary source of plantation labor, and new, black-majority slave societies began in the Carolinas and Georgia. Under the new paradigm, white equaled free, black equaled slave. White laws and leaders discouraged black manumissions and intermarriages. Slaves were still treated less harshly than those in the Caribbean, but in the Deep South, especially, white masters could beat or even maim them with little fear of consequences.

Yet the spread of slavery fostered more stable slave families and communities. Profits from plantation agriculture on the continent remained modest compared to those on the Caribbean, so owners in the American South had a relatively high financial interest in slaves' health and reproductive capacities. Slave women were more likely to both survive and to bear children than their counterparts in the Caribbean, a trend that led to much more even sex ratios. The number of males per female in a Maryland parish dropped from 1:8 in the 1690s to 1:5 a half century later, to 1:1 at onset of the American Revolution.[21] By that time, adults no longer outnumbered children. Chesapeake slaves reproduced themselves by the 1730s, though their rates of infant and childhood mortality remained higher than that of the whites. By the 1770s, African-born slaves constituted just one-tenth of the Chesapeake's total.

By the time of the American Revolution, most slaves lived in families. Kin ties also proliferated. In 1772, he master of Tom, a run-away slave of Caroline County, Virginia, thought it likely that he had fled to one of four places, as he had "many relations."[22] On larger plantations, individual cabins had largely replaced barrack-like structures, bequeathing individual slave families a degree of privacy. In coastal South Carolina sex ratios were highly skewed and children were rare early in the 1700s. Late in the century, most slaves lived in two-parent households on the larger plantations.

Of course, to document the emergence of slave families is to say nothing of the lives that they led and the horrible conditions they were forced to endure. But the emergence of African American slavery, of a labor force dominated by Creoles rather than by Africans, meant that most slaves would grow up and live among blood kin. Fictive kin—the creation of familial-like bonds with persons one did not share a common ancestor with—would remain an important part of African American slavery. But so would biological ties, familial relations that would constitute slavery's keenest cruelty and its most prized consolation. Brutalized fragments of dispersed and diverse African communities had, with their descendents, created African American identities, communities, and families.

* * *

All of North America's disparate groups showed a great deal of resilience in adjusting to the impact of colonization. Juana Hurtado was the daughter of a Zia (Pueblo) mother and a prominent Hispanic father who held *encomiendas* (rights to the labor of subject Indians.) Juana was kidnapped at age seven in 1680 by Indians. She returned to the Spanish community sixteen years later, with her two children. Her Dené (Navajo) kin continued to visit her. She gained a private land grant and had some children by a man who was married to another woman. Colonial officials wanted to punish Juana and her family for immorality. But the Zia Pueblo protected and defended her, and Fray Miguel Menchero praised her for helping him in his efforts to convert the Dené. One of her children became the *teniente* (assistant magistrate) of their district. Most of her descendants became Pueblo. Kinship ties were both complicated and potent in the Southwest.

North America offered the prospect of freedom for European colonists. "The conquistadores," notes Alan Taylor, "ultimately lusted for power over others that they might escape dependence upon a superior," an escape nearly impossible to come by "in European societies premised upon a strict hierarchy of power that obliged almost everyone to submit to a superior."[23] This lust for power disrupted or destroyed people's lives and kinship structures across North America and West Africa.

But most North Americans had at least partially recovered their social equilibrium by the 1700s. Native American nations that had been conquered were fragmented, and many of those who remained independent had been weakened by disease, stratification, and conquest. But such groups used flexible kinship structures to accommodate these unprecedented changes. African Americans recovered from the shock of Trans-Atlantic enslavement to invent and sustain new kin networks. Stable white communities became the rule rather than the exception on the Chesapeake, as indentured servitude faded and sex ratios evened.

The legacy of perceiving in America fresh possibilities, an escape from subordination and stasis, would continue to inform the American dream and reality. But by 1700, most American colonies had contained these hopes in familial and social structures of authority and obligation.

Chapter 3

Revolution and Continuity

Going to North America was something of a subversive act for Europeans. It entailed leaving established, hierarchical communities, and often families, for a chance at economic and social advancement. Even the Puritans, who succeeded at creating more stable communities than the ones they had left behind, fled the authority of Crown and established church, and it is surely no coincidence that pious New England produced some of the most radical political and religious minds of the eighteenth and subsequent centuries.

Radicalism ripened as the colonies stabilized. Economic development fostered confidence. Social hierarchies loosened. The American Revolution itself was the culmination of a broad set of developments that had in common the questioning of authority and the assertion of reason over tradition.

But social relations within families changed much more slowly than did North America's political allegiances. The American Revolution was bound up in a cluster of complex, interrelated changes, including a loosening of patriarchy. But the eighteenth century did not overturn traditional familial relations.

* * *

The Quakers, who began settling in North America late in the seventeenth century, created distinctive families that anticipated later developments among less progressive populations. The Quakers lived across much of North America by the mid-seventeenth century, but not until the wealthy William Penn founded the colony of Pennsylvania in 1681 did they flourish. Eastern Pennsylvania had fertile land, which industrious Quakers soon turned into profitable farms. This Protestant sect's members believed that Christians were obligated to create holy communities. Unlike the Puritans, they were optimistic about human nature and believed that everyone carried a spark of divinity, an "inner light." Quaker worship services consisted largely of listening for, or contemplating, this inner light: God communicated with them directly rather than through intermediaries.

This belief that Christians could live an essentially perfect, Christlike life affected social relations. Devout Quakers asserted that violence was both sinful and avoidable. Children were born innocent and perfect, not stained by original sin. Everyone was saved—or was at least capable of salvation. This universalism and optimism led Quakers to question social gradations between young and old, women and men, poor and wealthy that other people in the Western world took for granted. Indeed, Quakers would be the first white North Americans to begin the long process of ending slavery. Quaker farmers soon exported a substantial portion of their crops, and profits from these exports freed the women and the children from much of the tedious work that was still predominant in New England. Women instead focused on child nurture, and many became leaders in the church and community. They inspected engagements and marriages to ensure that these met the church's high standards for harmony and piety, a responsibility that impinged on the lives of men as well as of women. Women ministers traveled and spoke widely, a practice that many men respected and encouraged. The Quakers favored persuasion and nurture over coercion and violence in raising their sons and daughters, and their children tended to receive their inheritances much earlier than did their New England counterparts.

Pennsylvania boasted North America's most dynamic economy for much of the eighteenth century, but other colonies were not far behind. The thirteen colonies grew from roughly 250,000 in 1700 to 2,500,000 at the outbreak of the American Revolution. As in England a century before, increased trade lay at the heart of growth. The Southern colonies exported lucrative plantation crops such as tobacco, rice, and indigo to England, the Middle Colonies shipped grain and other staples to the slave economies of the Caribbean, and New England provided many of the ships and the merchants to prosecute the trade. A larger and larger proportion of colonial exports consisted of value-added products such as lumber, flour, iron, and rum, and colonial craftsmen were fashioning furniture, shoes, cloth, and even stoves for domestic consumption.

The great majority of people still lived in the countryside, and the products of most farms were consumed close to home. Indeed, the most impressive rates of population growth often occurred in the backcountry of the Carolinas and Pennsylvania, places usually far removed from navigable streams, at a time when it cost as much to move goods ten miles in a wagon as it did to ship them across the Atlantic Ocean. All of the colonies imported most of their finished goods. Manufacturing remained relatively modest, even close to the ocean. Dozens of iron foundries appeared across the colonies, and New England boasted a strong shipbuilding industry. But more typical were modest sawmills or small shops producing rudimentary goods, such as barrels or shoes. Much of the colonies' explosive population growth (tenfold in seventy years) came from immigration. Thousands of British emigrants continued to arrive, but so did those from the continent, particularly pietistic Germans, such as the Moravians and the Mennonites. The result was "a heterogeneous culture made up of homogeneous and largely isolated individual units."[1]

Prosperity spread across the colonies. In the Chesapeake, where slavery continued to expand, leading planters lived in stately brick or wooden homes. By the 1730s, their homes were filled with fine furniture and dinnerware. In rural Virginia, less than one in ten poor or middling households owned a table fork in 1700. Three quarters of a century later, one in five poor families and one half of middling ones owned that item, and nearly one-third of poor families in Massachusetts had table knives and forks.[2] Improved roads linked larger towns, places with growing numbers of artisans, merchants, innkeepers, and attorneys plied their trades. Agricultural products flowed from ports where more and more goods such as clocks, textiles, china, and other imports arrived. Philadelphia grew from 10,000 people in 1720 to 40,000 in 1775.

Rich and poor people became more numerous. This was particularly evident in the colonies' growing cities, which drew ambitious merchants and desperate laborers. The top tenth of Boston taxpayers owned 46 percent of its taxable property in 1687 and 63 percent in 1771.[3] The elite advertised their status by building expensive houses and purchasing luxury goods such as tea, carriages, and powdered wigs. Restrictive and expensive clothing illustrated that one did not need to use one's body to make a living.

Prosperity undercut some forms of community interdependence and deference. The social aspects of servitude receded. Domestic servitude, which bound individuals to labor for a particular family for several years, gave way to contractual arrangements that either party could break at short notice. Servants, like other actors in the new economy, were providing a service for a price, not joining a family. Respect for the elderly waned. Wealth displaced age as the main criterion for enjoying the most prestigious seats in church, for example. Litigation, which was frowned upon in early New England, grew. Urbanization created larger and more fluid communities in which kin, at least for the working class, were rarely present, sex ratios were seldom even, and disease and death were never far away. All of these factors, together with the frequent comings and goings of sailors, merchants, and working people, made community more tenuous.

Yet the bonds that tied rich and poor together remained strong, particularly in the countryside. T. H. Breen describes how indebtedness linked wealthy, middling, and poor Virginia farmers in a network of unequal mutuality. The wealthy felt obligated to lend money to their less prosperous counterparts, who paid their respects through acts such as removing their hats in the presence of their superiors or allowing the wealthy to enter church last and leave first. At the voting booth, great men stood as candidates and poorer men voted for them publicly, an occasion which, in the words of Rhys Isaac, "was less an opportunity to confer a favor than a chance to show gratitude or to secure the goodwill of a powerful neighbor."[4] Elite white males repeatedly reminded themselves that privilege bequeathed responsibility. "Live not for yourselves, but the Publick… [and] let your own Ease, your own Pleasure, your own private Interests, yield to the common Good," remarked the President of Princeton College to his students in 1761. College students practiced particularly elaborate forms of deference—and not just to their professors. Yale required its freshmen to "show all proper Respect to the Officers of College, the Residency Graduates and undergraduate Classes superior in standing to themselves." When traversing a stairway or narrow hallway, for example, they should "stop and give way, leaving the most convenient side" to others, and if even a sophomore entered a room, freshmen were to rise and stay standing until he left.[5] Courtesy manuals grew in number and influence during the eighteenth century. The young George Washington copied 110 "Rules of Civility and Decent Behaviour In Company and Conversation," including detailed instructions on how to walk in the company of a superior: "Walk not with him Cheek by Joul but Somewhat behind him; but yet in Such a Manner that he may easily Speak to you."[6]

Washington's earnest attempts at self-improvement were but one of many signs of a growing ethos of ambition and hope. Humanity finally seemed to be gaining control over a world in which wringing a living from the earth had been a backbreaking and uncertain enterprise that was punctuated by periodic plagues and famines. Improvements in agricultural production together with increased trade brought unprecedented comfort, even as scientists discovered how to counteract killers such as smallpox. Belief in humanity and its capacity to reason increasingly replaced faith as the organizing principle in educated people's lives. This movement of course had deep roots in France and England, and American intellectuals eagerly read political and moral philosophers such as Locke, Hume, Reid, Kant, Berkeley, Smith, Voltaire, and Rousseau. Benjamin Franklin, Thomas Jefferson, and many other leading American thinkers espoused a sort of deism. They believed in God and in right and wrong. But they distrusted religious beliefs that seemed at odds with reason. Deists were more apt to view Jesus as a great moral teacher rather than as their personal savior or the worker of miracles. God revealed himself not so much in the Bible or in the personhood of Jesus as through nature's natural law, for God had set a logical universe in motion and then stepped aside to allow humans to improve their societies rather than intervene directly in their affairs. "*God gives all things to industry*," observed Benjamin Franklin.[7] Smallpox could be defeated not by smearing blood over one's door, as in the Old Testament, or through prayer, but through scientific investigations that established that a small amount of the virus would inoculate one from the fatal strain of the disease.

The Enlightenment celebrated the seemingly limitless potential of the individual. The American Revolution itself owed much to these developments. But its intellectual roots in North America went much further back than the Declaration of Independence. Defoe's *Robinson Crusoe,* which appeared in England in 1719, and Samuel Richardson's *Clarissa,* which appeared in 1747–48 found eager and numerous readers in North America. Crusoe rebelled against his father and was, ostensibly, punished by being shipwrecked. But on his island he mastered a variety of mechanical arts, formed a group of followers, and developed a strong, individualized, relationship with God. Rousseau, the quintessential romantic individualist, drew this moral from Defoe: "The most certain way to raise oneself above prejudices, and order one's judgments on the real relationships of things, is to put oneself in the position of an isolated man, and to judge everything as that man should judge it himself, as regards to its usefulness to him."[8] *Clarissa* unfurls the tragedy of a young woman whose father tries to force her into a marriage with a brutish man. She disobeys him and dies. But the American editions of the novel presented Clarissa as noble martyr to a foolish patriarch rather than as a rebellious daughter who got her just desserts. Here, as in *Robinson Crusoe*, right seemed to be on the side of youthful initiative, not hoary authority.

Less well-read colonists also became more distrustful of authority in the decades preceding the Revolutionary War. Religious intensity declined in the late seventeenth and early eighteenth centuries, owing to progress made in science and reason, and greater prosperity. In urban New England, cosmopolitan-minded merchants (the sort of people whose ancestors had backed Anne Hutchinson in the Antinomian controversy of the 1630s) shifted to the Church of England and gained substantial political as well as economic influence. Many ordinary New Englanders moved away from the meetinghouses and tight settlements that the founders had required them to attend and to reside in, respectively. The qualifications for church membership loosened as religious fervor fell. Traditionalists soon detected this declension. "Let Merchants and such as are increasing *Cent per Cent* remember this," warned John Higginson in an election-day sermon, back in 1663, "that worldly gain was not the end and designe of the people of *New-England*, but *Religion*."[9] The proportion of white people who attended church fell across the colonies early in the 1700s. In the Chesapeake, which had started out with a relatively low level of piety, even relatively liberal—not to mention lascivious—planters such as William Byrd held daily devotions and repented of their sins. Their descendants seemed more immoral and less guilt ridden by mid-century; drunkenness, gambling, and fornication became both commonplace and acceptable. The Great Awakening of the 1740s prompted a different sort of challenge to tradition. Some converts burned luxury items such as jewelry and wigs. On the Chesapeake, argues Isaac, the emphasis on an immediate experience of the divine constituted a pointed rejection of the status quo: "Against the system in which proud men were joined in rivalry and convivial excess was set a reproachful model of an order in which God-humbled men would seek a deep sharing of emotion while repudiating indulgence of the flesh."[10] Then, as now, piety offered a refuge of sorts from economic competition and rapid sociocultural change. It also undermined both the religious authority of established church leaders and patrician social authority. Lukewarm Christians, regardless of their great positions or learning, did not deserve the respect of those who had been awakened by the Holy Spirit. A pure and simple faith counted for more in God's eyes than did education or wealth. Chesapeake Baptists disciplined members who fought, fornicated, and drank to excess, the very activities that prominent men so often embraced, and their simple dress and church architecture rebuked the Church of England's ostentation and hierarchy. This critique of wealth was sometimes blunt. Said a Boston revivalist of the rich, "Pull them down, turn them out, and put others in their Places."[11] Revivals especially attracted young adults and city residents, the people most implicated in rapid change. The Great Awakening was traditional in that it tried to create communities that were more austere and interdependent at a time of growing prosperity and individualism. But revivalists also encouraged individualism inasmuch as they critiqued inherited or established authority and hierarchies. Conversion required searching one's own soul. Like its opposite number, Deism, it encouraged people to think—and certainly feel—for themselves.

The family remained North America's fundamental social institution in the eighteenth century, the place where people received most of their academic, religious, and certainly, vocational instruction. It was also a factory, a retirement home, an orphanage, and an insane asylum, as local authorities routinely bound indigent people out to individual families or gave those families modest payments to care for them. Men still found it essential to marry or remarry if they were to have a functioning household to head, and religious and civic leaders alike continued to emphasize the importance of family stability and hierarchy. A Connecticut minister wrote his unmarried sister in 1762 that she should aspire to be the sort of wife whose husband "may say of you, . . . that he never saw your Brows wrinkled into a disagreeable Frown, or your Lips polluted by a peevish Syllable."[12] Samuel Cobb of Virginia in 1757 praised his wife for being ever "kind, loving, and obedient to me without affectation."[13] The increased life expectancy in the Chesapeake served to create much stronger kinship networks, for people were living long enough to reproduce and create generations of cousins and other extended family. The percentage of friendships among household heads that were based on ties of blood or marriage rose from 17 percent in 1687 to 64 percent in 1724.[14] Husbands and fathers also lived longer by this time, so women were less likely to experience the poverty and autonomy that often accompanied widowhood. Likewise, children were much less likely to be orphaned and, in the case of sons, more likely to wait longer into adulthood to gain their inheritances.

Yet even some Southern patriarchs were discomfited by the new century's ethos. Virginia planter Landon Carter chafed under the humiliations of British rule even as he railed against his daughter for marrying a man he did not approve of and against his son and his daughter-in-law for allowing their son to behave impudently. When Landon lashed the eight-year-old boy, his daughter-in-law "rose like a bedlamite that her child should be struck with a whip—and up came her Knight Errant [husband] to his father with some heavy God damnings, but he prudently did not touch me. Otherwise my whip handle should have settled him—if I could." Isaac explains that this "domestic gust," as Landon Carter termed it, revealed a liminal world in which patriarchs' expectations were increasingly frustrated. Landon could delay or even deny his children their inheritances. But he could not force them to love and obey him, a failure that was all the more painful because even the patriarchs were reading the new sentimental literature that prompted them to both demand obedience and crave "affection and companionship."[15]

The erosion of patriarchy was most noticeable in New England, where seventeenth- century fathers with long lifespans had been reluctant to relinquish control over their lands to their sons. But New England's poor soils and high birth rates, together with the availability of land or other opportunities away from home, prompted many eighteenth-century sons to strike out on their own—with or without their fathers' approval.

More and more young men made their own way in the world. Benjamin Franklin was a sort of Robinson Crusoe himself. He dreamed of going to sea, broke an indenture as a printer's apprentice to his older brother, fled Boston, and then became wealthy and famous on his metaphorical island of Philadelphia, where, like a castaway, he started from scratch. Indeed, colonists were much attached to engravings of the prodigal son in the late eighteenth century—and they depicted this wayward son as less and less abject as the century progressed.

Children seized more control over their marriages in the eighteenth century. Parents had married off their daughters in order, from eldest to youngest. But now, younger daughters commonly wed out of turn. This became part of a larger pattern of women marrying whomsover they chose to marry, and when they wished to do so, a choice they might exercise by becoming pregnant. In Hingham, Massachusetts, for example, 30 percent of brides were pregnant in 1750, up from 10 percent a half-century earlier.[16] As bearing a "bastard" was a great scandal for the entire family, parents who had heretofore resisted a match might suddenly become agreeable. New England county courts in the mid-1700s stopped punishing couples who had sex before they got married. Families had used their children's marriages to consolidate or expand their own economic power. By the time of the American Revolution, more and more of their children married for love.

Some women also enjoyed more influence after they were married. Beauty, charm, and love—a connection between two hearts—were shouldering aside more doughty virtues such as piety, humility, and industriousness. Spouses increasingly spoke or wrote to each other in terms that suggested friendship, of complementary rather than hierarchical relationships. Divorce, that handmaiden of romantic love, also increased during the eighteenth century. The rate remained extremely low, certainly in relation to today, but the number of divorce petitions, particularly from women, rose dramatically by the eve of the American Revolution.

The work of many colonial wives eased. White women did less field labor in the eighteenth century than they did in the seventeenth century, as slavery become more common in the South and agricultural advances made their labor less necessary in the middle and northern colonies. Women grew more educated and literate and as cities expanded, and more of them turned to teaching, shop keeping, or vending to make a living, particularly those who were single or widowed.

The religious influence of married women rose. They constituted a growing majority in New England churches by the late-seventeenth century. Male ministers relied on them more heavily and depicted them more favorably. If women were truly the weaker vessel and more prone to sin and temptation, how could one explain that their dedication to church surpassed that of men? Here, as in so many other elements of colonial life, people found it difficult to maintain the old orthodoxies in the face of evidence to the contrary.

Historians of the American Revolution now commonly point out that the causes of this political event cannot be understood without considering how colonists were questioning all sorts of authority, from the traditional church to patriarchal-minded fathers. A son who left home before his father wished him to was more likely to question the right of England to dictate policy to the thirteen colonies than one who did not, as was a Christian who sought God in an individual, unmediated meeting rather than in a hierarchical church. Patriot leaders tended to be younger than their loyalist counterparts. Thomas Hutchinson, the former governor of Massachusetts, sounded much like a traditional patriarch when he criticized the Declaration of Independence for advancing "the absurdity of making the *governed* to be *governors*."[17] Individualism constituted the common denominator in this bundle of intertwined economic, social, cultural, and familial developments.

But if changes in the family helped to prompt the American Revolution, the reverse was also true. The process of revolution served to undermine patriarchal assumptions. Hence a patriot remarked after the Boston Massacre of 1770 of his sovereign: "We swore allegiance to him as a *King*, not a *Tyrant*—as a *Protector*, not as a *Destroyer*—as a *Father*, not as a *Murderer*."[18] Like Clarissa before them, the patriots believed that they were the youthful victims of an abusive father who had betrayed their trust and thereby made a necessity of independence.

The war itself offered women lots of opportunities,whether they wanted them or not, to act autonomously. Women asserted themselves in the non-importation movements before the war by providing the homespun that symbolized patriotism and by policing merchants who tried to avoid the boycott. A group of Philadelphia women went door-to-door to garner support for the Continental Army, an activity that some criticized as unwomanly. Women such as Mercy Otis Warren and Abigail Adams joined the debate about the nation's political future and, like African Americans, drew parallels between the subordination they confronted within colonial society and Great Britain's abuses. "At liberty's spring such draughts I've imbibed," declared one in 1794, "That I hate all the doctrines of wedlock prescrib'd."[19] Few women—at least publicly—drew such a direct line between national and feminine freedom. But most women—patriot, Tory, or indifferent—became more autonomous during the war. Wives had long filled the role of "deputy husband" when their husbands were absent or incapacitated. When men went away to fight, women by necessity managed farms and other businesses and made decisions that had once been claimed by their husbands.

Thousands of other women became camp followers who washed clothes and otherwise supported soldiers.

The founders did not, as Abigail Adams urged, "remember the ladies" in formulating the nation's founding documents and its government. Virtually all women remained disenfranchised, and the American Revolution was much more political than social. But educated men and women alike championed the creation of "Republican mothers" who pursued more education than before so that they could better prepare their sons for citizenship in the new nation.

Postrevolutionary shifts in family relations tended to be more subtle than extreme. The great majority of Americans still lived in communities dedicated to the harsh requirements of wringing a living from the soil. Less than 5 percent of the new nation lived in cities of 2,500 or more. The intoxicating ideals of the Enlightenment and the American Revolution existed alongside the sober requirements of tradition and survival. "God grant me strength to bear my toil and affliction," prayed midwife Martha Ballard of Maine time and time again in the 1790s as she struggled with the pains of old age and the requirements of keeping up a home and a business. "I rose early, put on a kettle of yarn to boil, then milkt and got breakfast and did my washing, then went to the spring for water, but alass how fatagued was I when I reached my house," she recorded in 1800.[20] Post-Revolution magazines stressed romantic love much more than they had before the war. But more practical considerations continued to loom large in most people's marital choices. Authorities outlawed primogeniture in the 1780s and 1790s to equalize inheritance between older and younger children and between sons and daughters. Parents tended to strike their children less frequently and to speak of them more affectionately. But they still expected to be obeyed.

Freedom, moreover, did not imply the freedom to do as one pleased. This was, after all, a society still immersed in the rhetoric and examples of Christian piety. Thomas Jefferson, certainly a free thinker, revered the teachings of Jesus enough to cut and paste them together into his own version of the New Testament. These were men, in the words of Barry Alan Shain, who "felt that personal independence and some measure of self-renunciation before family, God, and community were perfectly compatible goals, even if difficult to achieve."[21] Hence the Virginia Declaration of Rights closed by asserting: "it is the mutual duty of all to practice Christian forbearance, love, and charity towards each other."[22]

When the founding fathers and other patriots spoke of their hopes for the young nation, they commonly employed the term "virtue," an ideal deeply rooted in the colonial period and drawn from the classical world. Samuel Johnson's *Ethica Elementa. Or the First Principles of Moral Philosophy*, appeared in Boston in 1746 and located virtue "in that Integrity, Firmness and Stability of the Soul, whereby we do honestly and stedfastly persist in Spite of all Temptations to the contrary, in the Love and Practice of *Moral Good*, and the Hatred and Forebearance of *Moral Evil*."[23] Virtue was both personal and social; it improved both the individual and the community. This ethical system did not preclude commerce or material aid, for wealth and distinction could and should serve the public good. Many patriots believed that the colonies should become independent precisely because doing so would serve to preserve their virtue. The patriots celebrated the freedom not to do as they pleased, but rather the freedom to *be* good and to *do* good. "Lose no occasion of exercising your dispositions to be grateful, to be generous, to be charitable, to be humane," admonished Jefferson.[24]

* * *

Abigail [Smith] Adams dedicated her adult life to family, god, and country. Born in 1744 to an ordained minister, she married an ambitious young attorney, John Adams, at the age of nineteen and immediately began bearing children. A devoted mother, she embraced the patriot cause before her husband had signed the Declaration of Independence, for England had treated the colonists with "Tyranny, oppression, and Murder." Her many letters to John included her well-known admonition to "Remember the Ladies," as "all Men would be tyrants if they could." But Abigail was not anticipating modern feminism, was not calling for full political equality. Rather, she wished her husband and his colleagues in Congress to realize that powerful men's capacity for evil and oppression was not limited to Great Britain's leaders, that men easily became familial despots. A deeply pious, liberal Christian, Abigail believed that her faith required her to sacrifice her personal desires for the good of others, including her country. The war brought the first of many long separations for the devoted couple. "I had it in my Heart to disswade him from going" to Congress, she wrote early in 1777, "and I know I could have prevaild, but our publick affairs at the time wore so gloomy an aspect that I thought if ever his assistance was wanted, it must be at such a time." She believed that women and men had different, complementary natures and callings. In 1809, she still referred to woman as "an helpmeet for man."[25] But she also asserted that being a good wife and mother required substantial education and deserved much respect.

Abigail Adams's life helps to explain the nature and the extent of the American Revolution. We find the founders wanting, if not hypocritical, in limiting the scope of the Revolution, in not expanding their vision of freedom to include slaves and white women, for example. But the founders and most of their more obscure contemporaries viewed freedom much differently from the way in which most of us do. Most patriots still believed in social and, certainly, familial hierarchies. They certainly understood freedom to be deeply implicated with obligation. They were obsessed with the young nation's virtue and deeply opposed to the development of adversarial political parties.

To be sure, the war was both cause and consequence of a broad, durable movement against established order and authority, against the notion that God had created a static and stable hierarchy of relationships that could not—and should not—be altered. The music that accompanied the British surrender at Yorktown was "The World Turned Upside Down." A ragtag collection of colonies had defeated the greatest nation in the world. Like Anne Hutchinson before them, they had "stept out of your place, you have rather bine . . . a Magistrate than a Subject."[26]

The founders—white men of property—generally succeeded in blunting the Revolution's radical potential. Some freed their slaves, others thought they should. But most did not, and slavery survived and soon flourished. New Jersey offered women suffrage—then changed its mind. Pennsylvania created a radical constitution—then soon made it much more conservative. Most of the young states retained property qualifications for voting, and the new federal Constitution put the levers of power in fewer people's hands.

Tradition proved still more tenacious within the family. Daughters and especially sons acted more autonomously, husbands less unilaterally. But making a living continued to tie the great majority of the young nation's people to well-worn patterns of family obligation.

The coming century would open up much greater possibilities for freedom. The nation was about to experience an industrial revolution that would offer millions of people new avenues for comfort and autonomy. Most would eagerly seek one, but not the other.

Chapter 4

Containing the Bourgeois Family

The American Revolution was a signal event in a broad movement toward freedom. But its impact was more political than social, its influence on the family modest. People continued to focus much more on familial responsibilities than on the pursuit of individual happiness, in large part because making a living still required the work of many hands.

The nineteenth century ushered in a revolution in economic production that eroded the structural foundations of middle-class families. Larger institutions assumed most of the responsibility of educating children and caring for the poor and the insane. Prosperity freed millions of women and children from economic production and prompted the birth rate to plummet. An increasing number of men sought and achieved prosperity and were no longer compelled by necessity to marry.

Yet the family became the central and most celebrated institution of middle-class Victorian life, in part because it so well served the new economy's requirements. The middle-class family became a workshop of character rather than a production center. Within its warm confines, wives turned their attention from spinning and cleaning to imbuing children and husbands with the habits of self-restraint that would bring success in public and private life. Indeed, this new ethos advanced most rapidly in the places where the new economy was strongest: the Northeast and Midwest early in the nineteenth century, then the West, and finally, by the century's close, the South. Faced with a choice between freedom and obligation, Victorians emphatically chose the latter, and women led the way.

* * *

A cluster of technological changes began transforming the nation's economy early in the nineteenth century. Improvements in transportation were critical. The young nation's ample waterways—particularly the Mississippi River system—reached many of its nooks and corners, but travel upriver remained difficult and expensive. Steam boats and canals helped. But it was the proliferation of railroads, beginning in the 1830s, that shattered the transportation bottleneck. Railroads could move goods quickly and cheaply, and they could be built just about anywhere. They didn't freeze in the winter or dry up in the summer. They reduced the cost of shipping by about twentyfold. A product that had cost a dollar to move by wagon could now be moved for a nickel.

The steam engine that powered railroads was soon put to other uses. Mill streams had run colonial saw and grist mills. But flows fluctuated, or might even disappear altogether, in seasons of cold or drought, and the power they offered was modest. Steam engines offered a seemingly infinite amount of power, and factories powered by them could be located anywhere—including in, or close to, growing cities that offered cheap and plentiful labor.

Other improvements in manufacturing ensued. Advancements in the tool-and-die industry—the creation of molds and other manufacturing parts—created much more precise products. A rifle that had once required weeks of work from a highly skilled craftsman could, by the 1830s, be easily assembled from interchangeable parts. Machines created better machines that in turn manufactured better products more efficiently and cheaply. Companies like McCormick churned out countless reapers and other animal-drawn agricultural implements that made farms much more productive, increasing by a factor of four the amount of grain that a person could cut in a day. Late in the century, steam-driven donkey engines allowed loggers to cut much more widely and cheaply than before, as logs were now yarded (moved) by machine onto railroad cars rather than dragged by oxen. Steel production boomed after the Civil War, and no product was more important than the steel rails that carried the new machines and products across the country. The predictability of railroads and factory labor rendered time more fixed, less elastic. Clocks proliferated as their cost fell twentyfold by the mid-century.

These technological changes multiplied and centralized production throughout the nineteenth century. Lowell, Massachusetts, became a major textile center in the 1810s. Boot and shoe makers, gunsmiths, iron makers, and many others engaged in industry followed from East to West. Bates County, Missouri, sent only 5 percent of its coal outside its borders in 1879: eight years later, after the railroad's arrival, 94 percent left the county. Factories shrank in number as they expanded in size. Missouri's cooperages (barrel-making factories) declined from 291 to 30 factories in the half-century after 1870, iron or steel factories from 61 to 5.[1] The number of subsistence farms shrank as the size and the number of market-oriented farms and ranches grew. Textile workers in New York, miners and steelworkers in Pennsylvania, cotton pickers in Mississippi, cowboys in Texas, timber workers in Washington, and wheat farmers in the Dakotas participated in a sprawling economy that transformed raw materials into food, building materials, clothes, and much, much more.

In the main, working-class people lost ground as middle-class people gained it. Machines assumed or "bastardized" valuable craft skills as middle-class occupations expanded. Large factories required managers, accountants, and secretaries. The number and proportion of low-paid factory workers grew. But so did the number and proportion of all manner of people who handled goods and money (store owners and merchants large and small, investors, financiers and insurers) and professionals (teachers, attorneys, doctors, and officeholders).

The new economy rewarded hard work and punished sloth much more directly than before. "Time is money," Benjamin Franklin had asserted. But in his day most farmers and artisans worked sporadically, and few of them produced goods for distant markets. As production and transportation improved, his aphorism made more sense for more people. Public land became available in smaller parcels, which allowed more and more farmers to purchase it. Indentured servitude withered and died. Business was booming. A shrewd and determined young man such as Andrew Carnegie rose from the lowly position of clerk to become the most powerful steelmaker in the world.

Yet Americans betrayed ambivalence over this new world of opportunity. Most Europeans, to be sure, had come to the thirteen colonies at least in part to improve their economic prospects. The American Revolution had been fought in no small part to throw off Great Britain's economic domination of those colonies, colonies whose manufacturers and merchants chafed under restrictions created across the Atlantic Ocean. Dreams of prosperity fired the thousands who streamed westward across the Appalachian Mountains after the war, just as they motivated the inventors, manufacturers, and merchants who were so forcefully and effectively thrusting the young nation into the industrial revolution. Yet America was not supposed to be just about getting rich. The founders had constantly reminded one another and the rest of the nation that success depended on virtue as well as ambition, that the naked pursuit of political self-interest would doom the Republican experiment. A fixation on wealth could be just as corrosive. Unprecedented opportunities for prosperity and the dissolution of social distinctions threatened to create a nation of crass self-aggrandizement, of ambition unredeemed by taste, deference, or morality. Therefore, "an almost wholly new genre of literature emerged to address concerns about youth embarking into the world of the market economy" in the 1830s and 1840s. Often authored by ministers, these books warned of the evils of drinking, whoring, gambling, theater going—and greed. Those who came to the nation's booming cities seeking "wealth for its own sake" would fall victim to an "absorbing passion" that would "benumb the conscience."[2]

Self-restraint flourished not simply because of religious and moral imperatives, but also because habits of thrift, industry, and deferred gratification served material self-interest. As factory owners liked to remind their employees, sobriety and discipline helped one to get to work on time and to work efficiently. They were productive virtues in an economy of production. Time spent idly was time wasted from the work of self-improvement and making money. Money spent on dissipation could instead be saved and invested. Capitalism would eventually, in the twentieth century, foster a culture of self-indulgence; but successful Victorians constructed a constrained and productive self. "All the real work of life goes hard until you have accustomed yourself to do it," a father advised his son, "and then work often becomes a pleasure."[3]

This emphasis on hard work and self-restraint was not just rhetorical. Alcohol consumption averaged nearly four gallons per person in the early republic but plummeted in the 1830s to less than one gallon.[4] The homicide rate declined after the Civil War in spite of the proliferation of cheap firearms. Violence toward wives and at least some forms of violence toward children (such as whippings in school) also became less common, as did dueling and capital punishment. Couples had far fewer children; the average child per white woman dropped from about 7 to 3.5 during the century. Greater access to contraception and abortion contributed to the declining birth rate, but sexual restraint also played a role. Advice books counseled limiting sexual intercourse to about once per month. The rates of premarital pregnancy also dropped dramatically, this despite the fact that youth enjoyed more independence than during the colonial period.

A widespread ethos of self-restraint constituted the common denominator in the decline in drinking, violence, and sex. The nineteenth century brought "the substitution of *personal* discipline for *community* discipline."[5] The spread of evangelical Christianity provided a strong, internal moral compass. Conversion initiated a lifelong process of sanctification, of disciplining and improving the self. Born in Massachusetts in 1824, Lucy Larcom recalled that the great majority of the children she grew up with "believed that to disobey our parents, to lie or steal, had been forbidden by a Voice which was not to be gainsaid," for "the heavens and earth stood upon firm foundations—upon the Moral Law as taught in the Old Testament and confirmed by the New." Her father quizzed the children on Sunday afternoons from his catechism book. Her more easygoing grandfather treated them "to raisins and peppermints," but also to "rules for good behavior." Even Lucy's name inspired her to do good, as she bore the name of an aunt whose "beautiful character was just such an illumination to my young life as I should most desire mine to be to the lives of others."[6] This emphasis on self-improvement infused middle-class culture throughout the city. A popular guide to literature published in the 1870s bore this title: *Books and Reading: Or What Books Shall I Read and How Shall I Read Them.*[7] The young nation's ambitious young men commonly construed their life histories not so much as a movement from rags to riches as "about the self made into a vehicle for constructive action," with success measured not simply by wealth, but by the capacity to govern or control one's emotions and behavior.[8]

Women played a special role in this work. Colonists had posited women as being a paler version of men: weaker physically, mentally, and spiritually. But the very forces that spread prosperity to the growing middle class allowed families to move women and children from economic production into other areas. Women of means paid more attention to their families' emotional needs, even as the number of children they bore shrank. Middle-class homes, like the women who ran them, became a sort of counterweight to and refuge from the market place. Set back from the street, these increasingly elaborate domiciles tucked their workplaces (kitchens) away from public view and offered parlors stuffed with ornate furniture and art, including perhaps some needlework produced by the women and the girls of the house. These households still demanded a great deal of work. Housewives who enjoyed the services of domestic servants had to supervise them, and most middle-class wives did a great deal of cleaning, cooking, and child care. Men, furthermore, retained a great deal of their authority within the middle-class home and were still deemed to be its head.

Middle-class wives' lives remained circumscribed. Popular novels, notes Barbara Welter, were hard on a woman who "debated her rights or bewailed her wrong in a public place." Such protagonists suffered "a short unhappy life, dementia, death, and a total lack of respect from men or virtuous women were among the milder punishments."[9] Women authors commonly felt a tension between domesticity and writing, for commitment to caring for and nurturing others was supposed to trump such acts of self-expression. White Southern women found it especially difficult to escape the domestic sphere. A woman who grew up in the Ozarks late in the nineteenth century recalled that she had agreed to marry so that she could get away from her parents and because she lacked more attractive options: "I didn't want to get married. I wanted to go to school—off to a girls finishing school. Father could have afforded it, but he would not."[10] The nineteenth-century gendered system of self-restraint consigned women to supporting roles, to raising virtuous sons and obedient daughters who would replicate, in their own adult lives and marriages, entrenched inequality.

But marriage became more companionate and complementary, and love played a larger role in both courtship and marriage for the growing middle class. This emphasis on romance owed something to the changing functions of the family, as emotional components replaced economic ones. Even men's commitment to the marketplace, to making a living, could be interpreted as a way of caring for their families and bringing happiness to their wives and children.

The cult of domesticity offered women some tangible rewards, including a major improvement in material comfort. The prosperity that accompanied and made possible the notion of radically different spheres for women and men brought better food and clothing, more comfortable homes, fewer pregnancies, and a longer and better life. It also offered freedom from some—though by no means all—of the endless round of spinning, mending, weeding, cleaning, and cooking that had made women so essential to colonial economies.

The ideal Victorian wife or mother was pious, pure, domestic, and submissive—and commonly wielded considerable influence through the exercise of these virtues. For starters, "the female world of love and ritual," to borrow Carroll Smith-Rosenberg's phrase, provided a same-sex refuge from men.[11] Daniel Scott Smith argues that middle-class women could use the notion of separate spheres as a sort of "domestic feminism" to limit the frequency of sexual intercourse and pregnancy.[12] The dramatic decline in births added years to women's lifespans and created space for a wider range of activities and interests.

Domesticity also gave women a platform from which to influence men. "Above all," notes E. Anthony Rotundo, "a boy learned from his mother to hold back his aggressions and control his own 'male' energies."[13] Middle-class youth and young men remained with their families of origin much longer than did their poorer counterparts, a strategy that served to lengthen the amount of time they could devote to preparing for a lucrative career rather than being forced at a young age to make a living. When these young men started families of their own, moreover, they were apt to express respect for and even deference to the moral sensibilities of their wives and to focus more on their families than on public service. Ellen Rothman suggests that men married and participated in the formation of families and homes so that "they could re-create the comfort, sympathy, and nurturance they had known in childhood."[14]

Nineteenth-century women, moreover, kept stretching the boundaries of the home. Most women reformers began their work at church. Maternal associations brought women together to pray for their children's salvation and nurturance. Church women might also sponsor missionary work or run an orphanage. Such activities required organizational and administrative skills and often entailed working with and advocating among male church or government officials, tasks that hardly seemed feminine. But the work of prayer, conversion, and child nurture was a logical extension of women's sphere. So was temperance, the most ubiquitous Victorian reform movement. Saloons threatened domestic life by drawing men and their incomes out of the home and fostering violence. Temperance literature featured besotted husbands who arrived home to attack their vulnerable wives and children. For middle-class housewives, then, temperance constituted both an attempt at self-protection and a vehicle for political assertion—all undertaken in the name of defending the home. Such efforts multiplied in the closing decades of the nineteenth century with the creation and growth of the Woman's Christian Temperance Union, whose thousands of chapters tackled everything from saloons to Sabbath observance to prison reform. The Federation of Women's Clubs in the 1890s shifted from "self culture" (teaching each other about great art and literature) to political advocacy in areas such as public health. Women constituted most of the local foot soldiers in the Progressive Era's struggle for improved sanitation, for better sewage treatment, pasteurized milk, and safe food. Again, all of these movements could be understood as domesticity writ large.

Harriet Beecher Stowe, whom Lincoln reputedly deemed "the little lady responsible for starting this war," is a particular strong example of the powerful uses to which domesticity could be put. Its reflexive racism notwithstanding, *Uncle Tom's Cabin* pricked the consciences of thousands of Northerners by describing slavery as an assault on black families. It also featured powerful women. Maternal suasion is a mighty sword in *Uncle Tom's Cabin*. "Her husband and children were her entire world," wrote Stowe of Mrs. Mary Bird, "and in these she ruled more by entreaty and persuasion than by command or argument." Mrs. Bird is appalled to learn that her husband, a Kentucky senator, has supported a law forbidding people to aid escaped slaves. Their argument is interrupted by the arrival of just such a pair, a desperate young woman and the child that she has just learned has been sold. The senator promptly realizes his error and helps the woman and child to escape. Simon Legree, the evil slave holder, is ultimately undone by his memory of "a time when he had been rocked on the bosom of a mother,—cradled with prayers and pious hymns."[15] God and mothers are the powers to be reckoned with in *Uncle Tom's Cabin*, and they do not require political offices to work their transformative power. Life imitated art inasmuch as this book by a wife and mother was the first in the nation's history to sell more than 1 million copies and played a major part in animating moral and political feeling against slavery. The novel, as Jane Tompkins observes, anticipated "the day when the meek—that is to say, women—will inherit the earth." Hence Stowe's *The American Woman's Home*, co-authored with her sister, Catharine Beecher, bore this dedication: "To the Women of America, in whose hands rest the real destinies of the republic." "The family state," asserted the sisters, "is the aptest earthly illustration of the heavenly kingdom, and...woman is its chief minister." Motherhood offered the opportunity and responsibility to shape children and thereby change the nation's trajectory from selfishness to Christian community, to prepare "our whole race for heaven."[16] For Stowe, marriage was a venue for "transcendence of self," even "a means to sanctification."[17] Her husband admitted to being her inferior in that work and confessed that he must learn from her how to contain his baser passions.

As the title of Ann Douglas's study of literature puts it, we can speak of *The Feminization of American Culture* during the nineteenth century, a time in which the writings and sensibilities of middle-class women weighed heavily on the nation's bookshelves and consciences.[18]

Some nineteenth-century women tackled gender inequality head on. Women were active participants in the abolitionist movement that blossomed in the 1830s, and many stepped out of the domestic sphere by organizing and speaking on behalf of slaves. Some drew parallels between the enslavement of African Americans and the slavery of sex. The Seneca Falls Convention of 1848, the first women's rights meeting in the nation's history, produced a document that identified and condemned a long list of inequalities, including married women's loss of property, unequal wages, and lack of access to many professions and the vote. "Nothing is so bad as to be made a thing, as every married woman now is, in the eye of the law," declared Lucy Stone.[19] Women's rights advocates had become bolder by the century's close. Charlotte Perkins Gilman in *Women and Economics*, published in 1898, asserted that the notion of separate spheres for women and men had distorted and impoverished the lives of each, and she anticipated a world in which white women would be freed from the domestic grind of child care, cooking, and cleaning to pursue more rewarding work and economic independence. Indeed, by that time, a substantial number of young women were choosing professional careers and deferring or eschewing marriage. Most worked as educators or nurses; hundreds were becoming doctors and attorneys. Eighty-eight women had graduated from the University of Michigan medical school by 1890, many more from women's medical colleges. Few of these women followed Gilman in explicitly condemning domesticity. But the mere presence of professional women implied an embrace of individual rights. After all, the nineteenth century brought not just domesticity, but the abolition of slavery, a decline in capital and corporate punishment, and more humane treatment of asylum residents and prisoners, developments that reflected a growing sensitivity to justice and even equality. Michael Grossberg argues that the nation's legal foundation shifted from a patriarchal view, in which the father represented and constituted the family, to a model more sensitive to the rights of discrete and varied family members.[20]

The limits of Victorian women's reform movements become clear when examining subjects related to sexuality. Few feminists asserted publicly a right to contraception in the nineteenth century—even as women privately succeeded in dramatically decreasing the number of children they bore. Lower fertility rates were to be achieved through controlling men's sexual tyranny, not by uncoupling sex from reproduction. Women's capacity to nurture constituted, even for most women's-rights advocates, the heart of woman's power. For the same reason, few middle-class women defended prostitution; they instead sought to restrain men's sexuality. At best, prostitutes were victims. At worst, they were part of the problem.

Even professional single women of the late nineteenth century gilded themselves with domesticity. Jane Addams was the unmarried head of Hull House, a settlement-house complex that eventually covered four square blocks in South Chicago. Though an adept administrator, publicist, and political activist, the nation knew this single, childless career woman as "mother of the world." Addams burnished her maternal credentials by answering the door to Hull House herself and working with the neighborhood's children at her skirts.

Women reformers who abjured marriage commonly formed very intense, family-like communities with other women. A study of single nineteenth-century women concludes that to them, "*liberty* conveyed neither a sense of libertinism or libertarianism." Rather, "freedom enabled her to commit her life and her capacities to the betterment of her sex, her community, or her kin."[21] Lucy Stone, who married only after years of resistance, had these final words for her daughter: "Make the world better." Susan B. Anthony believed that marriage inevitably interfered with women's ability to do the hard work of improving the world. She died with the names of the women she had spent decades working with on her lips. "Young and old, living or dead, they all seemed to file past her dying eyes that day in an endless, shadowy review, and as they went, by she spoke to each of them," recalled Anna Howard Shaw.[22]

For women like Addams, Stone, and Anthony, the cult of domesticity cheated women and the world, not by insisting that women focus on serving others, but by limiting the extent of that service. The purpose of life was to make the world better, and they undertook that work with a band of like-minded sisters—their families of choice. Many reform-minded women had attended women's colleges, institutions that grew throughout the nineteenth century, particularly after the Civil War. These schools, notes Robyn Muncy, engendered "a peculiarly female culture that emphasized humility, relationships, care, and service."[23]

Most middle-class women expressed satisfaction with their work within the home and found the work of nurturing their children to be a satisfying and important sphere. But married and single middle-class women alike agreed that service to others constituted the heart and purpose of life.

Middle-class men expressed much more ambivalence over the strictures of domesticity than did their wives or sisters. Until late in the century, intimations of this disease came out obliquely, in rituals and through literature. Victorian fraternal orders such as the Masons, Odd Fellows, and Improved Order of Red Men offered bloody, pre-Christian ceremonies that drew tens of thousands of middle-class men. The initiation ritual created in 1868 for the Red Men, for example, required the initiate to be apprehended by a sleeping band of "Indians," who threatened him with torture and accused him of being a fearful "squaw" who "fears a Warrior's death!"[24] They then bound the candidate to a stake and began a scalp dance. After proving his courage, he received an eagle feather and membership in the order. The Odd Fellows had initiates play the part of Isaac and then prepared to sacrifice them to God. Just as Abraham was about to put his torch to the altar, a gong sounded; God had decided to spare the victim. Much male literature expressed ambivalence or outright hostility toward respectability and femininity. Henry David Thoreau referred to a husband's house as "a prison, in which he finds himself oppressed and confined."[25] The men in Herman Melville's *Moby Dick* are solitary existentialists wrestling for meaning on a trackless ocean of complexities. Huck Finn sets out his raft to escape smothering women. The protagonist in Edgar Allan Poe's "The Black Cat," buries an axe in his wife's brain when she tries to stop him from killing a cat whose "evident fondness for myself rather disgusted and annoyed me."[26]

Indeed, it was outside marriage that males could most fully express their disdain for femininity and its associated norms of respectability and self-restraint. Middle-class boys maintained a culture of "sociable sadism," of brutal games and pastimes that ostentatiously violated feminine norms.[27] Bachelors eschewed the constraints of domesticity for gambling, saloons, and brothels—or at least for good food, books, and cigars. *Reveries of a Bachelor*, published in 1850, averred that a man should not trade the freedom "to chase his fancies over the wide world" for the toils of a "relentless marriage."[28] Unlike single, middle-class women, who commonly traded marriage for a more intense, often reformist, form of domesticity, bachelors embraced single life as an opportunity to pursue pleasure.

But men expressed this dissenting note sotto voce. It was not uncommon for respectable nineteenth-century men to sneak off to brothels and saloons. But they seldom disputed openly the dictates of domesticity. To do so would have involved more than insulting women and the family. It would have called the very foundations of prosperity and success into question. The so-called feminine virtues of self-restraint and deferred gratification served both corporate and private ends.

The antebellum South succeeded in being an integral part of the industrial world without participating very much in the bourgeois social and cultural revolutions that accompanied it. Cotton constituted a crucial and growing part of the nation's exports and was essential to Northern industrialization, for textiles constituted the heart of early manufacturing. But this manufacturing occurred outside the South, which remained overwhelmingly agricultural. In 1800, 70 and 82 percent of Northern and Southern workers, respectively, labored in agriculture. In 1860, the percentages stood at 40 and 84 percent. The South also lagged far behind the North in urbanization, immigration, manufacturing, and railroad construction. Its children attended school about one-fifth as often as did their Northern counterparts. Nearly one-half of its whites were illiterate in 1850.[29] The Second Great Awakening touched Southern as well as Northern hearts, but in different ways. Pious Southerners were much less attracted to moral reform or perfectionism. Temperance societies were rare, and abolitionists and women's rights advocates were actively discouraged.

Slavery played a crucial role in the traditional cast of the South. The ownership of slaves constituted a fundamental and growing economic divider. More than one-third (36 percent) of white families owned slaves in 1830, whereas just one-fourth (25 percent) owned them in 1860. The value of the average slave doubled in the 1850s; a person who owned two slaves and nothing else was as wealthy as the average Northerner. Southern slave owners controlled at least 90 percent of their region's wealth by 1850. Slave owners became less apologetic over their "peculiar institution" as slavery grew more profitable and Northern critiques of it more pointed. Slavery constituted a positive, moral good; it was part of a hierarchical society that was knit together by bonds of obligation and obedience characterized, in the words of Eugene Genovese, by "social stratification and interdependence." The language of personal rights—a concept that fuelled the abolitionist movement—sounded alien and subversive. Elizabeth Fox-Genovese notes that white, slave-owning women believed in an ordered community characterized by "an obliteration or softening of the boundaries between egos," of the "self as bound to others."[30] An Alabama pastor explained: "The *good* of the family limited the *rights* of each member."[31] Patriarchy entailed dominance over slaves and wives alike. "To submit to a blow would be degrading to a freeman, "wrote the prominent slavery apologist William Harper, "because he is the protector of himself." Women and slaves did not enjoy that status and therefore could not be degraded by physical discipline. Louisa Susanna Cheves McCord declared that "Enfranchisement of Woman" was "but a piece with negro emancipation." Southern "conservatives" accepted that there were "God-given distinctions of sex and race."[32]

The antebellum Southern home in fact remained patriarchal. Plantation owners "dispense with the whole machinery of public police and public courts of justice. Thus we try, decide, and execute the sentences in thousands of cases, which in other countries would go to the courts."[33] In the words of historian Steven Stowe, Southern patriarchs "exercised the power inherent in family position, not the intimacy that clouded judgment."[34] In theory, they were paternalists who cared for and protected the women, children, and slaves under their care. Husbands who neglected or abused their families were subjected to community discipline, including whippings. But community members—including law-enforcement officials—hesitated to intervene in the lives of prominent men, especially. Southern courts were less sympathetic than Northern ones toward incest victims. More than a few Southern men, rich and poor, were chaste and temperate, just as there were middle-class men in the North who were not. But Southern men had more latitude than Northern men did. Though their mothers and wives might not like it, most felt that they had tacit permission to fornicate, drink, gamble, and to enjoy dog and cock fighting. A pair of men in the Deep South happily proclaimed that they lived like "fighting cocks."[35]

Honor was the key characteristic of Southern manhood, and honor required exterior rather than interior validation. One must react promptly to any hint of disrespect, from being called a liar to suffering the humiliation of a man refusing to let you treat him to a drink. Gentlemen "settled" such insults through ritualistic duels. The aggrieved party demanded a public retraction or an apology. If his opponent refused, he could insist on the "satisfaction" of a duel. After often-lengthy negotiations that were carried on between friends or "seconds," the two parties would meet and shoot at each other (with identical firearms, or dueling pistols). These duels seldom led to death. One or both parties might fire into the air—or simply miss. But duels had to involve the risk of death, as it was the willingness (and freedom) to risk death that set white men of means apart from everyone else.

Men routinely averred that Southern white women were the opposite of their hot-blooded, virile husbands. "Evangelicals, particularly evangelical ministers, often spoke as though women could do little wrong," notes historian Ted Ownby.[36] But unlike Northern women, who parlayed their purported moral superiority into a larger role inside and outside the home, Southern women were expected to marry and to submit to their husbands, to bear many children, and to tolerate their husbands' infidelities and other shortcomings without complaint.

The white women of Virginia tended to enjoy more autonomy than did their counterparts of the Deep South. The white women of Petersburg, Virginia—a substantial city by Southern standards—had a distinctive culture. Those who wrote wills were more likely than men to play favorites rather than divide their estates evenly between their heirs, and they were more likely than men to free their slaves. The city's women organized an orphan asylum by 1814, a House of Industry in the 1830s, and a second orphanage in the 1840s. They constituted between 65–80 percent of the city's church members and organized several women's groups within those churches. But once married—and everyone was supposed to get married—they were at the mercy of their husbands. A more mutualistic marriage depended on husbands' "willingness to refrain from using the many clubs his society handed him."[37]

White Virginia women joined a growing array of voluntary associations in the early nineteenth century: church groups, of course, but also orphanages, temperance organizations, and even colonization societies dedicated to resettling African Americans in West Africa. By 1835, women comprised roughly one-half of the members of Virginia's hundred temperance societies.[38] But colonization and temperance groups subsided as sectional tensions increased.

The Civil War and its aftermath both underscored and undermined Southern patriarchy. The war required women to assume larger economic roles and more domestic authority than before, as did the poverty that persisted after the war for so many families. The war also revealed Southern white men's shortcomings and exacerbated their fears of reform. Even before the war, notes Anne Firor Scott, "Southern men often identified the work of the hated abolitionists with the work of 'strong-minded' northern women."[39] Southern white men's acute fears of black autonomy and sexuality led them to both lynch thousands of African American men and to restrict the movement of white women. Most of the adjustments in gender roles forced by the war proved to be temporary.

But the Civil War's outcome undermined much of the economic and social foundations of Southern patriarchy, and the region began to more closely resemble the rest of the nation. Governments increasingly assumed the power once wielded by family heads in areas such as education, labor, and health. Southern courts more frequently awarded divorced mothers custody of children, though they remained reluctant to grant divorces. Women's temperance societies and clubs appeared late in the century in some parts of the South. The numbers of women teachers rose as more schools opened. Southern states passed laws against drinking, swearing, and animal cruelty.[40] The abolition of slavery and associated economic shifts served to make white Southern families and society more like their Northern counterparts, though the region remained the nation's most conservative one.

Though settled later than the South, the Western United States more quickly adopted modern economic and social patterns—though not at first.

A masculine ethos dominated the most recently settled parts of the nation during the nineteenth century, from Illinois to California to the Great Plains. Most '49ers went to the California gold fields without their wives; the opportunity to get rich quickly justified leaving one's wife and children behind to fend for themselves. If husbands wanted their wives to come along to homestead, wives had little choice but to follow; those who stayed behind could be sued for desertion. Frontier women were outnumbered and often isolated. The hard work of making a living meant, as during the colonial period, that the great majority spent all of their waking hours keeping their families fed, clothed, and otherwise cared for. Men were much more likely than women to travel to other homes or to town. Abigail Scott Duniway, who would become the leading woman's rights advocate of the Pacific Northwest, recalled a life in the foothills of the Willamette Valley characterized by isolation and grinding physical labor. She "milked enough with my two hands to float the Great Eastern [a steam boat] and . . . made butter enough for market . . . to grease the axles of creation." She later averred that "a woman's right to butcher hogs was one which we would ever after willingly delegate to the men."[41] True, frontier women were more apt than their Eastern counterparts to operate lucrative businesses, particularly in mining areas where men were willing to pay a great deal of money for good food and clean clothes. But skewed sex ratios more commonly prompted vulnerability. During Virginia City's silver boom of the 1870s and 1880s, prostitutes outnumbered school teachers 9:1 and suffered from high rates of suicide, poverty, violence, and drug addiction. The majority of frontier women were of course not prostitutes, but they usually married very young, often to men two or three times their age. "What could a girl of 14 do to protect herself from a man of 44?" lamented an Oregon woman whose husband "used to beat me until I thought I couldn't stand it."[42]

Men liked the West more than women did. The overland journey was a male rite of passage, an opportunity to "see the elephant," to live among the buffalo, the Indians, and the mountains of the fabled frontier. For women, moving West meant leaving kin and neighbors, often with no hope of ever seeing them again. It also meant surrendering, for Lord only knew how long, the hard-won symbols of domesticity and swapping the conveniences of homes with wood floors and glass windows for months of travel in a bone-jarring, dusty wagon, which was followed by years in a cramped log cabin or sod hut. "When women wrote of the decision to leave their homes," observes Lillian Schlissel, "it was almost always with anguish, a note conspicuously absent from the diaries of men."[43]

But domesticity soon arrived across the Midwest and the West, and for the same reason that it had arrived earlier in the Northeast: the economy matured. In Sugar Creek, Illinois, farmers shifted from subsistence farming to market farming in the 1840s, and the birth rate fell from 8.2 to 5.9 in one generation.[44] The home manufacture of cloth declined as store-bought cloth became less expensive. Prosperous farm wives turned their attention to reforming men's most objectionable habits, particularly drunkenness and prostitution. They re-created the cult of domesticity that they had left behind.

The shifting nature of violence against wives underscores the transformations in gender roles that accompanied prosperity and domesticity. The captain of an 1845 wagon train responded to an argument between two women by advising their husbands "to give . . . his wife A good licking that nite not over the Back But not far from the ass and all wod bee well."[45] Husbands might cut a switch to punish their wives with, as if they were disciplining a wayward child. However, by the 1890s, Pacific Northwest husbands described themselves and were described by others as being much less ready to claim a right to hit their wives, and their violent acts seemed much less deliberate.

Western children's lives underwent a similar transformation. Children's labor, like that of their mothers', was extremely important to early settlers. But these settlers also asserted a right to beat children into submission. The directors of a Willamette Valley school told an applicant in 1865 that they were primarily interested in whether or not he could "lick the big boys." He proved able: "If the rod didn't do the work I used my fists or a club." Three decades later, community members expected more restraint. One teacher was fined $5.00 for slapping a student.[46]

Violence between men also declined in the West late in the nineteenth century, just as it had in the East. Tuolumne County, a mining district in California, was 95 percent male in the 1850s and had an extremely high homicide rate: 129 per 100,000. In the 1870s, men made up 71.5 percent of the county, and the homicide rate had fallen to 41 per 100,000. Two decades later men comprised 61 percent of the population, and the homicide rate fell to 26.6 per 100,000.[47]

Violence declined as sex ratios approached parity, not simply because women were less apt to use violence than men. Women's presence reflected broad socioeconomic changes, which stimulated an ethos of self-restraint, and women used their domestic credentials to demand that their communities become more humane and restrained. Growing criticism of violence toward women and children in the West and a declining homicide rate mirrored earlier developments in the East: an economy that required a more disciplined workforce and a society and culture that emphasized the domestic virtues of self-restraint and respect for women and children. The growing power of women outside the home—carried out in the name of protecting the home—feminized the West as it had feminized the Northeast.

* * *

Herman Melville did not fit comfortably into the Victorian middle class. His family of origin was downwardly rather than upwardly mobile. His father was fleeing creditors upon a death that cut short his son's education, and Herman went to sea for several years. Living on whaling ships and among aborigines of the South Pacific brought Melville out of the cocoon of middle-class life. His first book, *Typee*, expressed his attraction to freer forms of sexuality. He characterized a Yankee lady as "a milliner's doll" in contrast to the "savage maidens" of the islands.[48] But Melville returned to his mother and sisters and in 1847 married the very respectable Elizabeth Shaw before settling down to write.

Melville never got the South Pacific out of his system. He realized that the verities his religious mother had raised him with were bogus, that at the center of existence was the "howling infinite" rather than a just and benevolent deity. "The freshness of primeval nature is in that man," remarked Sophia Hawthorne. *Moby Dick* constituted Melville's greatest attempt to illustrate the problematic human prospect. His narrator speaks casually of going to sea as "my substitute for pistol and ball," for simply doing himself in.[49]

Few readers understood the impulse. *Moby Dick* is now widely admired as the great American novel. It brought Melville little money or fame in his day. "Try to get a living by the Truth—and go to the Soup Societies," he complained to Nathaniel Hawthorne.[50] Even Hawthorne, another author who delved into the underside of the American soul, found Melville too intense.

Melville struggled as a husband and as a father. His wife was devoted to him and, like many women of her station and time, not much interested in sex. Little firsthand evidence of their marriage remains, but many of Melville's protagonists are sexually frustrated, and Melville may have been attracted to men as well as to less inhibited native women such as the sensuous Fayaway of *Typee*. Descendants of the couple claimed that Melville struck and otherwise abused Elizabeth to the point that she twice planned to leave him. He was hard on his sons, the eldest of whom committed suicide at home.

Melville set aside his literary ambitions at the close of the Civil War to take a routine job for the U.S. Customs Service. He left behind, for subsequent and less-settled generations, a record of discontent with the intellectual and sexual strictures of his day and depictions of the human prospect that were at once exhilarating and terrifying.

A more feminine ethos dominated Melville's era. Mothers lost few opportunities to inculcate habits of self-restraint in their children, women authors did the same for a national audience, and thousands of women reformers applied domestic values to a widening public sphere.

These efforts could not have succeeded if they had not coincided with the requirements of larger interests, particularly the imperatives of industrial capitalism. Habits of self-restraint served both individual workers and the broader economy. In Marxist terms, the superstructure (culture) rested on a foundation (economy) that shared the same characteristics. Hence the antebellum South embraced both a traditional economy and society, and the West both rejected slavery and eventually embraced domesticity.

Yet many groups across the nation remained outside the sphere of these new, middle-class norms. Both culture and circumstance shaped their families.

Chapter 5

Necessity and Tradition

Prosperity fueled the transformation of the middle-class family during the nineteenth century. It shifted the structural foundations of the family by drawing men out of the home and reducing other family members' economic contributions. But wives' social roles expanded as their economic roles receded. The production-oriented ethos of self-restraint, a broad emphasis on morality and deferred gratification, gave women considerable influence inside and outside the family to create a nation of productive and virtuous citizens.

Families who remained outside the growing middle class relied on each other out of necessity and tradition. Racism, poverty, and other hardships commonly fragmented families and communities, but they also placed a premium on obligation and cooperation.

* * *

The fact of slavery dominated the lives of most black families for most of the nineteenth century. North American slavery differed from Caribbean and Brazilian varieties. By the mid-eighteenth century it had become a Creole institution; once the slave population reproduced itself, slaves became African Americans rather than Africans living in America. Slaves living in the United States were more apt than their Jamaican counterparts to speak English and to be Christians. Whites who owned a few slaves worked alongside them. On large plantations, white children commonly grew up being nursed and otherwise looked after by black women and playing with black children.

Slavery in the United States was more paternalistic than it was elsewhere. It was good business for planters to be concerned about their slaves' physical welfare; plantation agriculture in the United States tended to be less lucrative than it was in the Caribbean, where slaves could be profitably worked to death and easily replaced with newcomers from Africa. By the 1830s, slave owners in the United States commonly claimed to love their slaves and asserted that they treated them better than Northern factory owners treated their workers. Most slave states passed laws against the selling of children under the age of ten, thereby preventing a separation between them and their mothers. Slaveholders often ignored such laws, to be sure. But many slave owners sincerely believed that they held their slaves' best interests at heart. Historians have found that many slaves—in a variety of sources—expressed some affection for their masters, even as they, the slaves, condemned slavery.

Paternalism had an underside. Southern slavery was mild only in comparison to even more brutal slave societies, and expressions of paternalism did not preclude brutal acts. The same owner who lamented the death (in 1857) of Fanny, a sixty-eight-year-old slave who "was a good and faithful servant" and who left behind "many children and grandchildren to mourn her loss," had also sold Fanny's daughter away from her.[1] Southern slaves were commonly whipped or otherwise tortured, cruelties that were witnessed by traumatized spouses, parents, and children, who agonized over how to help their loved ones. A Georgia slave was bold enough to cut the ropes that bound his wife to the tree she had been whipped at—but he waited until dark to do so. Antebellum Southern slavery rested on an assumption of racial superiority and lifelong bondage. Slaves were ultimately property. Wrote David Gavin upon the death of a slave infant, "This is two Negroes and three horses I have lost this year."[2] About one-half of slave children died by the age of one, which was roughly twice the rate at which white children died in the South. Those who survived faced an abrupt, harrowing transition from relatively carefree childhoods, in which their masters might treat them indulgently and allow fraternization with their own children, to the day when they had to go to work for the rest of their lives. Robert Ellett recalled growing up "with the young masters," playing, eating, and even sleeping with them. Life changed the day that he refused to call his playmates "masters," and "the old master carried me in the barn and tied me up and whipped me…till the blood run down." Southern slavery carried itsown brand of cruelty. The relatively small number of large holdings meant that many slaves could not find spouses on their plantations. The fact that slave owners took an interest in slave children—by naming them, for example—angered slave parents. "During slavery it seemed lakyo' chillunb'long to ev'ybody but you," remarked one.[3] Historians disagree over the extent to which paternalism affected slaves, the extent to which they were able to lead lives in the cabin that were separate from their owners' lives. But certainly, Southern slaves had less privacy (including sexual privacy) than their counterparts in many parts of the Americas. White owners commonly tried to compel male and female slaves to breed with one another or forced themselves on the female slaves sexually.

Concubinage and rape exacted a terrible toll on slave marriages and slave communities. Nathan Sayre, who became judge of the Georgia Superior Court, kept his free African American mistress and their three children in a secret apartment and had the children educated. But this was exceptional. The great majority of white fathers did not acknowledge their black children and evidently felt no obligations whatsoever to them or to the children's mothers. Slave communities often integrated and accepted the children of these relationships. But then again, they might not. Patience M. Avery, whose biological father was white, claimed: "I ain't got no father," that the "buzzards laid me an' de sun hatch me; an' she [mother] came 'long an' pick me up."[4] Celia, a young Missouri slave, suffered from the attacks of a rapist master, Robert Newsom, and her slave lover demanded that she stop having intercourse with her master. She threatened to harm Newsom if he did not desist. He dismissed the warning, and she clubbed him to death upon his next nocturnal visit. The nineteen-year-old mother of two was hanged for this. Slave women were also vulnerable to the displaced vengeance of white wives. A former slave remembered a "white lady" who "slipped in a colored gal's room and cut her baby's head clean off 'cause it belonged to her husband.'" The husband nevertheless "'kept going' with the colored gal and they had more chillun."[5] Most enslaved husbands felt helpless to defend their wives. "What we saw, couldn't do nothing 'bout it," recalled one.[6] Another husband and father decided to run away, as it was "hard to see them [his family] in want and abused when he was not at liberty to aid or protect them."[7] Some husbands tried their best to shield their wives. Others took out their shame and frustration on them—or pursued their own extramarital sexual relationships, consensual or otherwise.

The constant threat of family disruption was the most harrowing aspect of Southern slavery. The invention of the cotton gin and the defeat and expulsion of indigenous nations opened up the Deep South to extensive settlement and slavery. Some 1 million slaves had forcibly migrated by 1860, movements that fractured countless families. Historians estimate that slave sales separated about one-third of spouses from each other and one-half of children from at least one parent in the Upper South. Virginia slave narratives indicate that 82 percent of slave children had regular contact with a mother for most of their childhood and 42 percent with a father, though about one-third of those fathers lived apart from the child. The move to the Deep South constituted a sort of second "middle passage" that tore families apart in much the same way that the trip across the Atlantic had done. Few who were sold "down the river" could hope to see their families, who remained in the East. "Every time we look back and think 'bout home,'" remembered a Texan sold from Virginia, "it make us sad." Another former slave spoke of "one of de saddest songs we sungen durin' slavery days":

> "Mammy, is Ol' Massa gwin' er sell us tomorrow?"
> "Yes, my chile."
> "What he gwin'er sell us?"
> "Way down South in Georgia."

"It always did make me cry," she concluded.[8] When a sale separated Moses Grandy from his wife, his "heart was so full that I could say very little" to her. "I gave her the little money I had in my pocket, and bade her farewell. I have never seen or heard of her from that day to this. I loved her as I loved my life."[9] Another man "trembled lest some day he should go home, and find one of his little ones gone or his wife sold."[10] The masters' sons might want to strike out on their own, to head West with some slaves. Masters could be tempted by the growing profits of the slave trade or die at any moment, eventualities that ordinarily meant dividing an estate that slaves were the most valuable parts of.

How did slaves, individually and collectively, come to terms with these cruelties? Certainly not by denying them. A minister who came to the Sea Islands of South Carolina in 1862 observed that "the wild, sad strains" of the slave songs told "of crushed hopes, keen sorrow, and a dull daily misery."[11] The blues are descended from this tradition of recording grief honestly and cleanly. On the other hand, Christianity—the religion that most slaves had embraced as their own by the nineteenth century—gave slaves hope: hope in a heaven in which they would be reunited with all of their loved ones; hope that there would come a day of reckoning and judgment in which the last would be first and first would be last. Slaves commonly asserted among themselves that they were the Israelites, God's chosen and wandering people, who could look forward to a special dispensation in the next world—and perhaps in this one as well. They created a form of Christianity that offered them a sense of dignity and purpose in the midst of their suffering. They also formed a separate community—physically and emotionally—from their masters. The "religion of the quarters" was different from the religion of the whites. Behind closed doors, away from the eyes and ears of white masters and overseers, slaves prayed, talked, and sang much differently than they did in the fields or in the big house. Julia Frazier of Virginia learned as a young girl that it was well and good to sing a song poking fun of the master "all roun' de cabin," but not in his company.[12]

The slave family stood at the heart of the slave community. The great majority of slaves lived in nuclear households and embraced marriage and parenthood—notwithstanding the inevitable and acute vulnerabilities that they entailed. "I sought to love...with a full knowledge of the desperate agony that the slave husband and father is exposed to," wrote Tom Jones. "I sought to become a husband and father because I felt that I could live no longer unloved and unloving."[13] The inherently unstable nature of slaves' romantic and sexual relationships put a premium on flexibility. Young slaves might engage in several years of "sweet hearting," a phase that could entail having children but not necessarily being monogamous. Or they might spend some time "taking up" or living together, instead of or before marrying.[14]

This is not to say that slaves did not take marriage and other familial relations seriously. Rather, less committed forms of coupling reflected the contingent reality of all slave relationships. Fathers, much more likely to live away from their children than mothers, commonly walked many hours every week to spend time with their families. Those who lived with their families might hide upon hearing word of a planned sale of their children and consent to return only if the sale was cancelled. Mothers were more apt to beg for mercy. Slaveholders might relent, not simply out of pity, but because bereaved mothers—and other slaves—could refuse to work or become violent or suicidal. Young Thomas Johns of Alabama told his new owner, who was about to take him to Texas, that he could not "leave de only mother I got. I jus' cain' do dat." His new master relented.[15]

Most masters were less accommodating, but most slaves persisted in taking their family commitments very seriously.

The flexible, matrifocal familial practices of West Africa were ideally suited to such circumstances. Slaves tolerated premarital sexual explorations. They expected fidelity after marriage—if their masters would permit it—but attached no great stigma to divorce. Several women commonly shared a husband in West Africa, and such women operated their households and raised their children with a great deal of autonomy. In the United States, husbands and fathers were often absent, but not by choice. But here, too, strong, capable women resided at the heart of the home, and the slaves celebrated their children and the women who bore them. The mother-child bond often trumped marriage, and slaves practiced extensive forms of kinship. Children constituted a gift to the entire community whom everyone could and should play a role in raising. If biological parents could not be present, aunts, uncles, siblings, grandparents, and fictive kin usually stepped forward. Historian Herbert Gutman estimates that most slaves had a grandchild named after them. Though most slaves lived in nuclear families, households with extended kin—particularly adult siblings—were not unusual. Community and kinship stretched beyond the walls of homes and even the boundaries of plantations. By the turn of the nineteenth century, the great majority of slaves had long ago ceased to be Akan, Ibo, or Fulani and instead identified themselves as a distinctive race of people whose home had become the United States. But it was families, in the words of Deborah Gray White, that "enabled slaves to create an identity that went beyond that assigned by whites."[16]

These families were often scarred by violence. Many slaves beat their children, violence that prepared the latter for lives in which failure to obey authority could bring death. Violence also underscored parent's authority and expressed their rage and pain. Whippings often continued after slavery ended. Sojourner Truth beat her children to make them quiet and obedient. Slaves who had witnessed and borne violence could not simply set such experiences aside. "There is evidence that the child abuse of slavery imposed enormous costs," concludes Nell Irvin Painter.[17]

The end of slavery underscored how dearly former slaves cared about their families. As slaves fled their homes to enlist in the military, notes Ira Berlin, "they insisted their families be freed."[18] Liberated slaves in Louisiana who were recruited by the Union insisted that a record be kept "of their wives [and] children . . . to prevent such a separation as will result in their not knowing where their families are."[19] Thousands of former slaves took to the roads of the South in search of children, spouses, parents, or other relatives whom they had not seen for years or for decades. They also battled with former slaveholders and Northern bureaucrats who tried to claim the labor of black youths. "[I]n every case where I have bound out children," complained an agent of the Freedmen's Bureau, "[s]ome Grand Mother or fortieth cousin has come to have them released."[20] The former slaves protested that their children were being consigned "back into slavery."[21] "The idea of 'freedom' of independence, of calling their wives and their children, and little hut their *own*, was a soul animating one, that buoyed up their spirits," observed a Northern missionary.[22] An 1866 census in a Virginia county found that more than one-half of black families included wives, husbands, parents, or children who had lived apart three years before that date.[23]

Freedom brought new forms of stress. Some spouses who had been separated by slavery found that one or both had remarried and had started new families. One such woman spoke ofthe heartache this caused: "White folk's got a heap to answer for the way they've done to colored folks! So much they won't never *pray* it away."[24] Husbands and wives had to learn how to live together under different circumstances. Most former slave women contested not husbands' authority, but their abuse of or neglect of that responsibility. One insisted that men "be made to help support" their families.[25] Rosa Freeman complained that her husband, David, "has abused me & refused to pay for the rent of my room & has not furnished me with any money, food or clothing." Indeed, David wanted a separation, rather than a divorce, as a divorce would cost him money. Rosa demurred: "if you want to leave me; leave me like a man!"[26] Violence remained common. A man born in Mississippi recalled that men at the turn of the twentieth century spent much of their time "knocking"—hitting each other to see "who could absorb the most punishment."[27]

Yet free blacks often tried to approximate the norms of middle-class domesticity. Men commonly attempted to establish themselves as household heads or even as patriarchs, a position systematically denied them under slavery. Women often avoided outside employment. Shunning domestic work in white homes removed them from sexual danger and enabled them to focus on nurturing their own families. "House servants are difficult to get out here," remarked a Georgia observer. "Every negro woman wants to set up house keeping." Keeping house, like dressing in fine clothes, expressed the freedom to make choices long denied. "The freedman," noted a Georgia newspaper in 1869, "have almost universally withdrawn their women and children from the fields, putting the first at housework [at home] and the latter at school."[28] The black fertility rate fell dramatically after slavery, from close to eight children per woman in the 1850s to less than six children in 1900 to less than four children by 1920. Like their white counterparts, free blacks associated the limiting of births with economic opportunity.

Poverty commonly drove black women into the workforce. Free Southern blacks before the Civil War had generally favored marriages in which husbands earned a living and wives remained in the home. But most free black women had then earned money, and households headed by them were often desperately poor. The overwhelming majority of employed black women worked as domestics at jobs that required them to be away from home for long hours or even for days at a time. Many husbands were uncomfortable with this. One father of six told his wife: "I workin' makin' enough to support you. All I want you to do is keep dis house clean and me and my chillun."[29] But his wife sometimes did wage work behind his back to augment the family's income without wounding his pride. Male-headed African American families were most common in the rural cotton belt, female-headed ones most common in cities where women could find more jobs. But black women commonly worked outside the home even in rural areas. Nearly 40 percent of black women did so in three Texas counties in 1870 compared to just 1 percent of white women.[30]

Flexible family forms remained a necessity for most free blacks. If black families were more apt than white ones to break under the strain of poverty and racism, they also reconstituted themselves in myriad ways. White Northerners who came South in the 1860s, "heard blacks calling each other 'aunt,' 'uncle,' 'brother,' 'sister,' or 'cousin,' seemingly at random."[31] Kin—biological and fictive—performed a wide range of services. Women opened accounts in Freedman's Banks for stepmothers and mothers-in-law. Black families were more likely than white ones to incorporate people who could not contribute much wealth to the household, such as elderly mothers or orphaned children or unemployed kin. African American families cared for the old, the infirm, and the parentless long after institutions had assumed those roles for whites.

Successful African Americans had championed the Victorian virtues of domesticity and deferred gratification well before the Civil War. A black newspaper in New York City urged its women readers in 1829 to "endear home by temper, order, and cleanliness."[32] Black leaders by that time were advising men to move beyond manual labor into skilled trades and other occupations that would cultivate "wealth, virtue, and honor."[33] Temperance became a key component of this endeavor. Austin Steward marked the final emancipation of New York slaves in 1827 by pointing out that "INDUSTRY, PRUDENCE, AND ECONOMY came with freedom. Alcohol undermined health, wealth and happiness." "How can we expect to rise in the scale of moral being," asked a trio of black leaders twelve years later, "unless we are a temperate, sober, and industrious people?" New York's Abyssinian Benevolent Daughters of Esther Association closed its membership to women who used alcohol. Northern whites abhorred black temperance societies precisely because of this association of temperance and respectability. After white Philadelphians attacked a black temperance parade and burned the Smith Beneficial Hall and the Second Colored Presbyterian Church in 1842, city leaders ordered that a brick building used for temperance meetings be torn down, for it represented "the social and economic progress of the black community" that many whites found intolerable. But African Americans persisted. By 1842 Philadelphia had ten black temperance societies. "No one who wished to lay claim to respectability would dare serve liquor at a public function or be seen at a tippling house," concludes historian Donald Yacovone. Boston's blacks became divided between those who lived in the rough-and-tumble North End and the more respectable, family-oriented families of "the hill." Hence a North-end man named Fletcher who had caroused in his youth changed his ways when he "got married, got religion and moved to the hill."[34]

Frederick Douglass, the most prominent black leader of the nineteenth century, presented himself as the quintessential self-made man. Like white men on the make, Douglass perceived temperance as part of a cluster of virtues that successful men must cultivate. He associated liquor with slavery. The slaveowners drank to numb themselves to the cruelty they inflicted on their slaves, and they plied the slave with alcohol "to silence or drown his mind."[35] Like Lincoln, Douglass spent much of his childhood immersed in books designed to inculcate character. His favorite was a collection of Whig oratory. Douglass's most popular speech, delivered more than fifty times between 1859 and 1893, was "Self-Made Men." He celebrated men who pulled themselves up "by their own bootstraps," men who were "not only without the voluntary assistance or friendly co-operation of society, but often in open and derisive defiance of all the efforts of society and the tendency of circumstances to repress, retard, and keep them down."[36] He became estranged from the Garrisonian wing of the abolition movement in part because they found him too polished a speaker and wanted him to keep "a little of the plantation."[37]

Booker T. Washington, who supplanted Douglass as the leading African American late in the nineteenth century, presented a more accommodating façade but also emphasized that hard work and discipline were crucial to racial uplift. His entrance exam to the Hampton Normal and Agricultural Institute took the form of cleaning a room (he swept it three times and dusted it four times).[38] At Tuskegee Institute he perpetuated this emphasis on hard work, moral uplift, and deferred gratification. By the century's turn, even impoverished black families tended to keep children in school longer than did their immigrant counterparts.

African Americans by the nineteenth century had developed a coherent culture that incorporated many aspects of mainstream culture, and once slavery ended, the great majority lived in stable families.

Immigrant families both resembled and differed from African American families. They came to the United States voluntarily, even at the cost of leaving family, and most brought with them high hopes. But most came to a place whose language and culture was alien and where they often faced prejudice and discrimination. Anglo Americans did not consider the Irish to be white for most of the nineteenth century, and by the late nineteenth century the former were still more alarmed about immigrants from Asia and Southern and Eastern Europe. Most immigrants found life in the United Stated to be very difficult.

Most immigrants were pushed out of their homelands by factors similar to the ones that had driven so many people to North American colonies in the seventeenth century: a concentration of land ownership and more workers than could be absorbed by agriculture and manufacturing. More particular, episodic hardships also prompted immigration, such as the potato famine in Ireland of the 1840s and the persecution of Russian Jews later in the century. British, German, and Irish immigrants predominated before the Civil War. A larger and more diverse stream of new immigrants appeared in the second half of the nineteenth century, beginning with the Chinese in the 1850s and followed by Central and Eastern Europeans (Slavs, Poles, Ukrainians, Russians, Italians), the Mexicans, and the Japanese. This second wave of immigration did not subside until immigration restriction in the early 1920s. Families predominated among those who came to stay. But many saw immigration as a temporary measure, a means of amassing capital that could then be used to gain a foothold in the old country. The new immigrants were therefore dominated by single, unattached men—not the stuff from which stable families or communities were made. Traditional familial structures often fractured under the stress of isolation. Early in 1914, a Polish couple received word that their daughter in the United States had married a young man from a different part of Poland. She begged them not to "be angry with me for marrying so hastily and a man from so far a country and for not even writing to you about it." But what could the parents do, thousands of miles away, but give their blessing? A wife struggling to raise children wrote her husband, absent in the United States: "I have only wasted my young years in longing and grief, alone with these orphans, and I have no hope that it will end soon."[39]

The Chinese constituted an extreme example of skewed sex ratios. Unlike Europe, where economic expansion fueled immigration, China suffered from economic decline and political fragmentation. Great Britain succeeded in forcing China to accept opium as a trade item by the 1840s, and the drug quickly fostered addiction, poverty, and brigandage. Poor families who could not feed or otherwise care for their children commonly sold them to wealthier people as indentured servants or brides; some became prostitutes. Young males were much less likely to be sold than their female counterparts, as they were more able to make money to support their families. Many chose to leave China, some for Southeast Asia, some, after 1850, for California and the rest of the West where they might make twenty times as much money as they could back home. Merchants soon operated as essential economic and cultural brokers between poorer Chinese and the Yankees who needed their labor. These merchants commonly embraced life in the United States, balancing the racial discrimination they confronted there with expanded opportunities for profits and status within the Chinese American community. However, until the radical restriction of Chinese immigration in 1882, the overwhelming majority of immigrants comprised young men who expected to work for a few years on the West Coast before returning to China with enough money to lift their families of origin from poverty, to buy land, and to erect an impressive house. Less than one in twenty Chinese immigrants was female in 1880. Some 86 percent of San Francisco's Chinese women worked as prostitutes in 1860, 63 percent in 1870. Some of these women eventually married well, but sex ratios remained skewed and families rare, in part because some of the immigrants had wives in China. Hence the 1870 census enumerated just 500 children born in the United States, less than 1 percent of the total Chinese American population. By 1900 the figure had risen to 10 percent.[40]

Italian immigration to the United States resembled the Chinese one in many ways. The push factors were less extreme in Italy than in China, and the sex ratios of the Italians in America were less skewed. But Italians also commonly hoped to spend a few years in the United States before returning to or starting families in the old country. Men constituted about three-fourths of South Italian immigrants in the early twentieth century. Indeed, some married men sent for their wives and children, not to make a permanent home in the United States, but so that the family could more quickly earn enough money to live well in Italy. From the 1880s to 1914, about one-half as many Italians went from the United States to Italy as vice versa.

But to focus on the male-dominated, transitory nature of Chinese and Italian immigrant communities is to miss the broader, familial context in which such immigration occurred. Such immigrants were in the United States precisely because their families expected a lot from them. Hence a Chinese miner wrote from Central Oregon that "I could not keep the tears from running down my cheeks when thinking about the miserable and needy circumstances of our home, and thinking back to the time of our separation." He recalled that it was "our destitution" that had driven him away "several autumns" past "to try to make a living"[41] Making and saving money proved to be more difficult than expected, and not a few sojourners fell prey to gambling or opium addiction. Others, particularly those who did well, were tempted to stay in the United States and to neglect their families of origin in China. But duty was not contingent on proximity, and the great majority of Chinese Americans continued to perceive themselves as implicated in a web of familial obligations. In the United States they organized themselves into kinship groups based on the part of China they were from.

Chinese men, especially, were alarmed by the liberal nature of North American society and culture. Scholars describe traditional Chinese culture as emphasizing "harmony within hierarchy," a world in which a "child learns to see the world in terms of a network of relationships."[42] They had for many centuries celebrated and emphasized filial piety, children's devotion to their parents. A commonly told story related how Han Boyu wept when his mother beat him—not from physical pain, but because his mother's weak blows connoted her waning strength. Zhang Yinhuan, China's minister to the United States in the 1880s, noted that an eminent elderly man's son did not help his limping father up and down stairs: "This is what the sentiment between fathers and sons is like in the West."[43] "Women got too much freedom, too much power over here," observed Ying Foy. "Break up lots of families."[44]

European immigrants shared the Chinese emphasis on family obligations. Most young men crossed the Atlantic not in search of individual fortune or fame but as family members deputized to make enough money to help the family at home or to begin the process of transferring a chain of other family members to the United States, where they could reconstitute themselves under more promising circumstances. Many immigrants were delighted to learn that children as young as ten could make good money and happily removed them from school. "We looked forward to the time when we... quit school and got a job because we knew the parents needed money," recalled a Pole.[45] Tradition-minded elders were dumbfounded by children who felt otherwise. Complained a first-generation Italian American father of a daughter who insisted on keeping part of her earnings for herself, "But then, why did I make her?"[46] Immigrant mothers had little patience with native-born reformers who urged them to be more considerate of their children. A social worker "doesn't have to depend on her children's wages" and therefore can "afford to be lax with them."[47]

Immigrant women did not work outside the home nearly as often as their African American counterparts. But many took in piecework that they and their children labored over at home, or they took in boarders. A 1901 study of Packingtown in South Chicago found that two-thirds of its families had one or more boarders.[48]

Immigrants grounded their conservative family beliefs in rural traditions. John Lukasavicius recalled a Lithuanian childhood in which his mother beat him and his siblings if they neglected their many chores. "The only time we did anything different from working and sleeping was when there was a dance at one of the neighbors' houses or a wedding."[49] Southern Italian girls prided themselves on becoming useful at a young age. "When I was five or six years old," recalled a woman, "my father gave me a small scythe with which to help harvest the grain." The girls also learned to help their mothers around the house. "There was never an idle moment for girls or women. We all wanted the reputation of being good workers."[50] Becoming a worker entailed the right to wear a shawl, an article of clothing that marked one as a woman rather than as a girl. Pascal D'Angelo, born in 1894 in rural Italy, recalled a childhood of poverty and hunger. Everyone "must help, down to the children barely able to walk."[51]

The United States exposed children to a much different environment, particularly in cities. Children usually adapted much more quickly than did their parents to the new culture and language, so much so that parents often found themselves relying on children to navigate a foreign and often hostile cultural landscape. Most of the immigrant children spent at least some time in schools, which encouraged individual achievement rather than the subordination of their desires to the needs of the group. They also soaked in mainstream American values through popular culture, including movies, by the century's turn.

Adults also encountered fewer social and community constraints in the United States than they did back home. The classic study of Polish peasants in the old and new worlds by William Thomas and Florian Znaniecki found that couples in the United States were much more likely to quarrel, separate, or divorce, in part because Poles were unable to recreate in the United States the sort of all-encompassing church-community structures that existed back home.[52]

But a great deal of traditional life persisted. An Italian American girl remarked in 1914 that she liked to go to the movies precisely because "We don't get no chance to live that way and you can pretend when you see the picture that it's you."[53] Immigrant communities formed powerful institutions. Chinese bachelors commonly lived together and formed tight-knit associations based on their place of origin or kinship group. Immigrant households commonly extended beyond the immediate family, and most groups organized fraternal organizations to assist with unexpected deaths and lesser tragedies. Chicago's Bohemian Americans in 1902 had 30 savings-and-loan organizations; 259 benefit societies; 35 gymnastics associations; and 18 singing, 4 bicycling, and 4 drama clubs. In addition, many ethnic groups had their own churches and schools. The great majority married someone from within their ethnic group. There were just 5 interethnic couples out of 284 in a South Chicago neighborhood dominated by East European immigrants. Just 9 and 17 percent of New York City's first and second-generation Poles, respectively, married outside their ethnic group from 1908 to 1912. In a rural Minnesota township, the intramarriage rate enumerated in the 1900 census for German Americans stood at 95 percent for the first generation and 92 percent for the second generation. Immigrants' children commonly left school early to support their families. Indeed, the children of African Americans had higher rates of enrollment in Northern, urban high schools than did many European immigrants. Children of immigrants in Philadelphia at the turn of the century were twice as likely to be a part of the labor force than were children with native-born parents and three times more likely in Boston. As late as 1911, children's earnings still constituted nearly two-thirds of the income of unskilled Irish American families.[54]

Jewish immigrants, by way of contrast, embraced education, but education had long been part and parcel of an intense community and ritualistic life. Rose Pesotta described the elaborate Passover rituals in her Ukrainian Jewish family of the turn of the twentieth century: "father was a king, mother a queen, and we children, princes and princesses."[55] Sholom Aleichem, whose stories would later provide the basis for *Fiddler on the* Roof, recalled "a continuous buzzing" in children's ears: "'Don't do that! That's no place to stand! No, don't go there!' Everyone buzzed: Father, Mother, sisters, brothers, teacher, servants, uncles, aunts, Grandmother—especially Grandmother, ..."[56] The segregated Eastern European ghettoes could not be replicated in New York City or in other parts of the United States, where people and ideas flowed more freely, and divorces could be procured from the secular state. A social worker observed that children who attended public schools often cast aside much of their religious belief and saw "no further use of Hebrew." Russian Jew Abraham Bisno noted that "a significant minority" of wage-earning children wanted to keep their earnings: "They acquired the *right to a personality* which they had not ever possessed in the old country."[57] Lincoln Steffens observed synagogues in which orthodox fathers worshipped while their sons sat outside "hatless in their old clothes, smoking cigarettes . . . rebels against the law of Moses; they were lost souls, lost to God, the family, and to Israel of old."[58] Perhaps. But if the familial and religious lives of young Jewish immigrants changed dramatically with emigration, they nevertheless retained much of their distinctiveness. Intermarriage rates among the Jews remained very low (1 and 6 percent for the first and second generation, respectively, around 1910 in New York City), and their sense of obligation remained high, particularly for daughters, who commonly deferred their individual aspirations for education or other forms of fulfillment in order to earn wages for their families or to help at home. "I felt a great deal of responsibility toward my parents," recalled one. "I sort of felt that I owed them something."[59]

Native American families encountered fewer opportunities and a much more determined program of acculturation. White reformers of the eighteenth and especially nineteenth centuries believed that Indians were capable of becoming like whites—and that this should be encouraged or even required. White educators focused much of their attentions on indigenous children whom they hoped would prove more malleable than their parents. Most schools were located within indigenous communities or reservations. But proliferating boarding schools separated boys and girls from their elders for years at a time. The goal, as Connecticut's Reverend Eleazar Wheelock put it in the mid-eighteenth century, was to isolate these children from the "pernicious Influence of their Parents Example," where "I can correct, & punish them as I please."[60] This impulse to educate and discipline indigenous children spread in the nineteenth century, when white, evangelical reformers argued that given sufficient opportunities Indians could become integrated into the nation's economy and society. The Dawes Act of 1887 promised to transform Indians into Jeffersonian yeoman farmers who put aside their communal economies to pursue prosperity on privately owned farms peopled by self-sufficient, nuclear families.

These educational programs were poorly executed. The Dawes Act served largely to transfer Indian land to whites, as indigenous families lacked the resources and the desire to become yeoman farmers. Most schools, Wheelock's included, spent as much time extracting labor from their Indian pupils as teaching them practical skills. Reformers hoped that the graduates of these schools would return home to set an example for and lead their people. But the paucity of employment opportunities on reservations and the cultural gap between youth who had been forced to surrender their language and culture and other Indians commonly left them both jobless and disoriented. Childhood had been a time of intense socialization to group norms communicated through example, stories, rigorous training, and spirit quests. Years spent at boarding school robbed children of these experiences and substituted skills that elders found superfluous. A young Hopi woman who returned home after years at a boarding school found that her family had no use for the pies and cakes she baked and found her "as foolish as a white woman."[61] An Apache who came home from Carlisle Indian School around the turn of the twentieth century found that if one tried to acculturate "the Indians branded you as being some kind of an outcast who no longer loved his own people."[62] Educated Indian women often ended up in cities as domestic servants or prostitutes. Educated Indian men enjoyed more options by the late nineteenth-century, particularly if they had gone to college. A few became professionals. But they, too, often found themselves alienated both from their kin and a white society that would never fully accept them.

Many of the Indians who left reservations intermarried and did their best to blend into white society. The thousands of white-skinned Americans now striving to recover traces of indigenous heritage testify to the dedicated efforts of their Indian ancestors to assimilate quietly into mainstream society. But some refugees clung to their indigenous identity. Carlos Montezuma, a Yavapais purchased and raised by a white man, was graduated from the Chicago Medical College in 1889 and eventually married a woman of Romanian descent. But he also became one of the first Indians to advocate for indigenous peoples on the national level and was a determined critic of the Bureau of Indian Affairs. When death neared he left Chicago for a grass shelter in Arizona, on the land of his ancestors.[63]

Few Indians enjoyed the options available to Montezuma. Confronted with death, dispossession, poverty, and determined programs of assimilation, they had to adapt to survive. Some appropriated parts of white culture. Handsome Lake, a Seneca prophet, urged his people at the turn of the nineteenth century to blend elements of traditional belief with white gender roles. He condemned divorce and abortion and supported Quaker missionaries who were urging men to take over and modernize agriculture. He charged older women who resisted these innovations with witchcraft. Several were executed. The Cherokee and other large indigenous nations of the Southeast continued to alter their kinship practices. Towns defined by matrilineal clans fragmented into homesteads populated by nuclear families. The Cherokee replaced town councils with a centralized, male-dominated government. Most groups changed less radically. But those aspects of indigenous life that most offended Caucasians, the two spirits (transgendered people) and polygyny, became rare.

Many traditions survived the nineteenth century. The Seneca of 1900 were much more likely than their non-Indian counterparts to live in extended families. Only 4 percent of Omaha marriages around that time occurred within clan groups. Most Crow women who died from 1910 to 1914 willed property not to their husbands but to other kin, presumably members of their lineage, and one out of five Crow adults had married four times or more. Indian societies remained focused on kinship.[64]

But the fact that so many Native women were divorcing or deserting their husbands suggests their vulnerability as well as their independence. Charlotte Smith—the daughter of Celiast, a Clatsop woman who had married a French Canadian and then a Yankee—used white courts to extricate herself from three marriages that she described as highly abusive. Alcoholism, violence, and other forms of sociocultural disintegration grew in Native communities along with poverty. A Plymouth colony official in 1654 reported that intoxicated Indians "commit much horrid wickedness, as murdering the nearest relations, etc."[65] Nearly two centuries later, a white woman living among the Cherokee remarked that their women "were chaste and very civil, but their husbands would drink to drunkenness, and were very cruel when under the influence of fire water."[66]

Conquest and colonization increased Indians' vulnerability. A San Francisco newspaper reported in 1856 that government employees on a Digger reservation were "daily and nightly…kidnapping the younger portion of the females, for the vilest purposes," and that the Indians "dare not resent the insult, or even complain of the hideous outrage."[67] Sexual assault spawned violence toward wives, venereal disease, and abortion, a cluster of intersecting problems that tore Indian families apart and made reproduction extraordinarily difficult.

By the dawn of the twentieth century, all Indian nations had become colonized, and all struggled with the costs of poverty, racism, and concerted assimilation programs. Traditional, flexible kinship structures remained crucial to their survival, but survival was very difficult.

Mexicanos also suffered from conquest and oppression. Some communities, as in New Mexico, had roots stretching back to the sixteenth century and had blended extensively with neighboring Native Americans. Other settlements, as in Arizona and California, were more recent. Most were rural peasants of mixed (largely mestizo) ancestry, though Mexican independence and the ensuing secularization of California's Franciscan missions encouraged the rise of powerful, often light-skinned ranchero families there. Even married sons were not to sit or smoke in the presence of their powerful Californian fathers. Poorer Mexican communities were stable and close-knit. Mexican families, in what would become the Southwest, had always been flexible and interdependent. They resided, after all, on a far Northern frontier, places where husbands and fathers were apt to die young and where young women had a great deal of work to do inside and outside the home and could not simply be locked up until marriage. Women might elope with suitors or take lovers. Furthermore, domination entailed obligation. Angustias de la Guerra, born in San Diego in 1815, recounted how the family of a poor bride would "ask the wealthy people," such as her father, "to help dress the bride." They would bring him gifts "of small breads and sweets," then return after the ceremony to "drink chocolate with him." The poor family thereafter referred to the rich patron as "my captain." Mexicans of high status had many godchildren to whom they dispensed favors. Apolianaria Lorenzana, born in the 1790s, had more than 100 godchildren, both Indians and "gente de razón" (people of reason, or whites).[68] But the Mexican War brought much dislocation and poverty. Anglos soon worked their way across what was now the U.S. Southwest and took most of their land and businesses. Increased immigration from Mexico to the Southwest's railroads, mines, and farms that began late in the nineteenth century exacerbated the Mexicanos' growing poverty and skewed its sex ratios.

Mexican American women's responsibilities grew as their families' fortunes declined. In New Mexico, women remained in the villages to run their families and to tend their gardens as men went further and further afield for seasonal work. Most families eventually lost their land, and more and more families had to seek work elsewhere, often in cities. Husbands were more apt to leave—temporarily or permanently—under these circumstances, often for cities. Most newcomers who came North from Mexico late in the nineteenth century were unattached men, so the proportion of Mexican American adults who married and lived with their spouses fell. As before, ideals often clashed with conditions. The editor of Tucson's *El fronterizo* opined in 1882 that a wife should be a "balm for" her husband's cares, "surrounding him with her tender sisterly soul." A year later, an anonymous woman countered: "Men are like lit cigars, they show more smoke than fire." Scriptural justifications for male superiority could be dispensed with, she explained, as the Bible had been written by men, and "all men were liars."[69]

But Mexican American communities remained tight-knit even as their economies and settlements declined and fragmented. Households commonly included boarders, servants, relatives, and friends. The proportion of extended-kin families in Los Angeles, Tucson, Santa Fe, and San Antonio fluctuated from roughly 10 to 20 percent from 1850 to 1880. Such families were most common among the poor, who leaned most heavily on one another for economic support. Richard Griswold del Castillo suggests that Mexican American wives born in what would become the United States commonly headed households and worked outside the home precisely because they had a strong local kinship network to support them.[70] Like the Native Americans whom so many Hispanic families had lived among or incorporated, flexibility and kinship proved invaluable in confronting poverty, racism, and dislocation.

Native-born working-class families experienced many of the same economic challenges that immigrant and minority families faced—but often without their kin and community networks. Life expectancy declined for much of the nineteenth century, particularly among the urban poor: about 28 percent of New York City's children died by the age of five in 1820, 52 percent in the 1850s.[71] The working class often relied on a "family wage" rather than on the earnings of the husband or father. The widespread destruction of apprenticeship caused by nineteenth-century industrialization delayed independence and forced many working-class children back into the homes of their parents. Craftspeople had enjoyed relatively high status and incomes during the colonial period. But the industrial revolution that expanded the middle class generally harmed people who worked with their hands, as specialized craft skills that took many years of training to acquire were replaced by machines and the unskilled workers who tended them. The industrial economy proved to be unpredictable, particularly for its operatives. One made money only while working, and if one could not work—even if one was injured because of negligence on the part of one's employer—one could not earn money. Several severe depressions threw many workers out of their jobs during the nineteenth century, and even during good times roughly one worker out of five could expect to be unemployed at some point during a given year. Industrialization proceeded fitfully. Skilled carpenters continued to enjoy high wages generations after looms made hand weaving obsolete. But, in the main, industrialization meant lower wages and less control over one's work as manufacturing moved from cottages to factories. Industrialization created many unskilled jobs outside of factories: building railroads; grading streets; and loading, unloading, and transporting goods, for example. But these jobs were also poorly paid, dangerous, and often short-lived. Poor people also suffered from the growing regulation of subsistence economies. City officials no longer let pigs and chickens roam at large, and new regulations in the countryside made it more difficult to hunt or fish on land that one did not own. A larger fraction of meager wages had to be set aside for food.

Declining real wages and economic instability were a recipe for social tensions and violence, inside and outside the family. Young, urban working-class men, especially, developed a reputation for fighting. This violent pose served both to denigrate the norms of middle-class domesticity and to offer a respite from the numbness of work. Brawling in New York City "fostered a distinct working-class male identity that was centered on the boisterous public assertion of physical courage, independence, class pride, and American patriotism."[72] Miners on the Comstock Lode "celebrated maleness, mutuality, whiteness, and the power of chance."[73] But working-class women did not necessarily accept the subordinate position that men assigned to them. They contested their husbands' claims to superiority and often banded together to aid one another when dealing with abusive husbands or simply the demands of housework and child care. Of course, many working-class couples lived together harmoniously. But the pressures of working-class life, the poverty, and the unpredictability endemic to most nineteenth-century wage work brought tremendous pressures to working-class families.

Employers and reformers alike commonly steered workers toward churches, schools, and temperance societies. "The effect of intoxicants on labour efficiency was the strongest argument that could be presented in support of temperance," remarked an early advocate. The police in Lynne, Massachusetts, an important shoe making center, turned their attention to alcohol-related crimes by the late 1850s: drunkenness, disorderly conduct, and illegal liquor sales. Education leaders pledged to teach "sobriety, industry and frugality, chastity, moderation and temperance" and to encourage "habits of application, respect to superiors, and obedience to law."[74] In 1851, Massachusetts passed the nation's first compulsory school law. Child-saving institutions proliferated in the second half of the nineteenth century and took tens of thousands of children from poor, urban parents.

Working people often resented these intrusions and the attitudes that lay behind them. The Democrats could count on most working-class people's votes precisely because they billed themselves as the party of individual freedom. Young men often evinced anti-domestic sensibilities. Young women, though more vulnerable than their male counterparts, flocked to growing cities throughout the nineteenth and early twentieth centuries in search of independence, and they often chose to live in rented rooms, boarding houses, or with one another, rather than under the watchful eyes of the well-to-do reformers who wished to shelter them.

Others saw value in middle-class restraint, though they believed that working people should be allowed to choose temperance, for example, rather than being forced to give up drinking. The Washingtonians arose in 1841 as a working-class temperance organization that proclaimed that alcohol use only exacerbated the difficulties of working people's lives. "I was a football when a drunkard," proclaimed Boston mechanic and temperance lecturer Sam Hayward, "kicked around by everybody." He converted to temperance when a Washingtonian challenged him: "Sam, don't you want to be a *man* again?"[75] "For Washingtonian women," notes Ruth Alexander, "the most promising guarantee of social and economic stability was the adoption of standards of behavior that reflected a sense of responsibility to the family and an emotional attachment to its members."[76] Like their middle-class counterparts, working-class women wanted their husbands to invest emotionally and financially in their families. Many working men, in particular, rejected domestic norms out of hand; the precariousness and humiliations of working life made cultivating habits of industry and self-restraint seem pointless. But many others embraced education and character formation as the key to socioeconomic mobility.

Working-class families commonly turned to kin for help, but kin were often missing or had problems of their own. A widowed or deserted woman might move in with a sister or her parents, who would watch her children while she worked, for example. Struggling mothers and fathers without such kin could turn to a growing number of orphanages or children's aid societies. Indeed, such institutions actively recruited children from the mid-century forward, as cities assigned special police officers to the work of discovering neglected or abused children whose parent(s) a judge might decide were unfit. Charles Loring Brace, the longtime head of the New York Children's Aid Society, entitled his account of that work *The Dangerous Classes of New York*. Poor, especially immigrant, parents were almost automatically suspect, particularly single mothers. These institutions enjoyed little or no government funding, so their directors were reluctant to accept the temporary care of children who could not support themselves. Parents who wished to retrieve their children from such institutions had to either provide monthly payments or to consent to the child being bound out to a family who provided food and shelter in return for the child's work. The trick for poor parents, then, was to use the child-saving institutions without losing control over one's child.

Working-class families had little choice but to rely on one another when they could. Individualism was an unaffordable luxury.

* * *

Sojourner Truth is famous for rising at a women's rights convention to deflate male ministers who were claiming "dat woman needs to be helped into carriages, and lifted over ditches" by pointing out that no man had ever helped her, a woman who "have borne thirteen chillen, and seen 'em mos' all sold off into slavery,...and ar'n't I a woman?"[77] But Truth almost certainly did not speak these words. A more faithful account of her speech does not render it in dialect and instead presents a Truth who spoke simply and earnestly about women's rights. Truth did not have thirteen children, and she did not see most of them sold into slavery. But slavery deeply marked her and her family.

Sojourner Truth spent the early part of her life as Isabella, a New York slave born around 1797. Her father had lost two wives to sale when he married Isabella's mother, and Isabella was the youngest of their ten to twelve children, most of whom were sold. At age nine, her owner sold her away from her parents and one remaining sibling to a couple who whipped her brutally, leaving lifelong scars. She also suffered sexual abuse. In around 1815, she married a slave on the same farm and had five children. When she learned that New York would free all remaining slaves in 1827, she left with her youngest child for the shelter of an anti-slavery man who paid her master $27.20 for them.

Like many people of that time and place, Isabella underwent a shattering conversion experience in which she realized that god "was *all* over" and that he was an "ever-present help in time of trouble."[78] She joined the community of the Prophet Matthias, though this authoritarian leader took her money and beat her. When the commune broke up, she moved to New York City and worked as a servant. The son who lived with her went to sea, and she never saw him again. Truth's poverty often kept her from being able to care for her other children. The traumas of slavery and poverty left her both thirsting for a familial community and separated from kin. In 1843, she became Sojourner Truth, a name that reflected her belief that our time on earth was but a brief interval before attaining the joys of heaven or suffering the torments of hell. She joined a Millerite cooperative in Massachusetts and later a spiritualist community in Michigan. These activities brought her into contact with white and black reformers, and by the time she dictated her life story in the 1850s Truth was a popular lecturer and advocate for abolition and women's rights.

White women reformers such as Harriet Beecher Stowe and Francis Dana Gage tried to depict Truth as an African Amazon. Truth instead presented herself as a lady.

Truth was unique among African Americans, but her attraction to middle-class norms was not. African American families commonly sought to keep wives in the home and children at school. Poverty and racism often thwarted them. Most blacks inside and outside slavery relied heavily on kin, even as slavery and then poverty fragmented kin relations. Native American, Mexican American, and white, working-class families also battled prejudice, poverty, and at times enforced acculturation and reacted with a combination of innovation and tradition. The most common solution to oppression and other hardships was to rely heavily on one another.

The coming century would bring some radical changes for marginal families, as oppression and poverty alike receded and as middle-class youth, especially, began to appropriate cultural forms from groups that they had ignored or shunned earlier. Prosperity would blur racial, ethnic, and cultural distinctions.

Chapter 6

The First Modern Family

Industrialization and the prosperity it fostered conditioned the nature of nineteenth-century families. It drew millions of immigrants to the United States even as the lives of working people became more tenuous. African Americans, Mexican American immigrants, and white working-class families relied heavily on one another out of necessity as well as out of habit. Middle-class people had more choices, but they chose, far more often than not, to form durable families, for the habits of self-restraint fostered in middle-class families dovetailed with the requirements of a production-oriented culture and economy.

The economy shifted significantly early in the twentieth century, and the nation's families followed suit. Modern prosperity and complex reactions to modern life reworked most families, and in similar ways. By the onset of the Great Depression in 1929 a new, more widely shared style of family had emerged, one based more on the pursuit of freedom and self-realization, less on self-restraint and character. An ethos of consumption shouldered aside the Victorian emphasis on production as Americans became the richest people in the history of the world. Not everyone shared in the new prosperity. But America's diverse families converged in the early twentieth century in the pursuit of freedom and self-realization.

* * *

The quality of life improved markedly during the early twentieth century. The per capita gross national product rose well over threefold from 1897 to 1921. Life expectancy and overall physical well-being increased dramatically, as investments in public health paid big dividends. Americans spent a much smaller proportion of their earnings on food than did their counterparts in Europe. The texture of the new prosperity rested on the widespread diffusion of consumer goods rather than on production-oriented staples such as textiles, steel rails, and farm implements that had dominated the nineteenth century. More and more people had the wherewithal to buy products ranging from recorded music to curling irons to automobiles.

This shift from production to consumption changed the nature of work for both sexes. The proportion of men who labored in agriculture continued to plummet as the proportion of men who worked in white-collar jobs grew. The assets of the growing middle class resided in salaries and specialized skills that were acquired through formal education rather than through land or farm equipment. Women constituted a large and growing proportion of clerical and sales employees as they moved out of domestic service, a sector that had absorbed one-half of females working outside the home in 1870 but just one-fifth in 1930. Men were much more apt to supervise women than vice versa, and they earned more money for the same work. But in many offices and businesses the sexes worked side by side. For housewives, who still comprised the great majority of adult women, shopping (and driving to shop) for ready-made clothing and food (meat, canned goods, butter, bread, and biscuits) replaced the work of actually making such items at home. In Muncie, Indiana, bakeries provided about one-quarter of the city's bread in 1890s and about two-thirds of it in the 1920s.[1] Housework became easier, if no less time-consuming, as indoor plumbing did away with the hauling of water and electricity brought in its wake washing machines, refrigerators, and vacuum cleaners.

The family became smaller and more isolated. The fertility rate fell from just over 3.5 children in 1900 to under 2.5 three decades later. Households had fewer extended kin and domestic servants; a Northern family was half as likely to have a servant in 1920 as it was in 1900.[2] These smaller families enjoyed more privacy. More working-class couples rented and even owned houses by the 1920s rather than crowding into tenements or boardinghouses. Los Angeles-area suburbs such as South Gate and Watts offered lots at low prices along with modest taxes and little regulation, practices that enabled more working-class families to grasp a piece of the American dream.

Prosperity lengthened childhood. The proportion of youth who attended high school rose gradually from 10 percent in 1815 to 20 percent in 1915, then shot up to 50 percent by 1928.[3] Young people spent less time doing housework and more time playing—learning musical instruments or participating in sports or the Boy Scouts, for example.

The state's role expanded. Taxation grew dramatically during World War I and reached a much wider proportion of the populace than before. The role of city and other local governments increased, and state government assumed more of the work of supervising schools and roads. Attendance at primary school became mandatory. Juvenile courts arose around the century's turn to establish an alternative to the mainstream criminal justice system. Mothers' pensions spread rapidly from 1911 to include forty states by 1920 and made it possible for more and more single women to keep their children—though the payments were meager and moral expectations were high. Subsidized foster care replaced the "putting-out" system. Private agencies still conducted much of this work, but they increasingly answered to state governments, which both subsidized and monitored their work.

In sum, government more actively supported and supervised families. Recipients of mothers' or widows' pensions had to convince case workers of their moral rectitude. Those who went to church and abstained from smoking and drinking had a better chance of receiving money than those who did not. The U.S. Children's Bureau began in 1912, and its "Infant Care" soon became the government's best-selling publication. Social work moved from an avocation of well-to-do women, such as Jane Addams, to a profession dominated by career women, and its basis shifted from a broad consideration of the social environment to the case-work method that emphasized the client's personality. Clinically-trained social workers catalogued individual traits of their clients rather than campaigning against poverty or poor housing conditions.

Modern life engaged Americans in a set of powerful but often contradictory developments. Prosperity multiplied chances for privacy and luxury even as more and more people surrendered chunks of their autonomy to large institutions: the businesses they worked for, the schools they spent more of their lives in, and the governments that insinuated themselves into their lives. Resisting and suspecting authority was one way to resolve this paradox, and it meshed with the era's individualism. In the words of Lynn Dumenil, big government represented people's fears of both "lost community and personal autonomy."[4] World War I exacerbated this suspicion of authority. A soldier in John Dos Passos's novel *Three Soldiers* of 1919 remarks that "I wouldn't mind the war if it wasn't for the army."[5] Dos Passos dwells not so much on the carnage of the trenches as on the regimented, soul-destroying routine of army life outside of battle. Anti-government rhetoric grew in the 1920s as resentment of taxation, bureaucracy, prohibition, and other forms of regulation grew. Popular culture celebrated business leaders as rugged and successful individualists.

The growing predictability and regulation of life, together with women's expanding role, the apparent closing of the Western frontier, and increased prosperity and comfort, created what some historians have referred to as a "crisis in masculinity." Well-to-do and then middle-class men turned to adventure to reinvigorate their manhood: warfare; violent sports such as boxing and football; and camping and other forms of outdoor recreation. Teddy Roosevelt transformed himself from a slightly built rich boy with a high-pitched voice to a "rough rider" who embraced and advocated a return to a "strenuous life" of frontier living, warfare, and hunting. Shortly before his death, the man who had been one of the most distinguished political leaders in the nation's history recalled that the day on which he had killed a Spanish officer, "was the great day of my life."[6]

It is no coincidence that the Western, as a literary genre, appeared at the same time that men believed the real West to be slipping away. Owen Wister, a friend of Roosevelt's, inaugurated the new literary form with *The Virginian,* in 1902. The son of a mother whose attentions he found suffocating, Wister created a protagonist who was in many respects the opposite number of the heroines who peopled Victorian novels. They talked and prayed. The Virginian acted and killed. They posited a world in which self-restraint and virtue triumphed. The Virginian knew that life was brutal and that nothing counted but the courage of a solitary, brave man. Westerns, in the words of Jane Tompkins, "stage a moment in the psychosocial development of the male that requires that he demonstrate his independence from and superiority to women, specifically to his mother."[7] This mentality spilled over into other genres, including male adventure writing, more generally, and into much of the higher literature of the period. Ernest Hemingway's mother had castigated him in 1920 for being "lazy and pleasure-seeking," and "neglecting your duties to God and your Saviour Jesus Christ." She signed the letter: "Your still hoping and always praying mother."[8] Hemingway, like his less gifted counterparts, used his life and his fiction to assert a more existential and manly vision. The culture of the nineteenth century had been feminine. In the twentieth it would be masculine.

The rhetorical embrace of primitive masculinity seldom interfered with the work of modern consumption. Advertising doubled in just two years after World War I, and it associated products with intangible qualities: status, power, and, especially, sex. *Vanity Fair's* editor observed that his magazine's advertisements offered women "happy dreams and illusions," that its pages were "magic carpets on which they ride out to love," prompting ordinary women to "see themselves daily as *femmes fatales*, as Cleopatra, as Helen of Troy."[9] This emphasis on expression through consumption fit the requirements and products of the new economy. If owning an automobile, for example, was simply a matter of efficient transportation, a single, reliable, reasonably priced car built to last for many years would suffice. But if style, appearance, and novelty counted, one must spend money more liberally and frequently. Advertisers worked to create itches that had to be repeatedly scratched, desires that needed to be satisfied time after time.

Bankers obliged by encouraging borrowing over thrift. At the onset of the 1920s, most people paid for their new automobiles in cash. But by the decade's close, most bought on credit—and added furniture, washing machines, and phonographs to the products commonly bought "on time." Buying goods with money one did not have constituted a fundamental shift in how people looked at the world. Zelda Sayre, daughter of a Southern judge and future wife of F. Scott Fitzgerald, chose these lines for her high school yearbook:

> Why should all life be work, when we all can borrow.
> Let's only think of today, and not worry about tomorrow.[10]

The bankers and the flappers were singing from the same hymnal. "The greatest single engine in the destruction of the Protestant ethic," observes Daniel Bell in his aptly titled *Cultural Contradictions of Capitalism*, "was the invention of the installment plan."[11]

Business's emphasis on quick gratification meshed with the era's products and priorities. Phonographs and radios appeared early in the twentieth century. They spread a new music, jazz, which embodied a joyful embrace of life in general and of sex in particular. Lurid paperback novels and popular magazines also proliferated. "*Live Stories* is interested in what we call 'sex adventure' stories," explained an editor. A competitor, *Telling Tales*, featured stories with such titles as "Indolent Kisses," "Primitive Love," and "Innocents Astray."[12] Movies were a particularly potent vehicle for spreading the ethos of romance and consumption. The Lynds found that ticket sales in Muncie were fully four and one-half times the city's population in December 1923. In November, a slightly slower month, a third of the city's high school students attended the movies at least twice a week. What they saw and learned at the movies clashed with Victorian norms. In "Why Change Your Wife," the male protagonist leaves his marriage with a dull young woman who castigates "physical music" and recoils at the revealing negligee he buys her. "I want a *sweetheart*, not a judge," he responds to her attempts to "improve" him. Morality is eventually served. But he returns to his wife only after she adopts modern clothing and music. "A man would rather have his wife for his sweetheart than any other woman," the film concludes, "but ladies: if you would be your husband's sweetheart, you simply *must* learn when to forget you're his wife." Leading movie makers of the late 1910s and the 1920s filled the screen with sumptuous homes, clothes, and other consumer goods. The leading men and women of the silver screen fought for the freedom to pursue marriages blessed by fun, intimacy, and wealth. "Advertising and movies, the emerging and increasingly powerful cultural industries of the period," notes Eva Illouz, "developed and advanced a vision of love as a utopia wherein marriage should be eternally exciting and romantic and could be if the couple participated in the realm of leisure."[13]

An ethos of pleasure and authenticity shouldered aside old-fashioned values such as responsibility. "In place of principles I would give us all a magnificent and flaming audacity," remarked psychologist Lorine Pruette.[14] Nineteenth-century feminists had sought to control fertility by containing men's sex drives. Margaret Sanger, by way of contrast, championed birth control as a way to decouple sex from procreation so that sexual pleasure for women could become an "energy enhancing their lives and increasing self-expression and self-development."[15] The adulterous protagonist in Sherwood Anderson's *Many Marriages* expressed the fear of "at last facing death and the end of life without having lived at all."[16] Freud—or, more accurately, popular interpretations of Freud—contributed a great deal to this preoccupation with the self. Hence a fourteen-year-old girl confided to her diary that she was "too self-conscious" and was burdened by "a foul inferiority complex."[17] Respectable Victorians had asserted that the natural self must be disciplined by a higher, godly morality. But with Christianity in disrepute and the self being celebrated, more and more educated people embraced instincts and desire as natural and healthy impulses. The middle-class of the nineteenth century had understood heterosexual love, as Illouz puts it, as "a means to the ends of self-knowledge and spiritual edification." Early in the twentieth century, romantic love instead became bound up in "personal happiness and the affirmation of self," states of mind associated more with the early stages of courtship than with marriage. "Now it was sexuality, rather than domesticity, that united and uplifted a couple."[18] Good sex came to symbolize the transcendent, a person's best shot at authenticity.

Authenticity required individuality. "Personality is the quality of being Somebody," advised the self-improvement guides that multiplied early in the twentieth century. As Warren Susman puts it, "Every American was to become a performing self."[19] Americans had plenty of models to draw from in this work. F. Scott and Zelda Fitzgerald were literary celebrities, Babe Ruth and Jack Dempsey sports celebrities, people famous not simply for their accomplishments, but for their style and elán. But no one topped the Hollywood celebrities, young women and men who appeared on thousands of screens and elicited thousands of lines of type in magazines and newspapers and millions of imitative fans. "I am a girl twelve years of age," wrote Martha Meadows of Montgomery, Alabama, to actress Clara Bow. "I am just wild about you. Your mouth, your eyes, and your hair. This craze for blondes never would last I knew."[20]

Many opposed the new morality. Traditionalists contrasted "the so called search for happiness" with "the old time search for character" and asserted that the "clamor for happiness" revealed "a childish dissatisfaction with life as it is."[21] F. Scott Fitzgerald, certainly no friend of the old order, worried that the new generation was "shallow, cynical, impatient, turbulent, and empty."[22] Consider this plaint from *The Great Gatsby*: " 'What'll we do with ourselves this afternoon,' cried Daisy, 'and the day after that, and the next thirty years?' "[23] Fitzgerald—the decade's icon, the man who invented the flapper—became ambivalent over the culture he had done so much to create: "the world romantically arrested, suspended in wonder and love, and the world in motion, filled with rootless, grotesque images of dislocation, fragments without order, a waste land."[24] Fitzgerald's reservations eluded most of the self-styled "flappers" and "sheiks" who sought to emulate his apparently carefree life. But other intellectuals of the decade shared them.

The new morality and culture were much more androgynous than their Victorian antecedents had been. Among the intelligentsia, the spread of Darwinism and Freudian theory served to break down long-standing assumptions about binary, "natural" gender roles. The worlds of women and men merged at work, at college, and at play. The quintessential "flapper" had a boyish, sticklike figure and bobbed, boyish hair and was much more apt to join the guys in drinking, smoking, and necking than her grandmothers had been. Virginia Gildersleeve, Dean of Barnard, charged her women students of the 1920s with "blasé indifference, self-indulgence, and irresponsibility."[25] Nineteenth-century women had sought independence as a mode of social redemption, a conduit for "doing good." The new woman saw independence as an end rather than as a means, and she paired it with comfort and material goods. "Today's woman gets what she wants," noted an observer. "The vote. Slim sheaths of silk to replace voluminous petticoats. Glassware in sapphire blue or glowing amber. The right to a career. Soap to match her bathroom's color scheme."[26]

Less well-to-do women also embraced independence. Single women were more and more likely to live independently in cities—and liked it that way. They turned up their noses at the highly regulated group homes offered by well-to-do reformers and instead shared apartments with one another, where they could come and go when and where they pleased. Those destinations were often dance halls, nickelodeons, or movie theaters, places where young women and men could socialize freely. "We're human, all of us girls, and we're young," explained one.[27]

Yet women still labored under a double standard. Teenaged Beth Twiggard of Ossining, New York, confided to her diary: "I love dates and boys and whoopee, road houses, smoke and jazz." She enjoyed listing the names of the boys whom she had dated. "Methinks Beth has been flirting! Well, we girls do want our fun!" But she became despondent upon learning that boys considered her too easy: "I am hurt, battered, wholly crushed."[28]

Male and female was just one of many dyads that became fuzzy without disappearing early in the twentieth century. The boundaries between urban and rural, North and South, East and West, middle class and working class, white and black, immigrant and native born also blurred. Automobiles made it possible for a much larger proportion of rural children to attend high school. They also enabled them to move their courtship *From Front Porch to Back Seat*, as the title of Beth Bailey's fine book puts it.[29] Automobiles brought farm people to town to watch movies, and radios, phonographs, and cheap paperbacks brought urban culture to the farm. Rural people listened to the same music, read the same stories, and watched the same movies as did their big-city counterparts.

Modern culture also reduced the cultural gap between black and white. Indeed, in some, albeit largely symbolic respects, white youth aspired to imitate the "Negro." Jazz, the era's theme music, was created largely by African Americans, and more and more whites crossed a symbolic or literal color line to listen to black musicians such as Joseph "King" Oliver, Louis Armstrong, Bessie Smith, and Duke Ellington on phonographs, the radio, or in venues such as the Cotton Club, one of several Harlem night clubs that catered to whites' newfound love for "jungle music." These people were attracted to African American music and dance for many of the same reasons that they were drawn to boxing, sex, and alcohol: it struck them as sensual, exotic, and primitive, as—in a word—authentic. Harlem represented a rejection of "sterility," an embrace of "pure sensation untouched by self-consciousness and doubt."[30]

Black communities divided over the new morality that whites associated with them. Educated African Americans had long embraced an ethos of respectability and self-restraint. Their poorer, more numerous counterparts, surmising that respectability was not likely to get them anywhere, often expressed admiration for the amoral, "bad nigger" of folklore who was simply too tough and mean to be taken advantage of.[31] World War I touched off the first large-scale migration of blacks from the South to the North, a migration that brought both opportunities and challenges. Women who went to Northern cities tended to be younger and better educated than their counterparts who remained in the South, and once in the North they continued to work outside the home at high rates. Black churches, fraternal organizations, and other forms of community life grew quickly in New York, Chicago, Detroit, and other Northern cities and emphasized racial uplift through the Victorian virtues of hard work and self-restraint. Acutely aware of the racial stigma that all people of African descent labored under, black leaders in the North and in the South criticized the boisterous "street culture" of less educated African Americans. "Don't stick your head out of the window at every station" or "talk so loud to your friends who may be on the platform that a person a block away may hear you" counseled "The Traveler's Friend," a pamphlet created by the Woman's Convention of National Baptist Convention.[32]

But young, urban blacks often listened to other voices. The intellectuals of the Harlem Renaissance ostentatiously rejected the Victorian respectability of their elders and sought in jazz, poetry, or unconventional life experiences the same authenticity so eagerly sought by their white counterparts. Langston Hughes went to sea at age twenty-one hankering not for a livelihood but because on the ocean "I felt that nothing would ever happen to me again that I didn't want to happen." Hughes and his peers embraced the "primitive," African past that their elder counterparts were much less comfortable with. "We younger Negro artists," he pronounced, "intend to express our dark-skinned selves without fear or shame."[33] Other young, educated blacks also expressed a desire for freedom. Students went on strike at thirteen or more black colleges from 1914 to 1929 in an attempt to win more power and autonomy. Others simply had a lot of fun. W. E. B. DuBois, part of the earnest old guard, lamented a "growing mass of stupidity and indifference" in his 1930 commencement speech at Howard University.[34]

Poorer African Americans reacted in complex ways to the emerging consumer culture of the urban North. The United Negro Improvement Association, headed by Marcus Garvey, arose among the growing black working class and stressed black self-help and nationalism rather than integration into white society. Their emphasis on discipline and rectitude put them at odds with the cultural norms of the time. But they favored flamboyant uniforms and "garish displays."[35] Likewise, Spiritualist, Sanctified, and other charismatic, store-front preachers both warned their congregants about sin and claimed that they could help them choose the right numbers in the widespread "policy" or numbers games. Many young migrants paid no heed to improvers of any stripe and simply sought the widely available pleasures of drinking, gambling, and other public entertainments.

Growing opportunities mingled with continued racism and poverty to increase generational tensions within black families. Many parents remained authoritarian. The father of a Georgia adolescent "got a switch and whipped me" upon learning that his daughter had not been able to escape a boy who had chased her. He then "told that boy if he ever seen him near me again, he'd beat him to death."[36] But such rigidity could breed a deep sense of resentment and alienation among children attuned to other voices. Richard Wright and his brother had to live in an orphanage for a time and later with a variety of relatives. They were still dogged by poverty and racism and, in

Wright's opinion, superstition and ignorance. "When I brooded upon the cultural barrenness of black life, I wondered if clean, positive tenderness, love, honor, loyalty, and the capacity to remember were native with man," he later observed.[37] Scholars have established that Wright exaggerated—difficult as that was to do—the disadvantages of his childhood. But he did so to make a larger literary and historical truth, namely that racism and poverty, like slavery, twisted and distorted the lives of black individuals and families. In *Native Son,* published in 1940, Wright would establish a new genre of black realism, fiction devoted not to racial uplift but to dissecting how the dehumanization of Bigger Thomas made his murder of two innocent women "as instinctive and inevitable as breathing or blinking."[38]

Robert Maupin Beck, the future pimp and novelist who would become famous as "Iceberg Slim," was born a decade later than Wright, in 1918, and his childhood was even more harrowing. His biological father threw him against the wall and deserted his mother after she refused to give six-month-old Robert away. Robert also had cause to resent his mother, for she left a doting stepfather whom Robert adored for a man who threatened "to beat your mother-fucking ass" and smashed his kitten's skull before his eyes.[39] Robert eventually understood "that the most hellish aspect of America's racism is that for generations it has warped and twisted legions of innately good black men, causing the vital vine of black family stability and strength to be poisoned, hacked down by the pity, fear and hatred of black children." He also observed that "the most efficient and brutal pimps I have known had mothers who were drunkards, dope fiends, or whores," and that some of "the cruelest pimps that come to mind were abandoned as infants."[40]

Racism distorted black families in subtle ways. Clarence Norris, born in 1912, grew up in rural Georgia and by the age of ten did the work of a man "or my daddy would whup me good." But he did not hate his father until a white man told his father that Robert and his brother had set a fire that had destroyed his beehives. "Daddy stripped us buck naked in front of this man and beat us like we was mules. I could never love him after that, not from that day to this."[41] Likewise, Martin Luther King, Sr., also the son of a Georgia sharecropper, incited his father's wrath by publicly disagreeing with the white landowner his father rented from, an act that got the King family kicked out of their home and earned Martin a blow from his father that nearly knocked him off their wagon. "I told you, damn it! I told you to keep ya mouth shut," his father exclaimed.[42] White racism bred black domestic violence, for black fathers were compelled to beat boys who wronged or contradicted white men, violence that debased fathers and sons alike. Poverty compounded these cruelties. Losing the farm caused Martin's father to drink still more heavily, and Martin's pursuit of an education took him further from his father's orbit and represented an indictment of that man's life.

Most poor black families survived—and many flourished. Their marriages were often contentious. "When the men go hunting the women go fishing," explained one woman. At the same time, "there is a very real love for children and a great joy in having them about," and many poor mothers, especially, sacrificed a great deal for their children's educations.[43] As before, flexible forms of kinship filled in the gaps of missing biological parents. Acute family fragmentation lay well in the future.

Mexicano or Chicano families also struggled to balance traditional strategies of survival with new opportunities and dangers. Thousands of newcomers from rural Mexico sought a better life in the Southwest from the 1890s onward. The number of people of Mexican descent increased nearly tenfold in Texas between 1900 and 1930. Initially drawn by jobs in railroad construction and maintenance, mining, or agriculture, the Chicano population soon became more urban and family oriented. The census counted 30,000 in 1920 Los Angeles and nearly 100,000 in 1930.[44] Roughly one-half of Mexican-born women in that city worked outside the home. The great majority knew English. The great majority of urban Chicanos remained poor and mobile, but by the 1920s, a growing minority was approaching the lowest rungs of middle-class status.

Young Mexican immigrants had many opportunities to soak up mainstream culture—whether their parents liked it or not. A Mexican immigrant noted that although she appreciated the freedom in Southern California to go where she pleased without supervision, "liberty" had been "contagious" for her daughters. Young Chicanas shopped, danced, went to movies, bobbed their hair, wore makeup, and of course dated—often away from the supervision of their parents. An eighteen-year-old lamented that her father "began to watch me" two years ago "and would not let me go anywhere or have my friends come home. He was born in old Mexico but he has been here long enough to know how people do things." A mother regretted that "my Juanita wants [to dance] because the others do...I know the things I was taught as a girl and right and wrong cannot change."[45] "This terrible freedom in the United States" made it difficult to keep girls out of trouble, lamented one woman.[46] "Whose life is it anyway?" their daughters often countered.[47] Indeed, young women often won such battles. One-third of Los Angeles-area women immigrants from Mexico married Anglos, and many were pregnant when they did so.

Racial distinctions hardly disappeared early in the twentieth century. Lynching continued in the South, and blacks in Chicago and Chicanos in Los Angeles faced discrimination in housing, employment, and education. Korean-American Mary Paik Lee recalled that during her first day in school at Riverside, California, early in the twentieth century, a group of girls surrounded the Koreans and danced in a circle, singing this song:

> Ching Chong, Chinaman,
> Sitting on a wall.
> Along came a white man,
> And chopped his head off.

Each of the girls then "came over to me and hit me in the neck."[48] But continued discrimination did not preclude interethnic social and particularly cultural mingling.

Ethnic distinctions among recent European immigrants softened, particularly in urban areas. A survey taken in Greenwich Village in the 1930s found that 70 percent of Italian Americans who were over the age of thirty-five disagreed that marriage should be arranged by parents as compared with 99 percent of those who were below the age of thirty-five. The older group was much more likely to agree that large families were a blessing.[49]

White working-class youth, like African Americans, did much to pioneer new cultural forms. Young working men and women had for the past century embraced the freedom of the street and other public spaces as their real wages and workplace autonomy declined. The early twentieth-century combination of rising incomes and shorter working hours provided more money and time for leisure. Kathy Peiss describes how young, working-class women carefully balanced their desires and reputations in trading a spectrum of sexual favors for various presents. These "charity girls" were not prostitutes; they simply aspired to be attractive enough to enjoy nights out on the town without having to pay for their meals or entertainment.[50]

The status of children had risen by the 1920s. Children from comfortable homes enjoyed more toys and more time in which to enjoy them. Child psychology became a well-established field, and a much greater proportion of the populace believed that childhood represented an extremely important, even sacrosanct, stage of human development, replete with its own culture and requirements. "I have to be a pal and listen to my children's ideas," explained a Muncie, Indiana, mother. Others stressed how devoted they had become to their children. "I accommodate my entire life to my little girl," remarked a middle-class mother. Such parents were often more tentative, less sure of themselves than their mothers had been. "In those days one did not realize that there was so much to be known about the care of children," explained one, adding, "I am afraid of making mistakes and usually do not know where to go for advice."[51] Patriarchy continued its long decline. "We are a gang," proclaimed one father. "And I don't insist on being the leader of the gang more than my share of the time…"[52] Prosperity and the expansion of high school and college served to prolong childhood—and to establish adolescence as a distinct and increasingly independent stage in life. In Muncie, the great majority of high-school students went to the movies without their parents, and about half were away from home on more evenings than not. Teenagers were the most skilled manipulators and consumers of new technologies and products: automobiles, music, film, and other elements of popular culture. A pious working-class mother who had helped her son buy his Ford lamented, "Now he wants a Studebaker so he can go seventy-five miles an hour." "He don't pay any attention to mom and pop," she added.[53]

Family life became more focused on emotional satisfaction as its economic functions receded. Fathers, especially, played more with their children. Spouses and lovers referred to each other in highly familiar, jocular terms: "dearest Daddy"; "sweet Daddie"; "Sis"; "papa"; "kiddo"; "sweetheart mine"; Billie Boy mine"; and "dear little baby." Husbands and wives expected, and often received, more love and consideration from each other.

A husband recounted his devotion to his wife not by establishing his success as a breadwinner, as his grandfather would have done, but by recalling that "I give you coffe on the bed every morning and I kissed good buy when I whent to work."[54] Some blue-collar men became less domineering, more willing to view their marriages as an economic partnership. The husband of a wife who worked with him in an East St. Louis meatpacking plant observed that "the couple have a comfortable home & have gotten ahead some because his wife was willing to help when she could." The same respect could translate to a wife who did not work outside the home. A San Francisco streetcar worker noted that if his wife "was not such a good mother, cook, seamstress, doctor, barber, and laundress, we could never make ends meet."[55]

But if the number of highly satisfying, reciprocal marriages went up, so did the number of those characterized by friction and dissatisfaction. Exhibit A was a rising divorce rate, as husbands and wives alike brought higher expectations to marriage. Women's increasing, if still modest, capacity for economic independence had something to do with this. "If a woman has ever worked at all she is much more likely to seek a divorce," observed an attorney. "It's the timid ones that have never worked who grin and bear marriage."[56] The modern woman expected much more than support from her husband. Complained one, "I never have any good time since I married." Husbands also craved romance. One, who was in love with another woman, echoed the Hollywood view of romance by telling his wife that she should be "more of a sweet heart & less of a mother," for "if a man hasn't a sweet heart at home he'll have one some place else." Marriage was supposed to be fun, and if it was not, more and more men and women felt that they had a sort of moral obligation to themselves to move on. Hence a woman married to one minister, but in love with another, described the latter as "my own Godgiven husband" whom she must "meet to part no more . . . on this earth. God must let us live and work together. *Yes he must.*"[57]

Other women worried that they would never meet their soul mate and that courtship and marriage seemed to be a pale and insufficient approximation of the enraptured sheikhs and flappers who populated the silver screen. "All the most blissfully peaceful and restful moments of a woman's life are those in the arms of him who loves her," wrote a young woman. When no such man materialized, she began a correspondence with an imaginary lover, a man she feared was "only a 'phantom of Dreams.'" She settled for a hard-working man she respected, though just weeks before the wedding she lamented that "I never 'fell in love.'"[58]

The hothouse nature of heterosexual society often harmed women. The rich, same-sex intimacy—sexual and otherwise—that had characterized so much of middle-class life in the nineteenth century faded early in the twentieth century, as young women spent more and more time in the company of young men. Even avant-garde men who championed androgynous, egalitarian partnerships ended up replicating male privilege. Many husbands simply embraced the cultural norm of freedom and dropped their sense of responsibility. A St. Louis man was content to let his wife work full-time in a garment factory and to keep house so that he could just "look nice all the time."[59] Men's ambivalence toward women seemed to increase as the emotional distance between them receded. Abusive husbands of the 1920s and 1930s were much more likely than their nineteenth-century counterparts to attack their wives' sexuality. Others expressed ambivalence over the home itself. A poor woman in northern California recounted how she had managed to get a tree and "a few things together" one Christmas. Her husband came home late and drunk, and "upon entering the house and seeing the little tree, all fixed up, he became so angry that he took the tree and tore it to pieces, took all the little gifts and presents off of the tree and mutilated and destroyed them." "Not being satisfied with this," and while "cursing and defaming" his wife, he deposited the table cloths, bed coverings, cooking utensils, and "all the food there was in the house," on the kitchen floor and then dumped soot over them. This man's contempt for everything that marriage and family stood for could hardly have been more complete or palpable. Yet such men could also seem to be abjectly dependent. One man who had struck his wife assured her that "with a little encouragement, I'd be the sweetest thing in the world to you cause to me you're the most perfect, sweetest, most beautiful little thing Ive ever known." His next letter began, "Dam your soul."[60]

Violence against wives evidently became more frequent and extreme even as homicides and other forms of violence outside the family became rarer. Women who confronted such violence had more support than before from police officers and judges. "No man has a legal or moral right to bruise or beat his wife, or compel obedience by physical strength or domineering force," asserted the Oregon Supreme Court in 1921.[61] Women, for their part, more readily left, resisted, or talked back to abusive husbands. When her husband persisted in calling her, her mother, and her grandmother prostitutes, a divorce-seeking wife recounted to the judge: "Well, I didn't take that, and I said, 'Well, you're a pimp.'" Her husband then slapped her, though not with the results he had hoped for: "It isn't in my disposition to give in," she explained.[62] But the dangers faced by such women were in fact increasing. Neighbors and family members had become more reluctant to intervene even in violent marriages as the home became more private and marriage more intimate. Roger Lane has established that the percentage of homicides involving family members rose early in the twentieth century even as the overall homicide rate continued to decline. After all, "the underside of love and affection is possessiveness, jealousy, and tension."[63]

Likewise, violence against children in the home evidently became more extreme even as children became more prized. Spouses described themselves as inflicting extreme, often gratuitous forms of violence on their children, a prime example of such behaviour being the husband who shook his five-day-old baby hard after declaring that "he wasn't going to have that brat squalling any more."[64] Violence might erupt over children's rising desire for independence, but some of it also arose from the higher emotional pitch of family life. Nineteenth-century husbands and parents had ordinarily struck wives and children, respectively, in a considered, deliberate fashion, to punish or to coerce particular behaviors. In families of the 1920s, violence erupted less predictably and more readily.

* * *

Clara Bow grew up under extraordinarily violent and trying circumstances. Born in 1905 to an impoverished and quarrelsome couple in New York City, one of her earliest memories was of her doting grandfather having an epileptic fit while pushing her on a swing. He died a day later. Her best friend, a young boy from the neighborhood, died in her arms from burns. Her feckless father beat and sexually abused her. When Clara began to shine as an actress, her mentally ill mother said Clara was "goin' straighta hell" and threatened to kill her.[65]

The movies had always offered Clara an escape from her tragic childhood. They soon offered an avenue to fame. She impressed directors with her beauty, earnestness, and capacity to express a wide range of emotions—a crucial talent in the era of silent pictures. "It was easy for me t'cry," she recalled. "All I hadda do was think of home." Selected as the "It" girl for the movie of the same title, she became the biggest name in Hollywood in the late 1920s by playing uninhibited, fun-loving young women who got their men. Fitzgerald himself dubbed her "the quintessence of what the term 'flapper' signifies."[66]

But Bow pushed her independence too far. She ran up gambling debts and went through a series of public and often messy romances. "If you can't be good, be careful," advised one movie magazine. Gary Cooper wooed her, but she was put off by his reticence: "The biggest cock in Hollywood an' no ass t'push it with," she liked to say.[67] Sexual scandal and anxiety over acting in the talkies prompted a retreat to a more private life in the 1930s. But neither marriage nor motherhood suited Bow, who attempted suicide and was eventually diagnosed as schizophrenic.

Bow both represented and outran her times. The emergence of Hollywood gave her a dream and a venue in which she could redeem her tragic childhood, as her expressive face exuded a sort of magnetic authenticity that millions of movie goers found irresistible. But even the "It" girl was supposed to contain her desires, to find sexual and personal fulfillment in marriage on and off the screen.

Judged by the standards of the late twentieth or early twenty-first centuries, the "flaming youth" of the 1920s seem tame. Most youngsters got married and stayed married. Researchers of Carolina mill towns of this period concluded that its residents were characterized by "a broad network of obligation, responsibility, and concern"—the temptations of salacious movies and popular music notwithstanding.[68]

But the culture of obligation was clearly under siege by a spreading ethos of self-fulfillment and pleasure. Three decades of depression, war, and readjustment would slow the permissive turn. But the cult of happiness that emerged from the 1920s set the template for modern life and would persist beneath the surface of more sober eras, reasserting itself with a vengeance after they had passed.

Chapter 7

The Family in Crisis and After

The roaring twenties ended with a thud late in 1929—with a dramatic stock-market crash followed by a deep and durable depression. Its full-throttled embrace of pleasure and freedom would not fully resurface for another three decades. But neither did it disappear.

Three distinct eras appeared between 1929 and the early 1960s: the Great Depression of the 1930s; World War II; and "the fifties," a sort of short-hand term for a period of consensus and traditionalism that lasted from the end of World War II to some point in the early to mid-1960s. The Depression and the war at the very least slowed the movement toward individualism that had gathered so much momentum by the 1920s, and the memory of hardship and privation would very much color life after the war. Yet a commitment to leisure, women's increased employment, and the growing role of the state persisted, and by the 1950s, many elements of the 1920s had returned: political conservatism, the pursuit of pleasure, and a growing sense of permissiveness. The three decades that separate the "roaring twenties" from the tumultuous sixties illustrate that economic and political crises could only temporarily and partially retard the forces of expressive individualism that had so brashly emerged earlier in the century.

* * *

The Great Depression hit families hard and for a long time. One out of five banks failed, and millions of families lost their life savings. Many also lost their homes or farms. Farm income in 1932 stood at one-third of what it had been in 1929. The average family's income declined 40 percent from 1929 to 1933, to $1,500. The unemployment rate, which had stood at just 3.2 percent in 1929, skyrocketed to 23.6 percent in 1932. Men often took the Depression personally; it undercut the essential element of being a good husband and a good father. In the Dakotas, where businessmen and successful farmers had long asserted that only lazy men failed, many lost their livelihoods and their land, and young men left in droves. "Sometimes I feel like a murderer," said a New York man who had gone without a steady job for two years. "What's wrong with me, that I can't protect my children?"[1] A Chicago investigator reported that some men were so humiliated at being unemployed that they put on their work clothes and stayed away from home all day. "The Polish family is based on authority, not on love," noted a priest. "The prestige of the former wage earner is lowered by asking working children or women for spending money—for beer, for cigarettes, for carfare."[2] Of course not all unemployed men had the luxury of asking their children and wives for money. Many watched them go hungry. New York City recorded 110 deaths by starvation in 1934, and more children than not were malnourished in the poorest parts of the country. In Harlan County, Kentucky, people lived "on dandelions and blackberries," and hungry children reportedly chewed on their hands to keep hunger at bay.[3] "Momma wouldn't eat, but watched us eat," recalled a Southern daughter.[4] Programs such as the Worker's Progress Administration offered employment, but the wages were low, and some men simply could not bring themselves to do the work. Decades later, my aunt Helen Nelson recalled the sense of hopelessness that she felt when her husband arrived home after his first day on a public-works project to announce that he had quit. The foreman had told him to slow down to make sure that the job would last, and he was not about to work for an outfit that told a man to slack off.

Many families fragmented under such pressures. Marriage declined by 22 percent early in the Depression. The rate of divorce declined during the Depression because families could not afford them; the rate of separations increased. Not a few of the men riding the rails or inhabiting hobo camps were husbands and fathers, men who could not stand the shame of living with a family that they could not support. The fertility rate declined from 2.45 to 2.0. Many families resorted to sending their children to orphanages or other institutions for what they hoped would be temporary stays. The number of children living in such places increased by 50 percent during the Depression's first two years.[5]

This sort of desperation blunted criticism of government's growing role in families. The Depression discredited both big business and laissez-faire economics. President Franklin D. Roosevelt won a great deal of popularity for arguing that government should help ordinary people come to terms with joblessness and other aspects of economic hardship. In reality, however, much of his program actually benefited wealthier people. The Agricultural Adjust Act, for example, paid generous amounts of federal money to big farmers to keep their land out of production, a decision that drove thousands of tenant farmers from their homes and livelihoods. But the New Deal's relief programs, particularly its work-relief programs, were very, very popular. The federal government also undertook an ambitious national retirement program (social security), a rural-electrification program, a federal home mortgage insurance that enabled many thousands of families to keep or secure a house, and unemployment and disability insurance. The number of clinics dispensing advice regarding birth control increased more than twenty-five-fold during the 1930s.[6] Conservatives such as Herbert Hoover worried that the arrival of the welfare state would kill American individualism and initiative, that it would ultimately harm people's capacity to help themselves and one another. But large Democratic pluralities throughout the 1930s revealed that his was a minority voice.

Government programs that would outlive the Depression were assuming more of the work that family and kin had once performed. In the short term, though, the Depression prompted more reliance on family and kin. Those rendered homeless often moved in with relatives. In Bell Gardens, a Los Angeles suburb, 15 percent of families provided homes for kin or for others. Working wives commonly sent part of their earnings to relatives who did not live with them. Housework again became more productive and less consumptive. As income declined or disappeared, women who had once purchased ready-made clothes now made dresses out of flour sacks; those who had purchased canned goods now preserved fruits, vegetables, and meat. Women's access to high-paying, professional jobs and to school teaching suffered a severe blow, as public opinion and often the law turned against married women working when men were unemployed. In 1939, nearly nine out of ten men—and most women—agreed that "women should not hold a job after marriage."[7] Yet the proportion of women—including wives and mothers—who worked outside the home grew substantially during the Depression. Women and children made money by cleaning, laundering, and doing other jobs that few men were willing to work at, income that was crucial to family survival when so many husbands had been idled. In sum, women's employment became more important to families than ever before, even as women had more difficulty getting or holding jobs that men were interested in. Women's lives focused more on the family and less on individual achievement. A national survey of well-educated families found that women were more apt in 1933 than in 1927 to say that marriage entailed sacrifice, and they expressed a high degree of satisfaction with family life.[8]

Children contributed more to household incomes than they had in the 1920s. In Oakland, one-half of teenage boys and one-quarter of teenage girls worked part-time. A Cleveland study found that just 3 percent of working sons and 2 percent of working daughters did not contribute money for family expenses and that children helped with housework more than they had done in the 1920s.[9]

The Depression compounded the difficulties faced by African Americans. They received less government support than did their white counterparts and faced greater unemployment. A Georgia resident reported to President Roosevelt that local relief officials "give us black folks, each one, nothing but a few cans of pickle meet and to white folks they give blankets, bolts of cloth and things like that." He could not sign his name for fear that "they will beat me up and run me away from here and this is my home."[10] African Americans suffered much higher unemployment rates than whites and received much less relief. A great deal of suffering lay behind these stale facts. Ossie Guffy's father, who had made a good living as a candy maker, died when she was one, early in the Depression. Her mother then had to become a live-in maid and left Ossie and her sister with her parents—until Ossie's sister burned to death because of her alcoholic grandfather's neglect. Ossie's enraged mother called her father "a murderer," a charge that prompted her mother to protest, "If you don't know by now that a black woman can get a job when a black man can't, you got a lot to learn. And natchully, he turns to the drink when he can't get nothing to bring home to his family."[11] Maya Angelou's childhood also blended tragedy with community. She bounced between the homes of her divorced parents and her grandparents, suffered rape by her mother's boyfriend at age eight, and endured segregation and other forms of racism even as she lived in a series of communities in which many adults cared deeply about her.

The Depression was particularly hard on Mexican Americans. Between one-half and one-third left for Mexico. Anglo-American community leaders in the Southwest and government officials had long assumed or asserted that Latinos flowed back and forth across the border as needed. With unemployment at unprecedented levels, they believed strongly that the "Mexicans" should "go home"—even if they were U.S. citizens with deep roots in what was now the United States. Officials forcibly rounded up some Mexicanos. They told many more to leave. Others went South hoping to find work in Mexico—and were confronted by a much stronger border patrol if they then attempted to return to the United States. The decline of tenant farming and growing poverty drove many from their farms. White migrants from the Dust Bowl displaced Mexican-American agricultural laborers in California. Government officials routinely assumed that Latinos could not really be Americans, so New Deal programs commonly excluded them.

Mexican American families that were forced or prompted to return to Mexico often struggled there. Youth who had grown up in the United States confronted strict religious and cultural mores, particularly in rural Mexico. "Here the girls all dress alike, in black," lamented one, and "when a girl is married, it's all over."[12]

But the Depression made the Mexicanos who stayed in the United States more family oriented, partly because repatriation bore most heavily on unattached men from Mexico. Native-born Mexicans outnumbered Mexicanos born in the United States in 1930. By 1940, the latter were a large majority. Tradition and economic privation encouraged mutualism. Frances Esquibel Tywoniak, born in 1931 in rural New Mexico, later recalled: "Everyone took care of everyone else.... There always seemed to be a lot of people around, all family.... People loved each other." Every morning she and her older sister greeted their grandmother the same way: "Good morning, grandmother. May I have your blessing?"[13]

The Great Depression ultimately had a conservative impact on the nation's families, as it commonly prompted its members to depend on and care for each other more intensively. Mira Komarovsky's study of native-born, urban families found that the Depression altered the husband's status only about one-quarter of the time. Wives commonly blamed a spouse's unemployment on circumstances beyond his control. "This depression proves to me how courageous and devoted my husband is to the family," remarked one. "He will go without food for the sake of the children."[14] Strong, well-organized families tended to work together to get through hard times and those with weaker structures—a relatively small minority—tended to fall apart. The Depression retarded the movement toward freedom and individuality.

Yet elements of the 1920s persisted. The nation remained, by many measures, prosperous. Studies conducted in 1918 and 1935 revealed that those living during the latter period had, on average, better diets and wider access to such modern conveniences as automobiles, electricity, indoor plumbing, telephones, and radios than did those who lived during the former period. People in the 1930s were much less likely to buy a new car than they were in the 1920s, but they drove more than ever before. Movies, radio, and recorded music remained popular. This was, after all, the era of the big band, of Bennie Goodman and jitterbugging. *Esquire* magazine appeared in the 1930s and legitimized, in the words of Bill Osgerby, "the growth of a consumption-oriented masculine self" by locating masculinity not in the world of "hard work, thrift and production" but in "a reverence for tasteful elegance," of fine clothing, food, and home furnishings.[15] Plenty of impoverished families had no time or money for such diversions. But for those with steady and remunerative jobs, the 1930s in many ways resembled the 1920s. A study of suburban life in Westchester County, New York, found that girls spent roughly one-third of their leisure time at the movies and that youth moved in parallel worlds from their parents. "Oh, yes, I've been home, and so has Father, but I haven't seen him for three days," observed one suburban daughter.[16]

World War II set a very different tone. Jobs were easy to come by, and the average wage or salary increased substantially. Despite the rationing of meat, coffee, gasoline, and some other staples, civilian purchases rose smartly. Workers, who were making much more money than ever before, headed for restaurants and movie theaters. Advertisers and industrialists defined the war as a battle for the freedom to consume. "The Modern American bathroom is an example of the highest standard of living ever known…A Standard of Living Worth Fighting For," proclaimed one advertisement.[17] The war brought a sense of national unity. Few protested the U.S. entry into the war after Pearl Harbor, and rationing, scrap drives, war-related work, and widespread military service lent a sense of unity to a nation that had suffered substantial economic and political divisions during the Depression.

But the war also brought a great deal of social fragmentation. Roughly one in five Americans migrated during the war, often repeatedly and over great distances. Millions of husbands and fathers joined the armed services. The federal government and private industry encouraged women to work outside the home during the war, particularly in defense plants. Unprecedented numbers of women made good money for the first (and, usually, last) time in their lives in welding and other occupations that had been off-limits to them.

The rate of women's employment outside the home jumped, particularly for mothers of young children. Even those who did not earn money found themselves taking on more and more responsibility because of absent husbands. Wages were way up, but so were prices, and housewives had to work around the rationing of sugar, coffee, meat, dairy products, canned goods, gasoline, and many other staples. Wives took up gardening or raising chickens out of necessity and patriotism. Children, particularly the youth, were often left to their own devices due to absent fathers and working mothers, especially when their families had moved away from kin to pursue job opportunities. The federal government opened thousands of day-care centers to encourage the mothers of young children to work outside the home, but they serviced only a small fraction of working mothers. Many older children left school early to work or to enlist. The number of employed fourteen- and fifteen-year-olds quadrupled between 1941 and 1945.[18] Those residing in rapidly expanding cities or near military bases lived in an exciting and often dangerous world. Cities of tens of thousands of people appeared in a year's time, and many small towns and big cities alike burst at the seams. The combination of autonomy, spending money, and new, often fleeting friends created a marked increase in venereal disease and premarital pregnancy.

These diverse changes put a great strain on families. The whole country seemed to be on the move, money was flowing freely, and who knew what the morrow might bring. Patricia Livermore moved from South Dakota to Omaha in 1943 and worked as a photographer in nightclubs there. The war was "a very hectic, exciting time," she remembered, "but there was always an underlying sadness, a melancholy." "Relationships were extremely intense, because you didn't know how long they would last." She "did a lot of crying in those years, a lot of crying. I wasn't the only one." This hothouse environment of fleeting romances and fear of impending death prompted many ill-conceived romances and marriages. Barbara Norek of San Francisco was just twelve when the war began and her father receded from her life as he started working the graveyard shift in a shipyard. At the age of fourteen, she "became the best churchgoer in the neighborhood," since "each week a whole new crop of sailors was coming in." At one point she was engaged to five men at the same time. "I was sailor crazy." There were some awkward moments, such as when a suitor returned from duty "with a big diamond engagement ring," only to find out that Norek was two years younger than she had led him to believe and that her mother was not prepared to let him "take me off to Ohio." But many young women and men took these wartime romances very seriously—at least at first. The marriage rate during the month following the attack on Pearl Harbor was 60 percent higher than it had been during the same month the year before. Virginia Rasmussen tried to follow her soldier husband as he traveled around the United States. She and the other young wives sat on their suitcases in the aisles of trains, and she recalled "being put off in a place called El Reno, Oklahoma, which to me was nowhere, and I had to fend for myself," get a hotel room and look for transportation the next day. "It was a tremendous lesson in growing up."[19]

Many families suffered much more. Henrietta Bingham was just nine at the time of Pearl Harbor, and at that moment "all the war meant to me...was excitement." In 1942 a brother, Gerald, lied about his age to get into the Army Air Corps. He died, and was followed by his younger brother, Gene, who also died. Her "young pretty mother had turned almost white" by the end of the war, and her father had become "an old man." By age thirteen, Henrietta "had lost my childhood."[20] Wives lost husbands, children lost fathers—and the husbands and fathers who survived were often much changed. Fighting in the "good war" commonly entailed a great deal of trauma that went largely ignored and untreated at the time and later. Alcoholism was rife among returnees, and by 1950, some 1 million veterans had divorced. Many were simply unprepared to deal with the demands of young children. "My desire was to get away from it all—away from restrictions," recalled one. "I looked forward to spending a lot of time on the beach. But we had to take the baby. Then we had to bring him back for lunch and a nap. We never could enjoy the beach." Other fathers resented that their children did not warm up to them. "Even when he was two or three years old he just wouldn't let me come close to him," remembered one. "I didn't like it. I didn't like it a bit."[21] The war's end brought an end to high wages for women. But many were reluctant to surrender the autonomy that they had exercised inside and outside the home. Dellie Hahne described herself as a "shrinking violet" when her husband left for the war, a "very strong oak tree" when he returned. Shirley Hackett had learned how to change tires and maintain the car in her husband's absence, "yet he treated me as if I were insane to think that I could do those things."[22] The men were different, too. They went off to confront life and death and returned to wives and sweethearts who "couldn't understand why their men had changed so."[23]

Japanese-American families suffered the most from the war. The federal government decided soon after Pearl Harbor to remove them from the West Coast. They had just a few days to sell those possessions that they could not take with them, and many turned over farms or other businesses to non-Japanese neighbors. Unlike Chinese Americans, most Japanese Americans had succeeded in forming families before immigration was dramatically curtained, in 1924. These families tended to be authoritarian. Fathers and husbands had a great deal of power. These Issei (first generation) ordinarily ran the family business, whether it was a farm or a shop, and they expected their wives and children (Nisei) to obey them. Shidzeú Ishimoto recalled her mother advising, "Endurance a woman should cultivate more than anything else. If you endure well in any circumstances, you will achieve happiness."[24] Internment changed this. Issei men lost their livelihoods, and they had little control over day-to-day life. Everyone ate together, and families had little privacy. The children were much more apt to speak English well, one of several skills that helped them to adjust to life in camp more readily than did their elders. Children had school to keep them busy, and wives still had housework and mothering to do. Jeanne Wakatsuki Houston later recalled that tensions and humiliations in their Manzanar camp drove her father to turn to alcohol in his isolation and anger. When he threatened her mother, Jeanne's brother punched him in the face, an act she likened to "bloodying the nose of God."[25]

Mexican Americans experienced opportunity rather than dispossession because of the war, but also a growing generation gap. The nation's labor shortage prompted its leaders to recruit Mexican workers just a decade after they had tried so hard to exclude them. The braceros worked one-year contracts, though many would make their home in the United States after the war. But the war also affected Mexicanos already living in the United States. Like African Americans and Native Americans, many left rural areas for well-paying jobs in cities during World War II. One observer concluded, "Family solidarity is decreasing. Lack of parental control and dissatisfaction with prevailing conditions have developed too rapidly for adaptation to take place, and disintegration has started."[26] The second generation of Mexican Americans, the children of those who had immigrated early in the twentieth century and who had survived the Great Depression, expressed more interest in and affiliation toward the United States than their parents had. Many joined the armed services, an experience that brought them into close and sustained contact with people from very different cultures. The adoption of so-called "zoot suits" was in some respects a reflection of young men's embrace of American, multi-ethnic youth culture—though many Anglos associated the distinctive style with Chicanos. Octavio Paz, who lived in Los Angeles for two years during the mid-1940s, described young, adolescent "pachucos" as characterized by a "furtive, restless air" befitting a generation caught between cultures.[27] Other rebellions were more subtle. Frances Esquibel had moved with her family from rural New Mexico to California as a child, and by the age of nine, she learned that the worlds of her Anglo schools (the family moved frequently) and home "didn't exist in a state of harmony." She resented having to speak Spanish at home; her father knew little English. They moved to a Mexican barrio, but at junior high she felt out of place. Her solution "was to move more toward the mainstream"—making friends with Anglo girls, for example. By the time she entered high school, in 1945, Frances had become more alienated from her parents and "could not empathize or identify with my mother's subordinate role." Upon graduation she would leave for the University of California, Berkeley.[28]

The close of the war offered sustained prosperity after fifteen years of trauma. The number of new homes increased dramatically. There were 114,000 single-family dwellings erected in 1944, 937,000 in 1946, and 1,692,000 in 1950, an expansion made possible by such time-saving innovations as bulldozers, plywood, and power saws together with government-backed mortgages for veterans and white families.[29] Electric refrigerators, washers, and vacuum cleaners became standard in most homes. Diet improved dramatically, as more families had access to fruits and vegetables year round.

A wider range of people joined the middle class after the war. The children and grandchildren of immigrants from Central, Eastern, and Southern Europe prospered, as did those of Japanese immigrants. Several million Mexicans entered the United States between 1945 and 1960, many illegally.

As before, these newcomers were often solitary and highly mobile young men, including those who continued to participate in the bracero program that had begun during World War II. But the native-born Latino community also continued to grow. Many gained a foothold in the middle class by taking advantage of expanded educational and employment opportunities. The same can be said of African Americans, who had left the rural South in large numbers during the war. The gap between white and black working-class families had narrowed dramatically by the 1950s.

This major expansion of the middle class, broadly defined, and the general surge in relative prosperity created a deep sense of contentment made sweeter by the fifteen years of suffering that had preceded it. "Assessing their situation against a backdrop of turmoil and privation," notes Stephanie Coontz, couples of the 1950s "had modest expectations of comfort and happiness." Hence "they were much more inclined to count their blessings than to measure the distance between their dreams and their real lives."[30] This explains the widespread tolerance or denial of child and wife abuse by family members and professionals alike during the period, she notes, and it strongly informed the nation's tone of self-congratulation and consensus.

As in the 1920s, prosperity prompted a celebration of consumption. People learned to buy their automobiles on credit in the 1920s. By the 1950s, about one half were buying major household goods such as refrigerators or furniture on credit. Family vacations—aided by the spread of paved roads such as the interstate highway system—became an annual landmark of many children's summers. Movies, radios, and record players proliferated. But the advent of television constituted one of the seminal developments of the postwar period. One-third of households owned a set in 1950, three-quarters in 1956. By then televisions had shouldered out pianos and hearths as the symbolic center of family life. (In a nod to tradition, some stations broadcast burning Yule logs on Christmas Eve.)[31] The arrival of television at the home's center signified a colossal shift in day-to-day family life. From the 1950s to the present, families have spent many hours each day passively absorbing countless messages from television advertisers and shows championing and describing the good life of consumption and pleasure.

Home life in fact became more focused on pleasure, less on responsibility. Alan Petigny locates a "permissive turn" in the postwar years and identifies Rogerian therapy as a leading cause. Carl Rogers's humanitarian psychology posited a very optimistic view of human nature that soon pervaded the rapidly expanding fields of secular and religious counseling and popular culture more generally. The percentage of Americans who regarded alcoholism as a disease (as opposed to a sin or a personal failing) rose from 6 percent in 1944 to 63 percent in 1954, for example. Slogans such as "authenticity" and "peace of mind" proliferated. Guilt and sin—emblems of repression—were out, self-actualization was in. Hence observance of the Sabbath declined even as church membership rose. In sum, the culture was moving "the individual further away from the goal of self-mastery and closer to the Romantic ideal of being unrepressed and unencumbered."[32]

The new therapeutic ethos penetrated far beyond urban and educated people. A sociologist who studied behavioral patterns in Wheatland, Missouri, found that younger parents assigned to their children far fewer duties than their parents had assigned to them. Children of the Depression had started bringing in kindling and wood at a young age, picked berries, gathered eggs, fed chickens, and tended vegetable gardens. Girls did dishes and boys milked by eight to ten and were soon doing nearly all the work of adults. These children were parents by the mid-1950s, and they wanted their sons and daughters to enjoy more comforts than they had enjoyed. "We used to whip hell out of 'em," the elders grumbled. "Today they just talk to 'em."[33] Some ethnic groups retained the traditional distance between parents and adults. Herbert Gans found that Italian-American parents seldom played with their children and that they expected obedience and respect from them. But this was becoming a minority view. More and more parents pampered their children. Toy sales shot up from $87 million in 1939 to $608 million in 1953, a seven-fold increase in just fourteen years.[34]

The postwar family was becoming much less hierarchical. Benjamin Spock's first child-care book appeared in 1946 and quickly became the standard. Spock advised parents (particularly mothers, who were by far his greatest audience) to avoid conflict with their children, to treat them permissively. Psychoanalyst Martha Wolfenstein found that in contrast with past experts, who warned against "giving in to impulse"—by picking up a crying baby, for example—the new conventional wisdom held that "early indulgence" would "make the baby less demanding as he grows older." She linked this to a broader cultural development, namely, "the emergence of what we may call 'fun morality.'" "Where formerly there was felt to be the danger that, in seeking fun, one might be carried away into the depths of wickedness, today there is a recognizable fear that one may not be able to let go sufficiently, that one may not have enough fun." "Fun and play have assumed a new obligatory aspect," she concluded.[35] Social critic William Whyte observed that promoters of a new Illinois suburb had initially "advertised Forest Park as housing. Now they began advertising happiness."[36]

The government heavily subsidized white families' search for happiness. The GI Bill educated a generation of middle-class men for free. Ambitious road-building programs, capped by a new interstate highway system, stimulated a boom in suburban growth and created millions of reasonably priced homes that brought families from the city and the countryside to residential neighborhoods. Federal mortgage programs (the Federal Homes Administration and the Veterans Administration) enabled most families to own their own homes. "Children and dogs are as necessary to the welfare of this country as is Wall Street and the railroads," pronounced President Truman in 1948. "Would it not be better to compete in the relative merits of washing machines than in the strength of rockets?" asked Vice President Richard Nixon of Soviet premier Nikita Khrushchev a decade later.[37]

The modern suburb afforded unprecedented comfort and isolation for ordinary families. Oil and natural gas provided heat in the winter, and air conditioners proliferated. Suburbanites seldom used the land surrounding their homes to supplement their larders after the war. Lawn mowers multiplied, and pets, plastic mushrooms, and pink flamingoes shouldered aside vegetable gardens and chickens. Attached garages and private backyards replaced front porches and community parks. Factories, offices, schools, and stores—often in the form of strip malls—also moved to the suburbs after the war, but they were usually separated from residences. White suburbanites tirelessly excluded blacks from their neighborhoods and schools, and they often associated civil rights with communism; each movement symbolized unwelcome and outside threats to their sense of community and safety. Moving to the suburbs almost always meant leaving kin—parents, grandparents, cousins, aunts, and uncles—behind. Mirra Komarovsky, studying a more urban and working-class population, found that more than one-half had lived with relatives since being married.[38] But the great majority favored more autonomous living arrangements, which of course was what the suburbs offered. Ethnic ties among second-generation immigrants weakened, as roughly half of Polish and Italian Americans married outside their ethnic group after the war. Suburbanites socialized at churches and clubs and with neighbors as kinship bonds loosened.

Postwar Americans pinned most of their hopes on the nuclear family. Three distinct trends emerged: a greater proportion of the population married; they married at a younger age; and, in a striking reversal of a long-term historical trend, they had more children. Of the generation that came of age during and after the war, 96.4 percent of women and 94.1 percent of men would marry, and they married sooner than their parents had. The birth rate shot up 50 percent from 1940 to 1957, to 3.52 children per family, about what it had been in 1900. Most women had children early and often; the average postwar mother had her last child at age thirty. Those who could not have children turned to adoption, which grew ninefold between 1937 and 1965—and would have expanded still more sharply if supply had kept up with demand. Indeed, by the close of the 1950s, white adoptive parents were turning to Korea for babies. Many sterile couples felt compelled to adopt. "There's nothing to talk about if you don't have children," explained one hopeful adoptive parent.[39] But most people's urge to parent ran much more deeply than that. For a decade and a half, the nation had suffered through the insecurities of a severe and prolonged depression and then a world war that brought death and uncertainty. Family represented, more than ever before, a return to normalcy.

Young couples seldom expressed reservations over marriage. Asked what they had sacrificed for marriage, husbands tended to answer with statements such as "nothing but bad habits" and "the empty, aimless, lonely life of a bachelor." Most wives who had given up careers for motherhood were quick to emphasize that they "preferred marriage." Marriage, remarked one, offered a "happy, full, complete life; children; a feeling of serving some purpose in life other than making money."[40] The realities of marriage often fell far short of the ideal, particularly for women. But wives seldom voiced discontent overtly, and postwar couples tended to persevere. The divorce rate fell dramatically after the war and then increased, but slowly, in the 1950s.

Postwar marriage bore much more heavily on women than it did on men, who, it was widely believed, best served their families by going out into the world and making as much money as possible. Many men, to be sure, felt "overwhelmed with responsibility" by the prospect of fatherhood.[41] But they also associated the home with recreation and relaxation. For women, it remained a place of work that was only partially eased by electric washing machines and vacuum cleaners. Standards for cleaning rose exponentially, and suburban life required considerable driving to shop, run errands, and transport children to and from school and other commitments. Mothers confronted rising expectations. Experts urged them to enjoy their children, but they also made it clear that "any mistake in mothering could scar a child permanently."[42] Even so, most mothers found in their children a strong sense of meaning and satisfaction. "For the first time in my life," recalled one, "I was absolutely sure of my reason for being alive."[43]

Women fit work around the family. Prosperity swelled the number of women who went to college, but the great majority soon married (two-thirds within six years of graduation, according to one study) and had children. The pattern that emerged in the 1950s was for brides to work outside the home until their first child arrived, then to stay at home until their last child was in her or his teens. By 1960, most women who worked outside the home had children under the age of eighteen.[44] The great majority of women workers, about four in five, labored in low-paying fields: clerical work, cleaning, waiting tables, or hair dressing, for example. Women's access to high-paying professions continued to lag, and college-educated women made less than high-school educated men. But this steady rise in women's employment fueled a great deal of the growing prosperity that so many families enjoyed and in fact played a crucial—and seldom acknowledged—role in the middle class's expansion and prosperity.

By the close of the 1950s, it was evident that the nation's housewives were not as happy as they claimed to be. Betty Friedan in *The Feminine Mystique*, published in 1963 but drawing on research that began in 1957, identified the "problem that has no name": highly educated, upper-middle-class wives were turning to alcohol, antidepressants, and therapy in large numbers because being a housewife was not all that it was cracked up to be. A study of upper-middle-class couples in Boston found that twice as many wives as husbands were discontented with their marriages.[45] The leading women's magazines of the time often acknowledged the tension between domesticity and self-fulfillment and prescribed a sensible solution: women should communicate more frequently with their husbands. But what if those husbands were not listening? Joe Benson, for example, told a researcher in 1955 that he was completely satisfied with his wife and his marriage, that marriage had brought him "the love, care, and attention of a wonderful woman" and "4 great children who will be a credit and comfort to me if I live to be an old man." His wife Margaret also began by singing her spouse's praises, describing him as "a real saint and, compared to other husbands, a perfect mate." But she then remarked that he "expends his energies on carpentry hobbies or such and never seems to need me more than to have a hot meal ready and to have his clothes in good repair." Joe "likes to have me within calling distance, but never seems to need the closeness I require." Another wife noted that she loved her husband, "devotedly and deeply, but as a sort of combination of child and friend."[46] Germaine Greer concluded that for men marriage constituted "companionship that requires no effort."[47]

If women had more reason to be discontented with the domestic arrangements of the 1950s, men were more apt to chafe against them publicly. Exhibit number one was Hugh Hefner's *Playboy Magazine*, which debuted to a wide readership in 1953. Hefner was out to undo the "conformity, togetherness, anonymity and slow death" of male domesticity. "All woman wants is security," warned an early article. "And she's perfectly willing to crush man's adventurous, freedom-loving spirit to get it." "The real message," writes Barbara Ehrenreich, "was not eroticism, but escape—literal escape, from the bondage of bread-winning"[48] Not that Hefner had anything against making money. But he urged men to spend it on themselves, not on women and children. At the other end of the cultural spectrum, and much smaller in number, the disaffected beats rejected consumerism but embraced "male adventure and irresponsibility."[49]

Youth culture also tweaked authority and embraced sex. Thousands of college students rioted early in the 1950s. They aspired not to seize control of universities or to end the Korean War. They raided sororities and women's dormitories in search of feminine undergarments. "We want girls! We want sex! We want panties!" chanted a group of Princeton students in 1953.[50] "Dennis the Menace" and *Mad Magazine* thumbed their noses at the established order. Being bad was becoming good. James Dean played the iconic role of a brooding, alienated loner. Likewise, Elvis Presley seemed quirky when he arrived in a Memphis recording studio with his unorthodox clothes, mumbling "I don't sound like nobody," when asked which musician he resembled. But Elvis soon enthralled millions of youth. His working-class demeanor thrilled young women and girls, who described him to their uncomprehending elders as "just a great big beautiful hunk of forbidden fruit."[51]

Elvis did not materialize out of thin air. The entire postwar era, like the 1920s, was awash in sexuality. To be sure, the youth of the 1950s were more apt than their parents to "go steady." But this term often served to sanction sexual experimentation without the stigma of being considered "loose." Birthrates outside of wedlock were up, and by the early 1960s, most married couples' first-born children had been conceived before the couple had wed. As in the 1920s, prosperity and sexuality flourished side by side, though for young women, especially, walking the fine line between prudery and notoriety could be challenging and confusing. "What does it do to the mind of a sixteen-year-old to be Marilyn Monroe one moment and Little Goody Two-Shoes the next?" recalled a former cheerleader. "Half the time in real civilian life I had to keep pulling those gray flannel skirts down, making sure 'nothing showed.' The other half the time, as a cheerleader, I dropped a skimpy red costume over only bra and panties and got out there in the middle of a gym full of screaming spectators to wiggle my hips all over the place."[52] Elvis was no disaffected beatnik. He was a momma's boy who loved gospel music and uncomplainingly served in the armed services when he was drafted. He dreamed of going into law enforcement and cherished Cadillacs and pliant young women. Like Johnny Cash, another iconic rebel of the 1950s, Elvis was a liminal figure, an entertainer steeped in rural Protestantism and nostalgia who nevertheless lived a wild life and prophesized a less inhibited era.

The more perceptive writers of the 1930s, 1940s, and 1950s detected throughout these diverse decades the golden thread of individualism that had surfaced so brightly in the 1920s. Carson McCullers, in *The Heart is a Lonely Hunter*, observed that the Depression did not deliver the residents of her Southern city from the dilemmas of modernity: "The people dreamed and fought and slept as much as ever. And by habit they shortened their thoughts so that they would not wander out into the darkness beyond tomorrow."[53] Saul Bellow likewise noted that World War II had not rescued his protagonist from the grips of existential ennui, a condition he located in a bogus expectation of "pure freedom." "We suffer from bottomless avidity," for "we have been taught there is no limit to what a man can be."[54] Faced with that terrifyingly tantalizing possibility, *Dangling Man*'s protagonist chooses instead to join the armed services. Sylvia Plath's highly autobiographical *The Bell Jar* likens the adolescence of a well-educated young woman in the 1950s to watching a fig tree with "a fat purple fig, a wonderful future beckoned and winked," ripening on the tip of each branch: domesticity, academia, editing, travel, exotic lovers, athletics, and "many more figs I couldn't quite make out." But she sat "in the crotch of this fig tree, starving to death," for "choosing one meant losing all the rest," and as she waited, each of the figs "began to wrinkle and go black, and, one by one, they plopped to the ground at my feet."[55] John Updike's everyman, Harry Engstrom, debuts at the close of the 1950s, intoxicated and befuddled by the freedoms of modern life. He leaves his wife and child for another woman, surprised that "the world just can't touch you once you follow your instincts." His mistress complains that "he's got the idea he's Jesus Christ out to save the world just by doing whatever comes into his head."[56] Harry—aptly nicknamed "Rabbit"—is drawn back to his family by his second child's birth long enough to contribute to her tragic death. At the book's end, he flees the infant's funeral, free to follow instincts that he can neither comprehend nor predict. " 'Maturity' was the albatross of the postwar [literary] generation," notes Morris Dickstein.[57]

The 1950s was a paradoxical decade in part because the contradictions fathomed by writers such as Plath and Updike eluded most others. Petigny argues that the era's values remained conservative even as its norms became liberal, that adults and youth alike embraced a pleasure-oriented way of living while espousing traditional verities. Hence President Eisenhower could both ask the nation to make the Fourth of July an occasion of "penance and prayer" and spend the day fishing, golfing, and playing bridge.[58]

Alan Ehrenhalt's *The Lost City: The Forgotten Virtues of Community in America* is a striking exploration of how authority operated in three very different Chicago neighborhoods in the 1950s. In St. Nick's, a working-class parish on the Southwest Side, conformity to community norms was enforced by a legion of vigilant, stay-at-home mothers and Father Lynch, who walked the streets on summer evenings on the lookout for teenage parties. Five miles to the East lay Bronzeville, a black ghetto "economically poor, but spiritually and socially rich." Billiken kids' clubs, modeled on the segregated Boy Scouts, aimed "to make boys and girls better sons and daughters and more useful to the community," explained the local *Chicago Defender.* Elmhurst, a prosperous suburb outside Chicago, also emphasized community and conformity. A variety of associations claimed the time of the new arrivals: the Parent Teacher Association (PTA), the Jaycees, the little league, and of course the churches. Elmhurst's homes and neighborhoods were less authoritarian than their poorer counterparts, but teenagers faced a steady diet of regulations and restrictions at York High School, a place that stressed "character and citizenship." Most of Chicago's diverse residents believed "there were natural limits to life...that choice and privacy were restricted commodities, and that authority existed, in large part, to manage the job of restricting them."[59]

But those beliefs were under siege well before the mid-1960s, and not just or even primarily by radicals.

* * *

Edward Hopper, the prominent painter, did his greatest work during the 1930s, 1940s, and 1950s, but often seemed to be hardly touched by these eventful decades. Born in 1882 to a middle-class family outside New York City, he was a gangly, awkward child who soon took refuge in art. He did not marry until his forties and had no children. His wife, Jo Nivis, resembled his mother in being strong and outgoing, traits that both compelled and frightened Edward. He was soon earning enough to insulate the couple from the dislocations of depression and war.

Yet the Hoppers' childless marriage expressed strains that characterized less artistic couples of these decades. Like many educated women, Jo had ambitions of her own that she continually set aside for her insecure husband. "The minute any slight breeze blows in my direction—he must act immediately, kill it dead for all time," she observed during World War II. Hopper painted many alienated couples, men and women who shared the same frame or room, yet remained remote from each other. "I can scarcely stand E.H.," Jo wrote in the 1950s, "but how possibly live without him."[60] Growing numbers of American women then shared Jo's frustrations, even as the great majority of them chose to put the needs of their husbands and children before their own.

Edward's work illustrated common and shared themes that united the diverse decades stretching from 1930 to 1960. His paintings commonly hinted at nostalgia, of old storefronts in small towns or street scenes bereft of skyscrapers or other modern elements. Indeed, the Hoppers criticized abstract painters. "The inner life of a human being is a vast and varied realm and does not concern itself alone with stimulating arrangements of color, form, and design," remarked Edward. But if Edward believed that there was more to life and art than "the inventions of the intellect," his rejection of formlessness did not add up to an embrace of the verities with which he had grown up.[61] Edward Hopper's buildings and couples share a sense of emptiness.

Traditionalists often overlook such indications of unease that appeared well before the age of antiwar protests and instead express much fondness for the years that separated the roaring twenties from the tumultuous sixties. During these years, they argue, Americans pulled together for the common good, licking the Great Depression and Hitler. The 1950s were the "last good time," the calm before the storm of the 1960s, the decade that has led us to rack and ruin.

This point of view is simplistic. It underplays the tremendous discrimination that people of color, women, gays, and lesbians faced. It also overlooks the ways in which the 1930s, 1940s, and 1950s perpetuated the ethos of consumerism that marked the century's first three decades—not to mention the continued growth of government. The postwar embrace of family, which was illustrated most vividly by an unprecedented spike in the fertility rate, represented a desire for stability. But that desire resided alongside a deepening search for pleasure that often loosened familial ties.

The retreat of individualism was in fact partial and short-lived and was the artifact of fleeting rather than durable historical trends. Americans continued to choose consumption and pleasure when they could, to go shopping or to the movies, to listen to music, or to take a drive for an hour or a week. The persistent beat of freedom pounded beneath the surface of depression, war, and conformity. By the close of the 1950s, the nation's decks had been cleared of the residual baggage left over from the dusty Victorians, the more recent convulsions of the Great Depression and World War II, and the decade and a half of adjustment and reorientation that followed them. Our history in the half century since has resembled the 1920s, only much more so.

Chapter 8

Freedom's Florescence

Postwar couples embraced stability after fifteen years of deprivation and dislocation. But they also pursued prosperity and, increasingly, pleasure. Their children would do so much more insistently.

This generation grew up unchastened by memories of depression and war and took comfort for granted. They embraced freedom much more exuberantly than their parents had done. Subsequent generations would clash less radically with their elders in large part because the baby boomers would parent so permissively. The cultivation of individual happiness had become a national obsession by the 1970s for children and parents alike.

This embrace of freedom and individualism allowed a much wider range of families to proliferate and to prosper. But it also signified that freedom had decidedly pushed aside obligation at the center of American culture and society, particularly for men.

* * *

The standard of living continued to rise in the United States in the 1960s and the 1970s. Per capita income tripled from 1940 to 2000, and life expectancy continued to climb steadily after its steep gains in the twentieth-century's first half. The percentage of families living in poverty declined from 22 percent in 1959 to 11 percent in 1973. Expanded federal programs lay behind much of this improvement: Social Security, Aid to Families with Dependent Children, unemployment insurance, Medicare and Medicaid, food stamps, and public housing. The proportion of overcrowded U.S. households fell from 16 percent in 1950 to 5 percent in 1976. Continued technological innovations and efficiencies meant that even lower-income families enjoyed a much wider range of goods and services than ever before, including automobiles, air travel, eating out, telephones, television, music, and other forms of entertainment. The average hours of household television viewing per day increased from just over five in 1960 to more than seven in 1995, and the number of video games played on television, computers, and hand-held devices has multiplied since then.[1] More and more families owned second cars and took vacations. Homes became larger and more comfortable, with improved temperature control. The great majority of families in the United States enjoyed a level of material comfort and forms of entertainment unimaginable to even the wealthy elite of the nineteenth century.

But even families living much better than their great grandparents did are apt to feel and believe that they are not doing well. There is often a material basis for this perception, as working-class people's real wages have declined in recent decades; in the 1970s and 1980s, the United States shifted decisively from manufacturing to finance, lowered taxes on corporations and the wealthy, and cut funding to many of the government programs that had lifted so many out of poverty during the 1960s. Economic inequality has become steadily more acute since then. The proliferation of television shows and movies showing highly affluent people, together with the growing chorus of advertisers selling expensive automobiles, clothing, jewelry, vacations, and other prized symbols of prosperity, has created a sense of relative deprivation among people who, objectively speaking, live comfortable lives. In *The Paradox of Choice: Why Less is More*, Barry Schwartz explores how our abandonment of "good enough" for "the best" has engendered a chronic sense of regret, as we quickly take each new pleasure for granted and continued to fret about and resent what we may be missing.[2]

This restless sense of discontent is bound up with what Daniel Bell calls the "contradictions of capitalism." Early capitalism required saving and other forms of discipline. But productivity created a plethora of consumer goods, of material comforts that undercut the very forces of discipline and self-control that had created the bounty. Capitalism had been "based on a moral system of reward rooted in the Protestant sanctification of work," a system that modernity rejected for "a hedonism which promises material ease and luxury."[3] Many people remain dedicated to their work. But the nature of work has shifted to encourage self-reflection and self-realization. The economy has continued to shift from production-oriented jobs in agriculture and manufacturing to the provision of services, occupations that—at least at the higher levels—put a premium on initiative and creativity. The new work, in the words of cultural critic David Frum, encourages people to strive "for identity and personhood, rather than for duty."[4] Robert Bellah and his associates make the distinction between the old-fashioned notion of work as a "calling" that linked one to other members of the community in a web of mutuality to the new definition of work as career, as part of the fashioning of a solitary and continually evolving self.[5]

Hence business leaders, people long associated with the "establishment" or the status quo, have commonly used self-indulgent, anti-authoritarian rhetoric. Jefferson Cowie observes that the economic elites of the 1980s embraced "privilege without responsibility; wealth without obligation; nobless without oblige."[6] But if the economic fruits of deregulated capitalism were being spread more and more unevenly, its culture was relentlessly inclusive—even of its putative critics. Advertisers referred to the young counterculture as "the Now Generation," youth "given over to self-fulfillment by whatever means necessary—which would, of course, ultimately mean by shopping."[7] The consumer-oriented economy cultivates a culture obsessed with freedom and happiness.

Our valoration of freedom has been in many ways a positive development. The civil rights movement went national in the 1960s and was followed by movements espousing the rights of students, women, gays and lesbians, Chicanos, and other marginalized groups. National legislation eased discrimination against African Americans and women and liberalized immigration policies. Oppressed groups stood up for themselves more resolutely than before, and growing numbers of people expressed much more concern over injustice than they had in the past.

But only up to a point. The idealism and hope that characterized much of the 1960s' counterculture took a serious hit in the wake of political assassinations and a resurgent conservatism led by presidents Nixon and Reagan. Oppressed groups such as African Americans, Chicanos, and women have continued to advocate for themselves, but their appeal has narrowed as leaders of broad moral vision such as Ella Baker, Martin Luther King, and César Chávez have been supplanted by the more particular concerns of interest-group politics. Moreover, modern people of various ideological persuasions simply lost interest in reform. "In a world where your only obligation is to do what you really want to do, to admit that one is sacrificing would be to invite the suggestion that one should simply stop and pursue what one really wants," observes Ann Swindler.[8] "Look to your own oppression" often morphed into "do you own thing." A participant in the antidraft movement recalled "a real concentration on life styles and new sexual forms, all these supposedly revolutionary ways of living that weren't tied down to the old modes... this gross kind of individualism. You just go ahead and do what you want."[9]

Second-wave feminism challenged this individualism. True, women's liberation entailed personal liberation. But its principal tool for effecting that transformation was consciousness-raising, moments of individual insight arrived at in a collective setting. In such meetings, Ellen Willis "felt immediately accepted. If I made a comment, people listened to it... which I was not used to in New Left Groups."[10] Like their nineteenth-century forbearers, feminists dedicated themselves to making the world better. They created a dense, grassroots network of health and rape-crisis centers, battered women's shelters, and other services for vulnerable women. Yet the women's movement soon fragmented over a growing number of issues, including: the needs of professional white women versus women of color; sexual orientation; political activism versus the cultivation of a distinctive but often reclusive women's subculture; sexuality as a locus of oppression or freedom; and, at least in academia, the amoral implications of postmodernism. Young third-wave feminists who emerged late in the century tended to embrace a more amorphous, unstructured style of feminism that redrew or erased altogether definitions of gender, oppression, and political activism that the older generation had worked so hard to establish. Germaine Greer dismissed her younger counterparts as indulging in "ostentatious, sluttishness and disorderly behavior."[11] Indeed, Susan Faludi reported that a scholar at a 2010 conference on the future of gender studies urged her audience to embrace a "[Lady] Gaga feminism" dedicated to committing acts of "disloyalty" and "betrayal and rupture."[12] This fixation with deconstruction and transgression tends to equate liberation with simply dismantling the status quo, particularly conventional sexual categories and practices.

But the younger generation was elaborating a tension that had appeared at the birth of second-wave feminism. As Sarah Evans points out, the movement's key insight was that "the personal is political."[13] Feminism spread so widely and quickly because it prompted women to take themselves—not just their responsibilities—more seriously. For the first time in American history, really, women were being asked to see their lives as ends in and of themselves, not as vehicles for supporting and nurturing husbands, children, other dependents, or social causes. Feminism changed everything, even for the many women who professed to abhor it, from how stewardesses who had tolerated endemic sexual harassment became flight attendants to the legal recognition of marital rape to trading in uncomfortable heels, girdles, and dresses for the convenience of pants. But it was difficult to base a coherent women's movement on a slogan that privileged personal experience and desires. If political choice rested on personal choice, what happened when women chose conventional gender roles, phallus-centered pornography, or simply the private pursuit of self-fulfillment at the expense of women's collective concerns? Feminism inevitably became about women doing whatever they wished to, and of course women made such choices in a popular culture saturated with both invitations to self-indulgence and stubborn assumptions of male privilege.

Left and right alike have become uncomfortable with limits. Hence intellectual historian Mark Lilla's survey of the nation's political landscape in the spring of 2010 identifies two strands of libertarianism that have emerged over the past half century: progressives who advocated for "a more tolerant society with greater private autonomy" and self-styled conservatives who "wanted to be free from taxes and regulations so they could get rich fast."[14] These varieties of anarchic libertarianism label any sort of restraint as fascistic and oppressive. "Pleasure," observes Pierre Bourdieu, "is not only permitted but demanded, on ethical as much as on scientific grounds."[15] Dr. King's "beloved community" has been supplanted by the individual's search for unfettered bliss. All that is required of us is to mouth platitudes about freedom, equality, and tolerance. Rules are bad. Apple Computer's classic "1984" commercial, honored by *Advertising Age* as the best of the decade, featured a red-clad woman who eluded riot police to pitch a sledgehammer through a screen on which Big Brother had been promoting the "Unification of Thoughts." The simple, practical act of using an effective (non-Apple) operating system for one's computer made one an Orwellian victim of "groupthink."[16]

Even the Republican Party, once home to Abraham Lincoln and Herbert Hoover, has reinvented itself as the party of irreverence, of a "new conservative libertinism."[17] Ronald Reagan, a divorced ex-actor, was a key figure in conflating constraints on individual liberty (taxes and regulation—the government itself) with assaults on America itself. He ran successfully against President Jimmy Carter (a man with much more convincing evangelical Christian credentials) under this simple slogan: "Are you better off now than you were four years ago?" But the key to Reagan's popularity was his capacity to equate self-interest with traditionalism and moralism. He "offered a restoration of the glory days by bolstering morale on the basis of patriotism, God, race, patriarchy, and nostalgia for community."[18] But this was a call to action that required, in the end, hardly any action and certainly no sacrifice. Reagan, notes Daniel T. Rodgers in *Age of Fracture*, appealed to "that ultimate state of boundlessness: dreaming." Consider his 1985 State of the Union Address: "There are no constraints on the human mind, no walls around the human spirit, no barriers to our progress except those we ourselves erect." It was a political vision that promised everything and demanded nothing but belief. Reagan and the new conservatives had a ready explanation for whom or what to blame when dreams failed to materialize: government became "the people's antagonist, the limiter of their limitlessness."[19]

This blending of conservative libertinism and libertarianism has become stronger in the new millennium. After the terrorist attacks of September 11, 2001, President George W. Bush urged Americans to go shopping and rejected calls to raise taxes to pay for the wars that followed the attacks. At the 2004 National Republican Convention, his daughters celebrated their fondness for "Sex in the City" to distinguish themselves and their party from the passé earnestness expressed by Senator Kerry's children. Now, in 2011, Republicans routinely label as fascists people who are concerned over the cruelties of a health-care system in which millions of people are uninsured.

The common denominator of conservative politics and radical culture is, as it was in the 1920s, individualism. But this is an individualism that goes far beyond what most people conceived of early in the twentieth century. Irene Taviss Thomson's comparison of commentaries on individualism in the 1920s and 1970s detects a shift "towards a less binding society and a more fluid self," that by the latter decade we conceived as "the self...as an entity apart from society."[20] Psychologist Martin Seligman refers to the emergence of "the California self—an exalted entity whose pleasures and pains, whose successes and failures occupy center stage in our society."[21] The signs of this are everywhere, from the popular magazines (including one actually entitled *Self*) to Hollywood movies to popular television shows. Wayne Dyer's *Your Erroneous Zones* sold 4 million copies in the late 1970s and castigated "musterbation," the notion that one should feel obligated to, for example, go to a wedding or a funeral. "Obligation breeds guilt and dependency, while choice fosters love and independence," he explains. A student of Penelope Russianoff, a psychologist who offered workshops on assertiveness for women, recalled in 1975 how she succeeded in taking over the family's living room as her painting studio. Her husband and children simply "had to accept it. There were some hard moments, but I knew I needed it. It was my life and my work at stake."[22]

By the 1990s, as Frank notes, "the defiant individualist resisting the mandates of the machine civilization" had become ubiquitous:

> "An athlete decked out in Mohawk and multiple-pierced ears, a policeman who plays by his own rules, an actor on a motorcycle, a movie fratboy wreaking havoc on the townies' parade, a soldier of fortune with explosive bow and arrow, a long-haired alienated cowboy gunning down square cowboys, or a rock star in a leather jacket and sunglasses, he has become the paramount cliché of our popular entertainment, the preeminent symbol of the system he is supposed to be subverting."[23]

Consider *American Beauty*, a film that won the Academy Award in 2000 and much critical acclaim. The film's characters are neatly divided into good guys (rebels) and bad guys (conformists). The good guys smoke dope, don't care about making money, and are sensitive to beauty. The bad guys are sexually repressed and worried about how the rest of the world perceives them. The leading villain is a homophobic, military man who abuses his family. The film presents us with this choice: "One can maintain one's adolescent rebelliousness (smoking pot, hanging out, ignoring all responsibility, not to mention all moral constraint) and remain free." Or one can "sell out" and "become a neurotic, superficial conformist incapable of experiencing true pleasure."[24]

To be sure, commitment to self could be socially constructive. It could challenge marginalized people to stand up for themselves, could prompt browbeaten or battered wives to start a new life for themselves and their children. The quest for what Peter Clecak terms an "ideal self" prompted millions of people to take their own happiness seriously, to try (and often succeed) at leading more productive and constructive lives, lives that have been more satisfying in the old-fashioned, socially informed, sense of the term.[25]

But more and more people choose a life in which obligations to others are minimized. The proportion of those with no one to talk to about important personal issues has grown dramatically since the mid-1980s, particularly among less-educated people. The bonds of kinship have become more attenuated. The percentage of people who were sixty-five years or older and who lived with extended family (most commonly their children) dropped from nearly one-half in 1900 to around one-third at mid-century to one-eighth in 2000. The percentage of women who were sixty-five years or older and who lived alone has more than doubled from 1950 to 1980, and the proportion of elderly people who saw one of their children at least once a week declined by 25 percent from 1962 to 1984. Prosperity (fueled by the steady expansion of social security) and individualism have served to separate people who used to rely on one another. A sense of commitment to others is declining with each generation. Hence adult children render less help to their parents than vice versa until the parents are very old. A broad range of collective activities have declined, from voting to bowling leagues to PTA membership to simply having people over for dinner. People, by 2000, reported having fewer friends than they did even a generation ago. People who live together are eating together less often than they did in 1975.[26] Many suburban communities of the 1950s shared back lawns. Fences are ubiquitous today. Children socialize, not in their neighborhoods, but via scheduled "play dates" with selected friends located miles away, and much play time occurs indoors, in front of television sets—often with complex video games—or computers. Attached garages and the spread of hired landscaping and gardening services has minimized the amount of time that people spend in front of their houses, and air conditioning keeps people indoors in the summer.

Tight-knit ethnic communities have fragmented since the mid-twentieth century. The Irish of South Boston's Upper End in the 1990s bragged, "Southie is still a real community. We know everybody in our neighborhood. We don't lock the doors at night." But they also acknowledged that local employment was much less secure, the role of the Catholic Church less pronounced, and kinship ties less consequential as the younger generation commonly married and lived outside the community. "By not caring for their relatives they are isolating themselves from the world," remarked one resident. "Even in South Boston some prefer paying more than $5,000 each year for childcare when their relatives are living close enough." An elderly woman observed that her children's generation "are leading a better life in the suburbs, but sometimes they appear to be just 'wandering,' I mean, still searching for something.... I feel that they are missing 'relationships.'... Well, I don't know. I don't know what they are thinking about."[27] The children of such women are often torn by the competing claims of family and career. A computer engineer remarked that it would be "a kind of shame to go back to a blue-collar job," that he needed to "keep pushing." Yet he turned down an attractive position in California as he did not want to "desert" his parents." "I fell into a big dilemma." As Yasushi Watanabe notes, these Irish American families must balance the tradition of "working-class virtues and neighborhood" with the "expectations and pressures to keep 'moving up the hill' for better opportunities and higher accomplishments."[28] Alane Salierno Mason, born into an intimate Italian American family in 1964, weighed her desire for independence and career against the social demands of her isolated grandmother, who assures her, " 'I don't want you to have to quit your job,' which means, of course, that in some part of herself she has already imagined, already wished that I will." "What's more important," Mason wonders, "freedom or love?"[29]

This trend has affected rural areas too. Ron Powers returned to Hannibal, Missouri, at the turn of the twenty-first century to find that his boyhood community had been undercut by the rise of agribusinesses and chain stores at the expense of locally owned farms and merchants. Suburbanization and dropout rates were up, whereas community pride and celebrations were down.[30]

Atomism contributes to acute social problems. The United States has had the highest rate of mental disorders in the Western world, and it has increased over time. Self-reporting of anxiety has risen. The homicide rate roughly doubled from the late 1950s to the mid-1970s, rising from under 5 per 100,000 to just over 10 per 100,000 at its peak in 1980. Roger Lane, the leading historian of murder, attributes this rise to postindustrialism. If the culture of self-restraint fostered by industrialization depressed homicide rates in nineteenth-century cities, its dissolution has contributed to their rise, particularly among the young, marginalized men, who are the most frequent killers. The suicide rate, which had peaked early in the Depression and declined during the 1950s, grew steadily in the 1960s and 1970s and much more sharply among the youth, who were three times more likely to kill themselves at the turn of the twenty-first century than in the early 1960s. In the realm of suicide, as in the realm of homicide, the United States has had much higher rates than other industrialized nations in the last several decades. Andrew Oldenquist attributes the rise in youth suicide in the 1960s and 1970s to broader social changes: "We have continually diminished the bonds of community and the range of demands, duties, and restrictions made on our citizens."[31]

Indeed, we often seek connection with others not in the prosaic relationships of family and friends but rather through what sociologist Anthony Giddens aptly terms "pure relationships" pursued "solely for whatever rewards that relationship as such can deliver." These intense interactions "can by definition no longer be anchored in criteria outside the relationship itself—such as kinship, social duty or traditional obligation."[32] As legal scholar Milton C. Regan Jr. puts it, romance has become "an individual quest for authentic self-definition rather than, as with the Victorians, conduct that occurs within the context of a set of relationships."[33]

Radical libertarianism makes all relationships contingent. "In lasting commitments, liquid modern reason spies out oppression; in durable engagement, it sees incapacitating dependency," Zygmunt Bauman summarizes.[34]

Perhaps the most obvious way in which choice has affected families has been our reluctance or our inability to form lasting ones. A growing proportion of people, particularly poorer people, have chosen not to marry since the early 1960s. Because marriage and child rearing commonly lead to further social contacts and commitments, the decline of the family has played a major role in the broader decline of sociality. Those who have married have done do, on average, much later in life, and they are much more likely than before to divorce. The spread of much-improved employment opportunities and birth control have combined to make marriage optional for a growing number of young women, especially. The median age, at marriage, stood at 20.3 and 22.8 for women and men, respectively, in 1950. In 1992 it had increased to 24.4 and 26.5. The divorce rate rose from just under ten per one thousand married women per year in the mid-1950s to about twenty-three in the late 1970s, after which it declined slightly. Childless marriages have also become acceptable. The fertility rate peaked at 3.6 in the 1950s and declined precipitously to 1.67 in 1985, as people no longer felt compelled to or required to have children. A whopping 82 percent of women in a mid-1980s survey felt that children were not essential to a happy marriage. In a society devoted to self-development, sacrificing hundreds of thousands of dollars and decades of one's life to the hard work of raising children made less and less sense to more and more people. As one woman explained, "Goodness, I've got my hands full nurturing the child with-in me!"[35] These choices have not constituted a rejection of marriage. Far from it. Right into the early twenty-first century, opinion polls showed that the overwhelming majority of couples expected to have very satisfying marriages. Unlike Europe, where couples often choose long-term cohabitation over marriage, U.S. couples seldom take cohabitation very seriously.

Americans are prone to give up on marriages that are less than ideal, often for reasons that seem trivial. A 1993 issue of *Redbook* reported a woman's pride upon terminating a marriage of twenty-one years "that didn't lack love but did lack passion. I'm not doing that again." A man justified leaving his wife and children for a younger woman he supervised by invoking a familiar mantra: "I decided I had a right to be happy."[36] "We are in the business of saving individuals, not marriages," remarked one therapist when confronted with a client who expressed a desire to rebuild his marriage. "The deeper logic of expressive divorce was the logic of capitalism," notes Barbara Dafoe Whitehead in *The Divorce Culture*.[37] Modern consumers are predisposed to embrace novelty over stability. "Much as consumer products may serve as the locus of amorphous yearnings that consumption never quite satisfies," Regan explains, "so the family may serve as a highly charged symbol of intimacy that actual family life rarely realizes."[38]

Modern adults commonly embrace youth and childhood as an Edenic state. This idea has roots in the nineteenth century, when the growing middle-class associated children and childhood with innocence. It has accelerated over the past several decades, as parenting, particularly among the white middle class, has become less and less authoritarian. President Nixon decried the "fog of permissiveness" that had enveloped the nation, but his wife, Pat, recalled that she and her husband "never said a harsh word to the girls" and "didn't try to dominate."[39] "Don't worry about 'spoiling' the baby," remarked Benjamin Spock in the 1980 edition of his widely read guide to baby and child care.[40]

Many adults are committed to prolonging or recapturing childhood. Children's literature and movies since the 1960s, and especially the 1970s, have commonly depicted children as being more capable than adults. The young boy in *ET* is left to his own devices, and the children in most any modern sitcom are at least as mature as their fathers. It is unclear whether people have created and consumed these sort of images as part of an embrace of childhood or as a half-conscious, guilty acknowledgement of the extent to which these caricatures resemble reality. Many adults by the late twentieth century were dressing, speaking, and playing much like their children. Clothes are marketed to "the mother who tries to look 15." Popular culture became obsessed with shallow celebrities and adolescent themes. The most popular Google searches for 2004 were, in order: Britney Spears, Paris Hilton, Christina Aguilera, and Pamela Anderson. The top two movies were *Shrek 2* and *Spider-Man 2*. Cultural critic Benjamin Barber argues in *Consumed* that this form of capitalism essentially seeks to infantilize adults, to foster "a culture of impetuous consumption."[41] People are continually encouraged to choose impulse over deliberation, feeling over reason, dogmatism over doubt, play over work, private over public, and so on. Any thoughtful person who spends an hour, let alone a day, sampling modern television will have a hard time disagreeing with this.

Children have come to symbolize and to embody our deepest aspirations and fears. Reports of child abuse skyrocketed in the 1960s and especially 1970s, rising from less than 10,000 in 1967 to nearly 700,000 in 1976 and 2 million in 1985, when concerns over missing children peaked. Social scientists have identified this widespread, exaggerated fear of child kidnapping and molestation as a form of "moral panic" that commonly accompanies acute "social strain." The belief that our children are at high risk of being harmed by "predatory deviants" serves to express our "doubts about the modern world."[42] "When a child is abducted," observes historian Paula Fass, "not only is the future we envisage for the child gone . . . , but so is the very dream of our own future with and through the child."[43] Well-to-do parents commonly speak of wanting their children "to be the best that they can be," of being "the best" rather than "normal." They claim that affording children a sense of privacy and uniqueness will foster achievement. Likewise, Annette Lareau's in-depth observations of a dozen families revealed that middle-class parents commonly encourage their children to negotiate with them—both because they believe that these qualities will lead to success and because they are not confident that they are right and their children are wrong.[44] Modern, "liquid" life pairs unprecedented freedom with widespread uncertainty over how to use it.

Our unwillingness to impose boundaries on our children reflects our own desire for perfect freedom, for if children cannot be free, what chance do adults have?

It is highly ironic, then, that children's welfare has in many ways declined over the past few decades, and for reasons that are much more prosaic and controllable than is child abduction. Child poverty has risen, and children's health has deteriorated. Parents are spending less time with their children. Parents, by the 1980s, were expressing less concern over their children's futures than they did before. The percentage citing "aspirations for children" as what they most wanted in life dropped from 35 percent in 1964 to 8 percent in 1981. Only about one-quarter of children see their divorced fathers once a month, and by the time the children reach the age of fifteen, divorced fathers live, on an average, four hundred miles away. This is not always the choice of the father. But one's own happiness commonly comes first. "To follow one's bliss is in my opinion the single most important example a father or a mother can set for their child," remarks radical environmentalist Paul

Watson. "I would never abandon my dreams for domestic enslavement." In "The Real Thing," Kenny Loggins explains to his hurt and confused daughter that he is leaving her mother "for you, and for me" because "love" is the "only one thing, [t]hat you can never give up." This is no longer a deviant point of view. The proportion of people who agreed that a couple should not stay together for their children stood at 51 percent in 1962 and shot up to 85 percent in 1982.[45]

Childhood has become particularly difficult for poor children, especially the children of parents troubled by addiction and alienation. Remarked a young delinquent in Bergenfield, New Jersey, in the late 1970s, "Our parents are just like us!"[46] Powers aptly terms the intensely alienated delinquents of Hannibal, Missouri, as "feral children"—youth that have been essentially unparented and unsocialized.[47]

But not all of the feral children are from poor or even divorced families. Consider Bernard Lefkowitz's exploration of a rape committed in 1989 by popular high school boys in Glen Ridge, a prosperous New Jersey suburb, or Alexandra Robbins's account of sorority life at Southern Methodist University in the late 1990s. Or talk to teachers or counselors at upper-middle-class high schools. All tell the same stories of casual sex, widespread drug and alcohol use, and a sense of privilege often nurtured by parents who assert that their progeny should not be subjected to ordinary social constraints. Many people who have come of age since the 1960s recall an acute sense of disorientation. Philosophers Joseph Heath and Andrew Potter observe that "the sexual revolution had the effect of destroying all of the traditional social norms that had governed relations between the sexes, without replacing them with any new ones." "The result," they conclude, "was not liberation, it was hell."[48] Elizabeth Wurtzel writes of a generation "born into homes that had already fallen apart, fathers on the lam, mothers on the floor, no sense of security and safety, no sense of home at all."[49]

Divorce has become so widespread in part because people bring such high expectations to marriage. Popular music and movies commonly depict romantic love as both transcendent and ephemeral. Advertisements commonly show love—like consumption—transpiring outside the realm of everyday life: in nature, for example, where the couple is socially isolated. Indeed, nearly all of the people interviewed in one study identified their most romantic relationships as being intense and short-lived. But marriage is seldom a series of intensely romantic moments. It is much more likely, in the words of Marilyn Monroe, to be a "crazy, difficult friendship with sexual privileges."[50] Modern prosperity and conveniences notwithstanding, marriage still largely consists of the mundane, shared work of running a household and often of child rearing.

People's expectations for and capacity to tolerate marriage has headed in opposite directions. Certainly the skyrocketing divorce rate is evidence of that. The children of unmarried parents in Sweden are more likely to stay together than the children of married couples in the United States. Even marriages that have survived have evidently become less close and satisfying.

Sociologist Norval Glenn examined a broad set of data from the early 1970s to the late 1980s and concluded: "The probability of attaining marital success, in a first marriage *or* at all," had declined.[51]

The prevalence of divorce would be much less problematic if children were not so conservative. The impact of divorce on children has been a contentious field of academic and popular study for decades. But a rough consensus has emerged. Children of divorced parents are more likely than those in more stable homes to exhibit a wide range of social and personal problems, from suicide to low achievement in school. Their own marriages are more likely to be problematic and to end in divorce. These are tendencies, not predictions, and most children of divorce are productive citizens. Divorce in fact tends to improve the lives of children with highly combative or abusive parents, for it removes them from a stressful environment. But both statistical and anecdotal evidence suggests that children would be better off if parents who simply felt unfulfilled by their spouses stayed in the marriage and in the home. As Avner Offer puts it, "it is the amicable divorce that breaks up an apparently successful household, and delivers a shock to unsuspecting children."[52] Those who leave a serviceable spouse in search of a soul mate may well become happier, but at the expense of their children.

The proliferation of blended families illustrates the possibilities and pitfalls of our more fluid families. On the one hand, when parents—particularly single mothers—marry, their children are offered households with higher incomes and many more kin for everyone—additional parents, grandparents, children, siblings, aunts, and uncles. Yet researchers find that remarriage, in the main, does not compensate for the traumas of divorce. Remarriage, after all, brings its own set of challenges, and remarriages are more likely than first marriages to end in divorce, particularly double remarriages involving stepchildren. Hence children frequently lose the kin temporarily acquired through remarriage.

Andrew J. Cherlin in *The Marriage-Go-Round* lays out a strong case for choosing single parenthood over a succession of partners. Eight percent of children in the United States have lived with three or more stepfathers or their mothers' live-in boyfriends by the age of fifteen. This is four times the rate than for any other country apart from Sweden, where the corresponding statistic is just 3 percent. Children born to single mothers commonly do better at school and have fewer behavior problems than do children who have suffered through a series of family transitions. "Children living with married stepparents don't do better, on average, than children living with lone parents," concludes Cherlin, "and children living with cohabiting stepparents may do even worse."[53]

Cherlin aptly captures Americans' unique attachment to marriage and freedom. People in the United States remain much more likely than do Europeans to marry and divorce. Cherlin suggests that these two trends in fact help to explain each other. Early marriage is a strong predictor of divorce (which is why Republican, Bible-belt states have such high divorce rates), and the same idealism that prompts couples to marry before they are ready can prompt them to divorce before they should.

Our marital struggles also owe much to men's inability to come to terms with both obligation and androgeny. Masculinity, as traditionally understood, has become something of an anachronism. The new economy favors communication and collaboration rather than upper-body strength and competitiveness. Ever-rising expectations for families' material quality of life, coupled with falling wages and rising unemployment in occupations dominated by men, has drawn more and more women into the workforce. Women constituted 46 percent of the labor force by 1994.[54] Women from poorer families are much more likely than men from poorer families to go to college, and elite colleges have quietly undertaken affirmative-action programs for men to ensure that gender ratios do not become too skewed. Traditional notions of domestic divisions of labor no longer make sense. It is both sensible and fair for husbands and fathers to surrender the traditional male prerogatives associated with being the breadwinner and to shoulder their fair burden of bathroom cleaning, clothes folding, diaper changing, and even birthday planning.

This has not happened. Husbands' contributions to housework rose significantly in the 1960s through the mid 1980s, when it topped out at about one-third or one-half of what the average wife did. Men, moreover, tend to gravitate toward more recreational forms of housework, such as yard work and playing with the children, while wives are far more likely to do the essentials: cooking, cleaning, dishwashing, and laundry. Wives are also much more likely to be in charge of organizing and planning family life, creating menus, arranging for child care, making doctor and dentist appointments, and keeping in touch with kin, for example. "It's like I run the whole show," complains a twenty-eight-year-old factory worker. "If I don't stay on top of it all, things fall apart because nobody else is going to do it. The kids can't and Nick, well, forget it."[55] Husbands are much more likely to view their homes as a lair or recreational center rather than as a workplace. "Everybody needs a wife," remarks sociologist Miriam Johnson, "but it is men who get them."[56]

Much male privilege remains, and most men do not want to give it up. As husbands do more housework and child care, they tend to become less happy whereas their wives become more happy. Women are more likely to prefer shared decision making, to work as a team. Most men still prefer to be the family's main wage earner and to emphasize that part of their role. They tend to be happier and to change less in their marriages than women do.

Andrew Hacker's *Mismatch: The Growing Gulf Between Women and Men* makes a strong case that the sexes are in fact becoming less, rather than more, similar. "We are witnessing," he remarks, "a *women's liberation* which grows from taking on obligations, while its male counterpart is based on abandoning them."[57] For men, marriage tends to be about fun, not work. Larry Colton recalls being a father in the last half of the 1960s, of giving his little girl "piggyback rides, reading her Dr. Seuss bedtime stories, quacking like

Donald Duck, staying up until 5 A.M. on Christmas Eve desperately trying to assemble 'Clyde,' her super-deluxe rocking horse. But I also wanted to jump bones on every woman who walked by, be one with the sexual revolution."[58] John Updike's Harry Engstrom or "Rabbit," who debuted in 1960, returned to his wife and surviving child in a subsequent novel, but by his mid-40s had concluded, "The entire squeezed and cut-down shape of his life is her fault; at every turn she has been a wall to his freedom."[59] Despite the lamentations over the impact of feminism on the family, the modern cult of self-indulgence has affected men much more than it has affected women. Hence mothers are much more likely than are fathers to try to gain custody of their children in the event of a divorce. Men tend to link fathering with marriage, to view being a husband, father, breadwinner, and home owner as a "package deal."[60] Close to half the total number of children in the United States spend at least part of their childhoods apart from their biological fathers.

Gender differences emerge well before marriage. Sharon Thompson's interviews of hundreds of teenage girls conducted from 1978 to 1986 found that they commonly embraced sex within a romantic, mutually respectful relationship, an expectation that almost inevitably brought disappointment. A 1991 Gallup survey found that nearly twice as many young men as women welcomed "more acceptance of sexual freedom." An experiment from 1978 to the late 1980s entailed research assistants propositioning attractive members of the opposite gender. Virtually none of the women agreed to have sex, and more than half of the men did.[61] Young men commonly spend much of their time playing video games, viewing pornography, and pursuing promiscuity, while their female counterparts wait for the men, in the words of one young woman, to "grow up a little."[62]

Women and men agree that gender equity is a laudable value. Studies from the past few decades reveal a steady increase in the proportion of people who believe that women and men are equal and that couples should share decision making. But the reality is commonly at odds with the rhetoric. My wife, a mental-health therapist, sums up the differences between how her male and female clients approach their families: "I versus we," respectively. Indeed, researchers who probe beneath the veneer of mutually assured equality find that husbands continue to enjoy and exercise substantial privileges, from where the couple lives to what television shows they watch.

"Almost all of us describe our marriages as equal," remarks social commentator Susan Maushart. "The evidence indicates that nine out of ten of us are lying."[63] For more educated couples, to admit to being in a relationship in which the man does not pull his weight is to acknowledge having failed. Arlie Russell Hochschild cites the case of Nancy, a social worker, and Evan, a salesman, whose quarrels escalated when Nancy resolved that Evan should do his fair share of the housework and child care. After contemplating separation, they resolved their impasse by having her "do the upstairs and Evan does the downstairs and the dog."[64] The upstairs included everything but the garage.

Gender differences have also proved to be very stubborn in parenting. Fathers tend to approach parenting far more differently than their wives do.

They commonly devote more time to play than to care, and this play is often secondary to (accompanied by) watching television or doing chores. Such fathers, notes sociologist Ralph LaRossa, are "technically present but functionally absent."[65] A survey of scholarly literature by Timothy J. Biblarz and Judith Stacey that was published in 2010 suggests that women tend to be more effective parents than men. Fathers are, on average, less engaged with their children, less adept at disciplining, and more likely to treat their sons and daughters differently. Fathers are also more likely (relative to the time they spend with their children) to abuse them physically and sexually. Of course children tend to do better when there are two engaged parents in their lives. But fathers' capacity to parent actually increases when they are single parents, in part because they feel compelled to take on some roles that are considered feminine. By the same token, gay men do better, on average, than heterosexual men. The children who are most likely to have the fewest behavior problems and to manifest the highest degree of attachment are those who have been raised by two mothers, pairings that "typically bestow a double dose of caretaking, communication, and intimacy"—of, in short, what is commonly known as mothering.[66] This finding of course goes against the common assumptions that children—particularly boys—founder without fathers. But Biblarz and Stacey point out that researchers commonly conflate the presence of two parents with heterosexual parenting. Having two parental figures is very important, but so is the quality of their care, and women tend to be more effective parents than men.

The appearance of gay and lesbian families is one of the signal developments of modern life. Until early in the twentieth century, Westerners associated homosexuality with same-gender sexual activities rather than with a durable or inherent gay or lesbian sexual identity. Even as gay and lesbian communities arose—both discursively and socially—gay and lesbian relationships did not and could not resemble heterosexual marriage; such relationships were illegal, and the medical and psychological professions stigmatized homosexuality as they "discovered" it. Even as the growth of cities and urban subcultures abetted the spread of gay and lesbian culture, durable gay and lesbian relationships became in some respects more difficult than they were during the nineteenth century, when same-sex couples were more able to live together without suspicion or comment. Buffalo's postwar lesbians who were married (to men) and who had children waited until their children were grown to divorce their husbands. One recalled that her girlfriend lived with her and her husband and children and that her husband "didn't know the relationships.... It was like two lives I had to lead, without hurting one or the other." Among lesbians who were not tied down by children, on the other hand, love reigned supreme in the 1940s and 1950s, a preoccupation that frequently led to the same "system of serial monogamy" that characterizes so many modern heterosexual marriages.[67] Many gay and lesbian radicals have associated monogamy with heterosexuality and oppression. Couples might even have sex with others out of a sense of "political duty." "We wanted to create a new society," one woman recalls, "though I don't think anybody was very comfortable with it—and it just didn't work."[68] Gay men, like men in general, tended to embrace promiscuity with more enthusiasm. A major survey conducted in the early 1980s found that just 36 percent of gay men who were in relationships reported that it was important for them to be monogamous, which was half the rate of lesbians who were in relationships.[69] Philip Gefter recalled the New York gay scene in the 1970s as a kaleidoscope of drugs, music, and frequent and varied sexual encounters, including an early morning encounter when he and his fellows streamed out of a disco to dance "under the stars as the sun was coming up. And I believed at that moment in time that we were having more fun than anybody in the *history* of civilization had ever had."[70]

But as the twentieth century drew to a close, more and more lesbian and gay couples were fighting for their right to marry and to have children. Gay Pride marchers chanted, "We're here and we're gay and we're in the PTA."[71] This embrace of stability owed something to the horrible toll that the AIDS epidemic inflicted on the gay community. A growing sobriety (much traditional gay and lesbian culture had focused on bars) movement also nurtured a general emphasis on self-restraint. The growing tolerance toward gays and lesbians in the broader culture has made it easier—though by no means easy—for same-sex couples to live openly in stable, committed relationships and to have children. By the twenty-first century, most American agreed that a same-sex couple living with children constituted a family, and the percentage that felt so was rising. By the 1990s, many parented high-needs foster children, and a growing number of agencies allowed gay couples to adopt. Even radicals, who associate family life with oppression, commonly argue that those who wish to marry or to have children should be free to do so. Activist Tom Stoddard in 1996 described the gay movement as working for "a richer, more diverse, more compassionate culture, in which everyone feels the possibility of self-expression and self-actualization."[72] As with modern feminism, self-expression and self-actualization can take myriad forms. For a lesbian couple I know, who met at an evangelical college, it has meant largely devoting their lives to their adopted children. To a young *boi* (boyish) lesbian who was overheard at the Meow Mix bar in New York, it means adopting the same sort of attitude to femmes that feckless heterosexual men commonly express: "I fucked her and that was cool. But now she's like, *e-mailing* me and I'm just like, chill *out* bitch!"[73] Modern life has presented gays and lesbians with unprecedented choices to pursue meaning inside and outside committed relationships.

Gay and lesbian people and couples have been both on the leading edge of and a counterweight to a society that is based on the pursuit of pleasure. The broader society's embrace of sexual relations as an end in itself rather than for procreation and marriage owes something to the example of gay relations. Gay, lesbian, and transgendered people and communities have long dropped rigid judgements and have accepted people as they are. They have also personified the individual's search for his or her true self. When gays and lesbians speak of the struggle to live truly and authentically, their words resonate with most straight people and dovetail with an embracing of freedom and a shedding of "hang ups." But gays and lesbians also commonly form tight kinship networks in a fragmented society. As Kath Weston points out in *Families We Choose*, urban lesbians and gays create communities characterized by fluidity, breadth, and intensity in which sexuality and friendship overlap, and ex-lovers commonly remain friends.[74] Gay men find most of their friends within gay communities, and their friendships are both more numerous and emotionally richer than the friendships of heterosexual men. The small number of straight men with gay friends find these relationships "to be less instrumental, less rigid, more intimate, and more open than their friendships with other heterosexual men."[75] Gays and lesbians now face less oppression, but not to the extent that they have become like, say, third-generation Polish Americans, who have largely dissolved into the larger and highly atomized whole. Gays and lesbians often reside in intense, rich communities of fictive kin.

The past half-century has also created unprecedented opportunities for people of different ethnic groups to form families. Racial categories such as "white," "black," "Indian," and "Mexican" have always been culturally constructed and problematic. Most people who are considered "black" in the United States have had some white or Native American ancestry, for example, and the term "Mexican" subsumes a mestizo nation of intermingled indigenous, Spanish, and often African ancestry. But these categories, their artificiality notwithstanding, have had considerable historical weight, and not until 1966 did the United States Supreme Court overturn state laws forbidding racial intermarriage. Intermarriages increased sixfold from 1960 to 1980, when they constituted nearly 2 percent of marriages, and they have become much more common since then. Asian Americans and Latinos are the most likely to marry outside their ethnic group, but growing numbers of African Americans and whites are also making that choice. That people who were once forbidden from marrying are now able to do so is another manifestation of the expanded choices of modern life, is an expression of, as the leading scholar of intermarriage puts it, "Love's Revolution."[76]

The decline in racism has also multiplied the number of white parents who have adopted darker-skinned children. The movement began in earnest with the adoption of Korean children in the 1950s and expanded to African Americans by the 1960s. These adoptees were joined by thousands from Central America and China later in the century. Many white parents prefer a child who resembles them. But a shortage of adoptable white infants from the United States, coupled with a softening of racial prejudice, has afforded more and more people with the opportunity to parent.

More and more people are also raising children on their own, without a partner. By the early twenty-first century, roughly one child in three was born to a single mother. Single mothers are able to have and to raise children because the social stigma against their doing so has declined dramatically and also due to the expansion of the welfare state in the 1960s and enhanced employment opportunities for women. Families that are headed by single mothers are at a very high risk of poverty. Only about one-half of divorced fathers regularly support their children, just one in seven fathers who do not marry.[77] Most single mothers would like to be married. But they see marriage, like child rearing, as a choice rather than as a necessity, a choice that will not necessarily improve the lives of their children.

A very significant and often overlooked aspect of the nation's embrace of freedom and choice, then, has been the acceptance and proliferation of new forms of families. The spread of personal rights, women's increased economic autonomy, and the uncoupling of sexuality from reproduction have enabled families and households to assume many new forms. People who were once barred by poverty or prejudice from forming lasting commitments are now able to form them. Surely this has been a very positive if often contested development, and one that must be laid largely at the doorstep of our larger embrace of freedom of choice.

But our valoration of freedom has undermined the foundation of all families even as it has allowed new types to appear. Of course instability is nothing new for families. Death and migration commonly fractured families of the past. But modern families are both weaker and more isolated from the broader forms of kinship and community that used to cushion such losses. Nuclear families are both more isolated and more apt to fragment than they were in the past.

* * *

The young Kurt Cobain had loved being with his parents so much that he fought off sleep to prolong their hours together. When his parents divorced, nine-year-old Kurt saw all that was dear to him "unravel in front of his eyes," as an aunt observed.[78] Kurt eventually funneled this trauma and anger into Nirvana, a band whose "Nevermind" zeitgeist articulated a generation's disgust with the pieties, artificialities, and hypocrisies of the "Morning in America" Reagan years. "Punk rock is freedom," asserted Kurt, who promised to be the sort of father to his young daughter that his own father had failed to be. But Kurt Cobain chose to commit suicide before his daughter had reached her second birthday, leaving her with a larger burden than his parents had bequeathed him with. Cobain's suicide replicated the family fragmentation that had damaged his own childhood, and his compelling music, like his life, constituted a damning indictment and deconstruction of modern pieties without offering a workable alternative for the child and fans he left behind. As Ryan Moore puts it, for Cobain's generation "the rejection of dominant values and identities cannot be matched by an investment in any alternatives."[79]

This chapter emphasizes the costs of individualism. Yet the search for freedom has bequeathed many impressive gains inside and outside the family. Women whose grandmothers faced a choice between poverty and an abusive marriage are now much more able to have satisfying lives as single adults and single parents. Many couples have used the freedoms and opportunities of modern life to craft relationships that are characterized by high levels of respect, affection, and flexibility and homes in which kin and neighbors are made welcome and children are nurtured and challenged. Many of these strong, loving families, moreover, were not tolerated until recently. If freedom has made family and obligation optional for most of us, it has also made such loving choices possible for a growing range of couples and individuals, from lesbian and single mothers to interracial couples, families, and beyond.

But these diverse people and families confront a challenge that is arguably just as insidious and corrosive as are prejudice and poverty: the florescence of a pleasure-oriented popular culture that touts freedom as the one good thing. The libertarian ethos of continual self-gratification is no longer a radical or countercultural notion. It has gone mainstream, has become the default value that so many of us gravitate to when familial and other social commitments begin to bind.

The hippies, campus radicals, and other idealists of the sixties believed that they were creating a radical, new counterculture that just might transform the Western world. A half-century later, "do your own thing" and "question authority" have become clichés of Hollywood, Madison Avenue, and even Main Street. The rebel has become everywoman, and certainly, everyman.

The rebel has become trite. Today's counterculturalists are striving not for still more freedom and transgression. They are instead struggling to establish warm, meaningful networks of obligation in a world that has grown hostile to any limit of the self whatsoever.

Chapter 9

Countercultures?

The twentieth century spawned a pair of closely related trends: the spread of prosperity and the pursuit of pleasure and freedom that overturned the nineteenth-century culture of self-restraint. These trends quickened in the 1960s and after.

The impact of prosperity on poor and minority families has been complex. On the one hand, rising incomes—often supplemented by federal programs—have removed, or at least eased, some elements of economic and racial inequality and discrimination that had long harmed marginal families. On the other hand, prosperity has made reliance on family and kin less necessary. More importantly, especially for African American males, modernity has eroded traditional, obligation-oriented cultures. The modern culture of self-fulfillment is explicitly multicultural and multiracial. Some of its leading icons, from Muhammad Ali to Oprah Winfrey to Tupac Shakur, are black.

To be sure, many minority groups have maintained subcultures and societies that are characterized by a strong sense of obligation. But such groups usually comprise recent immigrants steeped in traditional cultures. The organizations that have succeeded best at warding off the pervasive charms of modern individualism are both conservative and highly organized: evangelical churches.

* * *

The black middle class grew dramatically during the 1960s, a product of both sustained prosperity and advances in civil rights that bequeathed political power and educational and occupational opportunities. However, progress slowed in the 1980s, and by the twenty-first century's turn, about one-half of African American children lived in poverty, another one-quarter in near poverty, and the last one-quarter well above the poverty line.[1]

Middle-class black families are both similar to and different from their white counterparts. The great majority of middle-class black children have two parents, both of whom work outside the home. African American women's growing educational and occupational attainments have been fundamental to the rise of the black middle class. They constituted about six out of ten black college students by 1982. Middle-class African American couples are somewhat more likely to experience a divorce and less likely to remarry than their white counterparts, but they are also more likely to share housework and practice more flexible gender roles.[2]

Black middle-class families are more economically vulnerable than white ones. In most cases, theirs is the first generation of the family to enjoy economic security. These family members' parents were usually unable to pay for their tuition or to bequeath to them substantial inheritances. African Americans are often deeply in debt upon finishing college, and even those with middle-class incomes tend to lag well behind their white counterparts in wealth. By 1995, African Americans with college degrees had 77 percent of the income of their white counterparts, 23 percent of their wealth or net worth. Since wealth is ordinarily accrued over generations, black professionals have much more difficulty in transferring their status to their children than do white professionals. Though formal structures of housing segregation became illegal in the 1960s and 1970s, de facto racial segregation remains commonplace in both housing and education. Middle-class black families, including those that have moved to black suburbs, are much more likely than are whites to live in or near areas with lots of poverty, crime, and poor schools. A resident of Groveland, a black, middle-class Chicago neighborhood, both complained of a group of young men congregating or "gangbanging" on her corner and explained that she would not give the ringleader's name to the police "because his mama is such a sweet lady."[3] Black, middle-class children are much more likely to be exposed to the social problems associated with poverty, and their parents are much more likely to be asked for money or other forms of economic assistance by family members and friends.

Poorer African Americans face many more hurdles than do poor whites. Urban de-industrialization inflicted great harm on black men, who depended heavily on blue-collar work. They have been twice as likely to be unemployed than their white counterparts. Between one- quarter and one-third of African American men are jailed at some point of their lives, usually for relatively minor drug offences. Nearly one black child in five had a parent in prison in 1999. The pervasive unemployment and incarceration of black men has played a major role in their shrinking role as husbands and as fathers. In 1964, 24 percent of black children were born to single mothers. By 2001, this figure rose to 68 percent. Most of these mothers were poor and often depended more on government programs such as Aid to Families with Dependent Children, food stamps, and Medicaid than on the fathers of their children. From 1970 to 2000, the percentage of white women who were married fell from just over 80 percent to just over 60 percent. For black women, the percentage plummeted from 60 percent to 30 percent. Put another way, in the 1980s, the average white woman could expect to spend about 43 percent of her life married, whereas the average black woman could expect to spend only about 22 percent of her life married.[4]

Some poor families did better in the 1990s, when welfare reform and a growing economy put single mothers of all ethnicities to work and moved some of them above the poverty line. But most single mothers who left welfare joined the working poor, and a significant minority fell into extreme poverty, suffering from both unemployment and a fraying welfare state. Racial inequality is particularly acute among the poor. African Americans in the lowest fifth of income earners have a much lower average net worth than their do their white counterparts.[5]

Racial inequality is closely related to our highly segregated and unequal education system. In 1997, just 25 out of 11,000 elementary and middle school students in a New York City district were white, and their teachers made barely half of what their counterparts in white schools did. Mireya, an ambitious student at Los Angeles's Fremont High School, hoped to go to college and wanted to take college-preparation courses. She instead had to settle for sewing and hairdressing in order to graduate. A weeping Mireya explained, "I don't *want* to take hair-dressing. I did not need sewing, either. I knew how to sew. My mother is a seamstress in a factory.... I hoped for something else." She realized that the children of factory owners had opportunities to "grow beyond themselves," while "we remain the same."[6]

Such assertions anger conservatives, who argue that a culture of poverty has more to do with inequality than does racism—past or present. Their arguments are not without merit. Certainly, elements of African American culture discourage academic achievement. Geoffrey Canada, the distinguished educator and social activist, explains:

> "Many children feel that their lives are so harsh, so uncertain, that when they see a child doing well in school and adopting middle-class norms and attitudes it triggers the reaction 'You think I'm going to suffer and live a life of fear, fear for my future, fear for my safety, fear for my very existence, and you're gonna just waltz through life and make it out of here? No way. You ought to feel pain and fear and doubt just like the rest of us.'"

As one of his classmates put it to him at their New York junior high school in 1966, "We'll fuck all of you up. You, that sissy I just fucked up, and all the rest of you eggheads."[7] Nathan McCall recalls how in the early 1970s the movies and soundtracks to "Superfly" and "The Mack" prompted a "fashion revolution," as "brothers shifted from Black Power chic to gangster buffoon." Politics became more personal, as the films inspired "cats who wanted to be players, cool and confident dudes who lived life on their terms, not the white man's." But they channeled this rebelliousness into drug dealing and pimping, "preying on their own people."[8]

As sociologist Orlando Patterson points out, young black men are susceptible to an ethos of under-achievement, not simply or even primarily because they reject the norms of mainstream, white culture, but because so much of white, mainstream culture constructs and perpetuates an ethos of black irresponsibility. Whites have always imbued or associated blackness with passion and with emotionalism. In the nineteenth century, that association was no compliment. But since then, whites have increasingly embraced a black culture of emotion and excitement. Young black men, commonly depicted as rappers, thugs, and pimps, are now the leading icons of cool. Patterson points out that many young black men choose "hanging out on the street after school, shopping and dressing sharply, sexual conquests, party drugs, hip-hop music and culture" over grinding away at their schoolwork both because of the intrinsic pleasure of the "cool-pose culture" and because it grants "them a great deal of respect from white youths." Young black men generally have high levels of self-esteem—regardless of their academic performance. They are enmeshed in a "Dionysian trap," a subculture that both nourishes their self-respect and exacerbates their economic and social marginalization.[9] The cool-pose culture has a wicked underside. The homicide rate among black males has remained several times as high as it is among whites, and the overwhelming majority of black victims are killed by black men. White youths usually participate in the cool-pose culture more selectively than do their black counterparts, and police officers, judges, and others forgive and forget their transgressions more readily. Moreover, though street-savvy black men may be lionized on MTV, the association of blackness with violence and emotional expressiveness has much less cachet among employers—let alone wives, children, and other kin. The black man, notes David Marriott, is commonly represented as "a being incapable of inhibition, morals or ideas;...a being whose violent, sexual criminality is incapable of any lasting, or real relationships, only counterfeit, or trickery; a being who remains a perpetual child, rather than a father."[10] All black men are limited and damaged by this stereotype, particularly those who try to live it out.

Independence, irresponsibility, and short-term pleasure are all the more compelling when the alternatives to them are remote. Elliott Liebow pointed out in the 1960s that "the constant awareness of a future loaded with 'trouble' results in a constant readiness to leave, to 'make it,' to 'get out of town,' and discourages the man from sinking roots into the world he lives in," from putting money in the bank or committing to a wife and children. Indeed, "marriage is an occasion of failure," since it requires one "to live with your failure, to be confronted by it day in and day out." Black fathers commonly gained more status through supporting the children of other men rather than their own; the community respected men who offered even modest gifts of time and money to the children of another man. Much higher, seemingly unobtainable expectations adhered to biological fatherhood. Many poor men instead turned to the male conviviality of the street corner, a place where a man is reassured that "his marriage did not fail because he failed as breadwinner and head of the family but because his wife refused to put up with his manly appetite for whiskey and other women."[11] Lee Rainwater found similar dynamics at work in St. Louis's massive Pruitt-Igoe housing project. A husband's familial status rested "narrowly on his ability to bring money into the household," and wives were "often ready to blame an unemployed husband for his unemployment." Husbands often reacted to these expectations "with prickly self-defensiveness"; violence and arguments often erupted when men lost their jobs. Young men, especially, sought status not through work and marriage but via sexual conquest ("one of the few resources for self enhancement that is plentiful in their environment") or by pimping or " 'running games' on friends and strangers of both sexes." None of these activities abetted in ensuring that marriages or families endured. But the whole concept of calculating long-term rewards of any sort made little sense at Pruitt-Igoe. Poor people, noted Rainwater, "cannot choose between immediate and deferred gratifications; the only gratifications available must be taken when they occur or must be forgone entirely."[12] Elijah Anderson described young black men in the 1990s who were obsessed with sexual conquest, with various strategies of "getting over" young women's defenses without "playing house" (getting married).[13] Again, this was, in some respects, a rational response to a situation in which being a successful father (making a good, steady income at a respectable job) seemed out of reach. Low-income, poorly educated young black men could pursue low-paying service jobs, many of which entailed expensive and time-consuming commutes to white suburbs where they felt unwelcome. Or they could sell drugs, live off the earnings of women, or construct some other sort of hustle. Warren Kimbro, a former Black Panther, who in the 1990s ran a halfway house for former convicts, noted that he could not find his clients "a job that pays them as much as they make dealing drugs." Yet drugs are "a new form a slavery," for cocaine has been able to "destroy a culture, a people, a way of life."[14] They have exacerbated crime, imprisonment, poverty, poor parenting, and the flight of middle-class families even as they have become many black men's best chance at making a decent living.

Poor black men face many barriers to being effective fathers. A turn-of-the century study of thirty-six low-income African American fathers living apart from the mothers of their biological children in Milwaukee found that all of the men tried to keep in contact with those children. Many of the young fathers, especially, asserted that they did not want to be absent, as their own fathers had been. They or their kin often contributed at least sporadically to their children's upkeep. However, all but three faced criminal or civil actions in a two-year period, and eleven were incarcerated for not paying child support. Only one father had completely paid his child support. Two had been murdered.[15]

Simply urging a poor black mother to find a husband has seldom worked. Journalist Katherine Boo, early in the twenty-first century, chronicled the dogged attempts of two women in Oklahoma City to follow the dictates of the Bush administration's "marriage cure" for poverty. The course's teacher, a pastor, conceded privately that the odds were stacked against Kim Henderson. "She lives in an isolated neighborhood where most of the males have abandoned hope in schools, legit jobs, the system," he summarized. "The way they tell it to me, they [the men] see three ways to get out of the ghetto: through professional sports, through rapping, and through crime." Indeed, on her way home from the marriage class an older man presented himself: "Now, for my part, I believe you have a beautiful face and a nice body. Are you over eighteen? I'll be getting out of the halfway house in several months and I'd like to buy you a steak."[16]

If poor black men are often seduced by the culture of the "cool pose" to live up to their image of America's quintessential individualists, their female counterparts reside near the opposite end of the spectrum. Rainwater found that the families of the Pruitt-Igoe project had a "pervasive matrifocal emphasis" in the early 1960s—whether or not husbands were present. Carol Stack's study of poor African Americans in a small, southern Illinois city in the late 1960s and early 1970s described a world of highly interdependent mothers who relied heavily on female kin—actual and fictive—to support their families. Ruby Banks, who had just traded hot corn bread and beans with her baby's aunt for diapers and milk, put it this way: "You have to have help from everybody and anybody, so don't turn no one down when they come round for help."[17] The high stakes of these intensely reciprocal relationships often made them volatile, and sharing could keep everyone alive, but poor. Stack conceded that the expectation that financial windfalls would be widely distributed often kept families from bettering their condition—by investing in better housing, for example. But it also kept everyone alive and fed. Shaquena, raised by her grandmother since the age of ten, described a kin network in Harlem in the 1990s as including an aunt across the street, a "guy down the hall" who "give us stuff," and a best friend who lived upstairs with her grandmother, who "keep a kitchen full of food."[18]

Motherhood makes perfect sense in this context. For poor women, "the road to adulthood, success, and social membership seems out of reach in almost every way—except through the fulfillment of your role as a mother."[19] As a low-income, African American mother of three young children recently put it, "I'm complete, and I've done what I am supposed to do." "I don't see myself as being an individual anymore, really," she continued. "Everything I do is mostly centered around my children, to make *their* lives better."[20] Their parenting styles tend to be old- fashioned. Adrie Kusserow's examination of neighborhoods around New York City reveals that poor parents tend to both nurture a sense of toughness in and demand respect from their children. One espoused the widely touted ideal of encouraging her child to "be her own person" before shouting, "because I'm your mother and you do what I tell you to do" at her child.[21] Motherhood constitutes for such young women a rare opportunity for both status and satisfaction and often, in the words of anthropologist Katherine Newman, "catalyzes a sense of responsibility, of having someone important to provide for."[22]

Providing for one's children has become more difficult over the past generation for poor and working-class people of all ethnicities. By 1990, children were more likely to live in poverty than were the elderly. Globalization moved many manufacturing jobs overseas, and the arrival of millions of immigrants willing to work for relatively low wages resulted in their being fewer manufacturing jobs available for unskilled, native-born workers. Many poor and even middle-class families found themselves without medical coverage. Indeed, major illness joins unemployment and divorce as the three crises that most commonly plunge working families into poverty.

Working-class men have had a particularly difficult time adjusting to these challenges. Their wages have steadily declined since the 1970s as their wives have entered colleges and the workforce. Most of these wives work at jobs that offer little pay or satisfaction; they would rather work fewer hours outside the home, or not at all. Since that is usually not a viable option, they expect their husbands—who commonly work and earn less than they do—to shoulder more of the work at home. Yet white, working-class husbands commonly resist that expectation. "I just want him to help out a little more," remarks a thirty-five-year-old office worker. "But every time I try to talk to him, you know, to ask him if I couldn't get a little more help around here, there's a fight."[23] A recent survey of marital satisfaction concludes that of five major types of couples, young, working-class, dual-earners "appeared to be the most troubled, with a below-average level of marital happiness and modestly elevated levels of marital conflict, problems, and divorce proneness." Husbands commonly complained about their wives' work outside the home, and wives commonly complained of husbands' lack of work inside the home.[24] Middle-class husbands can afford to at least pay lip service to the new, androgynous gender norms because their remunerative jobs offer them a stable source of income and masculine status inside and outside the home. Men with less education and job security are acutely aware that their position in both the community and their families has declined and requires them to be on the cutting edge of shifting gender roles, which many of them resent and reject. Jefferson Cowie's *Stayin' Alive: The 1970s and the Last Days of the Working Class* details how the working-class drifted from collectivist unions to dreams of "individual emancipation" articulated by artists such as Bruce Springsteen.[25] Confronted with boyfriends or spouses who commonly lack both the capacity to earn good money or to engage more fully with their families, many poor white and black mothers alike have concluded that they are better off single—even after the extensive cuts in social welfare instituted over the past generation. One-third of marriages of women without high school diplomas end within five years, a rate nearly triple that of women with college degrees.[26]

A century ago, poor working-class people were apt to be recent immigrants from Europe. Most of their children and grandchildren lived much more comfortable and less traditional lives by the last half of the twentieth century. Second, and particularly, third-generation Italians, Poles, and other immigrants from southern and eastern Europe commonly climbed onto at least the bottom rungs of the middle class, moved away from ethnically homogeneous neighborhoods, and married outside their ethnic groups. By the 1970s, celebrating one's (often highly selected) European ethnic heritage through crafts, holidays, and bumper stickers had become commonplace—a sure indication that more substantial aspects of ethnicity had vanished.

Jews represented something of an exception for most of the twentieth century, as they constituted a highly distinctive ethnic and religious subculture.

But the decline of anti-Semitism and the spread of prosperity eroded Jewish communities after World War II, and by the 1970s, a sociologist remarked that Jewish families were on the "SCIDs," as they were "*s*ingle, *c*hildless, *i*ntermarried, and *d*ivorced."[27] Jewish American families had become all-too-American. A growing minority of Jewish families turned from reformed to Orthodox Judaism to connect with a tradition, a sense of "belonging to a people," as some women put it.[28]

Asian immigrants have resembled Jewish Americans in many ways. They were much more coherent and discriminated against than were most European immigrant groups, tended to focus on educational attainment, and enjoyed much more tolerance and economic success after World War II, when intermarriage and other signs of acculturation rose. Asian immigration surged again in the 1960s, after the federal government reversed the system of racial and racist quotas that it had instituted in the early 1920s. Over the past forty years, the descendants of immigrants from China, Japan, and the Philippines have been joined by millions of newcomers from Vietnam, India, Cambodia, and elsewhere. Like their nineteenth and early twentieth-century counterparts, these newcomers have generally come from highly traditional cultures to one of the world's most uninhibited ones. A Taiwanese who came to the United States to attend college, and who babysat for a family over the Christmas vacation around 1970 was appalled at the treatment of an elderly woman who had traveled 1,000 miles to be with her family, but was soon consigned to watching television by herself in the basement "to avoid disturbing her children and grandchildren." "That Americans are polite to strangers and to ordinary friends but cannot maintain courtesy to the elders of their own family leaves one dumbfounded," she concluded.[29]

These recent immigrants have been the most successful ethnic groups at creating substantial and viable subcultures of familial obligation. Chinese (largely Taiwanese) mothers, who lived in the Los Angeles area in the early 1990s, expected more of both their children (respect and self-control) and of themselves ("a high level of maternal involvement"), than did their white neighbors.[30] A Vietnamese American college student explained in the 1990s: "To be an American, you may be able to do whatever you want. But to be a Vietnamese, you must think of your family first."[31] Putting your family first meant associating only with those whom your parents approved of, following their wishes about what one studied, marrying within one's ethnic group, and giving money to one's relatives. "Your family is your social security," asserted Nghi Van Nguyen, whose family combined its earnings to buy a home near a good school in a San Diego suburb. "We know that we need each other to pull ahead."[32] Individual dreams and preferences count for little. Ying Ying Yu, a thirteen-year-old immigrant from China, shared that she used to dream about being a gardener, for "the gritty feel of dirt was much more tangible than a bunch of flimsy words strung together." But her family wished her to become a lawyer. "Here in America," she observed, "there is almost a pressure to follow your dreams." But: "I believe in the power of duty to impel. Only duty will offer me something true, something worthy of my effort and the support of my family and country. Duty can bring me to an achievement that is greater than I am."[33]

The Khmer of Cambodia, who came to the United States early in the 1980s, have tried especially hard to get their children to conform to traditional family and community norms. Those who commit sexual improprieties, for example, might be blamed for a relative's misfortune, as their transgression angered powerful ancestors. A mother remarked that children who addressed others properly would bring credit to the entire family, for observers would say: "Oh, that family is very good, they know very good words, they know about hierarchy and the proper status of people." Parents are one's "first gods," or "gods within the house," to whom one owes a debt "so great that it can never be fully repaid." "Buddhist doctrine doesn't want all people to be equal," for if "everybody is equal, then who listens to whom?"[34]

Such people view American schools as incubators of selfishness and acculturation. Children are exposed to the English language and other elements of mainstream American culture much more extensively than their parents are and must constantly negotiate their way across dissimilar cultures. "Here in America," laments a Vietnamese man, "my wife and I will die a lonely death, abandoned by our children."[35] Asian American families also suffer from the usual challenges facing people of color in the United States: racism and poverty. "The whites will not let us catch up with them, nor will they let us join them," observed a Punjabi (Sikh) parent in California in the early 1980s.[36]

Yet recent Asian immigrant families and communities have often succeeded in blending economic success with social stability. It helps that many have come to the United States as part of intact family groups, and Vietnamese immigrants enjoyed a great deal of support from the federal government. But they have had to adapt. As in the nineteenth century, the new immigrants often shifted from depending largely or entirely on the father's income to a strategy in which mothers, and often children, contributed. The result was a synthesis that combines "the traditional belief in mutual protection and support" and "the American ideal of equality in family relations."[37] Women and children gain some autonomy and respect, but within a cooperative socioeconomic framework. Vietnamese American women attempt to "take advantage of their new resources" and status as well as to try "to protect the structure and sanctity of the traditional family system," to both preserve that way of life and "to moderate their position of subordination to men within it." They "spoke approvingly of how according to the dictates of Vietnamese culture, in contrast to those of U.S. culture, men were expected to devote themselves, at whatever personal cost, to provide economically for their families."[38] Likewise, young Vietnamese Americans both desired more freedom than their parents wished to give them and expressed pride in the strength of their familial obligations. "I really can't feel free to do things I like," remarked a U.S. born sixteen-year-old, but added: "Young people can easily get lost in a maze of confusing values and norms in America. I think the control is necessary and good for you after all."[39] Young Vietnamese Americans who have sacrificed a great deal to achieve their educational or occupational goals may defer the attainment of these goals to send money to a family member in need. "We're different from Americans because our families are much closer," explained one. "I think that's the biggest difference between Americans and Vietnamese."[40]

Native American families, particularly those living on reservations, continued to be characterized both by high rates of social trauma and social solidarity. Up to one-third of Native American children were taken from their families well into the 1970s, and most went to non-Indian families. The federal government changed that policy, but Native American families continue to suffer from very high levels of unemployment, suicide, and alcoholism. Around 1980, Indians were three times more likely to be in a motor vehicle accident, four times more likely to die of tuberculosis, and six times more likely to die from alcoholism than was the rest of the nation. Less than one-half were graduating from high school. Unemployment rates on many reservations have long exceeded 50 percent.[41] They can reach as high as 90 percent. Such acute levels of economic and social suffering created high levels of trauma within families, including fetal alcohol syndrome and many forms of abuse. Sherman Alexie, the distinguished Washington writer, describes two uncles who are "slugging each other with such force that they had to be in love. Strangers would never want to hurt each other that badly"[42] Yet Alexie's stories also speak of children struggling to forgive absent fathers, parents, determined, against steep odds, to offer their children hope, spouses giving each other another chance, reservation residents—the ravages of poverty, racism, and alcoholism notwithstanding—being family, being kin. Indigenous people never created utopian societies, and many modern reservations are among the most impoverished communities in the nation. But they continue to confront mainstream American society with a more collective way of finding one's way in the world.

So have Latino families. The term "Hispanic" or "Latino" obscures a great deal of diversity and complexity. Hispanic families have been in what is now the United States longer than Anglo families have, and their numbers steadily swelled in the twentieth century until they now represent both the largest non-Euro-American population group in the nation and, in the case of Mexico, the largest number of recent immigrants from any country. But Mexican Americans have become a shrinking majority of Hispanics who live in the United States. Many have also arrived from such diverse places and cultures as Puerto Rico, Cuba, the Dominican Republic, and Central America. Latinos varied in their appearance, ancestry, economic circumstances, and legal status. Latin America has also changed dramatically. Mexico was an overwhelmingly agrarian society until the 1960s, when a cluster of changes pushed people off the land. NAFTA (the North American Free Trade Agreement) has devastated Mexican farmers since its implementation in the early 1990s, as it flooded Mexico with cheap U.S. corn. The birth rate plunged from 7.0 in 1960 to just 2.6 in 1997; a nonagricultural society required fewer children.[43] The commercialization and mechanization of farming made it more difficult for peasants to live off the land as better transportation and manufacturing jobs offered other options, in Mexico or in the United States. Many Mexican villages are now populated almost entirely by the very old and the very young. By the late twentieth century, unmarried or divorced Mexican women were often going North on their own. Much the same pattern has prevailed in Central America and parts of the Caribbean.

Though these migrations have sundered family ties for months, years, or even decades, most Latin Americans come to the United States for their families. "I did *not* leave my mother," explains a young man living in Brooklyn. "I *had* to go. There wasn't anything to eat. There was no work. I went because I had to take care of my mother, and I couldn't take care of her in Mexico...."[44] Millions of people are weighing this choice. Lourdes, a young single mother from Honduras, left her son and daughter in 1989, trading the certain poverty of scrubbing clothes and peddling gum and cigarettes for the possibilities (depicted on television) of obtaining well-paying work that would hopefully mean that her children could go to school for more than a few years and have a good future. Rose Chávez, a few years later, contemplated the dangers of joining her husband in St. Louis or remaining in her southern Mexican village of Cherán, where she would "Stay at home, mend clothes, stitch doilies that won't sell at market...mind a store that has no customers....watch her daughter, Yeni, grow up, attend a few years of elementary school, and get knocked up by a local boy who will surely run away to the north himself."[45]

Living in the United States, even temporarily, changed familial relations in unforeseen ways. Mexican women gained more autonomy and influence in their families of origin and marriages as they worked outside the home in Mexico or in the United States. Hispanic households in the United States have been marked by two broad trends since 1960: falling birth rates and rising divorce rates, both of which attest to women's growing autonomy. Women who moved to the United States were freer to dress and to leave the house as they pleased, to have their husbands arrested for wife beating, to earn their own money, and to refuse a husband's sexual overtures. Even Catholic confessors in the United States were reluctant to pry into the sexual lives of their parishioners. Not surprisingly, then, men were often more eager than were women to return to Mexico, to use their earnings to live more comfortably in a place where male dominance seemed to be more secure and racism toward brown-skinned people seemed to be less acute. But the shifting dynamics of Mexican American gender relations were often complex. Jennifer S. Hirsch's masterful *A Courtship after Marriage: Sexuality and Love in Mexican Transnational Families* finds that the older generation of women she spoke to in the villages and towns of Jalisco and Michoacán understood marriage to be a "a cross" characterized by "endurance, not pleasure or intimacy." The young women of today, they complained, "don't have any shame."[46] This concept of *vergüenza* (shame) can be defined as "the inability to respond (or at least the willingness *not* to respond) to male anger, the male gaze, or other exercises of male power." This concept of feminine honor "requires a woman to feel shame for being female in the presence of males."[47] Hence young women in small towns were expected to sequester themselves from the street and other public areas and to guard carefully their virginity, for this would illustrate their honor and the honor of their families. "When women reject physical advances," explains Hirsch, "they are demanding respect." Upon marriage, the good wife would let her husband determine when she left the house, what she wore, and when they had sex, and she would not complain if he hit her for arguing with him. She "was to wash, mend, and iron clothes; keep the house and children clean; cook food and serve a hot meal to her husband in the morning and in the afternoon; raise the children to be polite (*bieneducados*), God-fearing, and respectful of their elders; and make sure that however much money her husband gave her to buy food lasted for the whole week." Adherence to these demanding requirements brought "a certain amount of leverage." Well-behaved women were more than justified in turning to their neighbors, parents, their husband's parents, the church, or local authorities if their husbands did not treat them honorably—by submitting them to unprovoked acts of violence or harsh words, for example. "Even though they are men, they still have to show respect for their wives," remarked one.[48]

Younger women, particularly those who spent at least some time in the United States, acquired different and in many ways higher standards for marriage. Like their Anglo counterparts, they expected suitors and husbands to be romantic and their marriages to be companionate. Hence when Hirsch asked her subjects to illustrate the key moments in their lives, the older women always drew a picture of their homes, often without even placing themselves in the picture. But the younger women "depicted themselves as the central character of a story," of a series of events in which they had starring roles: "First communions, quinceañeras, graduation from school, a first job, a first boyfriend, a first child." But romance and love could be ephemeral, and modern husbands felt less obligated to remain married than did traditional ones. "Privileging emotional satisfaction over men's responsibility to support their families," notes Hirsch, "leaves women on shaky ground."[49]

Young Mexican American husbands, for their part, embraced affection, but not equality. They both desired marriages that were more companionate than those of their parents and asserted that the men "should have the last word." Young Mexican American men commonly associated being macho with being outdated and ignorant. Modern forms of power and prestige rested less on physical power than on a mastery of "new technologies" In western Mexico, "men dangle large key chains from the pockets of their pants," icons that suggest their freedom of movement. In Atlanta, cell phones and pagers became the "tokens of masculine power"; status comes from controlling information rather than from machines and buildings.[50] The new economy offered more money, and money brought status. Don Emiliano recalled how in Mexico "I worked like a man, leading an ox team, working with material."

In a New York restaurant he was handed an apron. "I felt humiliated, getting screwed where I came to be the one giving it.... I felt that I looked like my pants had fallen down." But he changed his mind when cooking earned him $70.00 in his first week. The money erased his shame, and he concluded that the men in his native pueblo who thought less of him for doing the work of a woman were mired in "machismo or ignorance."[51]

Hispanic families in the United States commonly suffer from a set of daunting and interlocking problems. Most immigrants from Latin America are not proficient in English. Many are here illegally, which means that they cannot access educational and social services and that employers can exploit and cheat them. They usually live in poor, violent neighborhoods that have poor schools. Vietnamese and Cuban Americans have done so well in part because the federal government has assisted them so much, and the Cuban American community in Florida is large and prosperous enough to provide both employment opportunities and a buffer from Anglos. But most Hispanics, including those who are born here, face discrimination in housing, employment, and daily encounters if they are dark-skinned or speak with a Spanish accent. Though most come to the United States for their families, that choice brings separation and, often, alienation. Lourdes left a young son and daughter in Honduras so that she could give them a better life. That son, Enrique, several times ran a gauntlet of beatings and privations to join her in the United States, only to find himself enraged with the woman who, from his perspective, "abandoned me," who "forgot about me." Lourdes cried herself to sleep at night and protested, "I killed myself trying to help you."[52] A psychologist with the Los Angeles Unified School district estimated that only one in ten of such students eventually accept their parents' reasons for leaving them behind.

Families that survived poverty in Latin America often came apart in the United States. Luis Rodriguez noted that the girls from Mexico at his Los Angeles junior high school in the late 1960s came from families that "still had strong reins on many of them" and that they were "mostly traditional and Catholic."[53] But the ratio of single-parent families had become very high among third-generation Mexican, Dominican, and Cuban families. Second- or third-generation Mexican Americans referred to successful newcomers as "wannabes" in much the same way as African American students accused their academically oriented peers as acting white.[54]

Both economic success and failure can lead to cultural fragmentation. "By leaving Mexico and being left by her, our forebears had meant to free us from that ceaseless cycle of sacred duties to dance and chant and make sacrifices and pilgrimages, so that the cosmos would continue to exist," concludes John Phillip Santos. "The world we lived in now didn't require anything of us to keep the great movements and cycles of the earth and the universe in perpetual order."[55] Raúl Tapia first came to the United States in 1968, picking grapes in California and tomatoes in Arkansas, before bringing his wife and children to the United States from Cherán. They wandered and struggled for a quarter of a century before settling in Warren, Arkansas, where Raúl got a job working for the city. Their home is expansive and well appointed, their children have been, or will be, college educated. They will also leave Warren, for their small town holds few opportunities for well-educated professionals. Raúl seldom returns to Cherán. His life is in Warren. "But what," asks Martinez, "will be left for him here when the children move away?" He "came to American alone to give his children a future. He just never thought about how that very future might swallow them up."[56] It was not unusual for the same immigrant parents (who pushed their children to succeed in school in order to take advantages of the opportunities they never had) to feel hurt and abandoned when that search for success flung them to alien universities or careers.

Hispanic families have more commonly worried about their children being swallowed up by gang life, particularly the majority who lived in cities. Esmeralda Santiago recalled her mother's instructions on the rare occasions when she was allowed to venture out in Brooklyn: "Keep to the avenues. Don't talk to anyone. Don't accept any rides. If there are too many people milling around a sidewalk, cross the street and walk on the other side." "We lived separated by thick doors with several bolts, windows with iron grates, peepholes," she remembered.[57] Parents did not simply fear that their children would be attacked by gangs. They feared that they would become part of them. The great majority of newcomers from Mexico and the Caribbean had to live in poor neighborhoods and to send their children to poor schools where gangs predominated. The parents were commonly absent, working long hours or even remaining in Latin America. These conditions, coupled with racism and cultural dislocation, led to alienation, and alienated youth were highly susceptible to the sociability and excitement of gang life and culture. "I'm just a thug... living a thug life," boasted Toño, a young Mexican raised in New York, who then splayed his fingers out like a rapper to legitimize his claim.[58] Such youth adopted the uniform of inner-city protest—the baggy pants, languid walk, ostentatious jewelry, and rapper music and speech—that spread across North America and the rest of the world. Gangs offered "friendship, emotional support, and a sense of security and protection in the face of unpredictable, 'crazy' street pressures."[59] They reflected both the breakdown of traditional families and communities and constituted a highly problematic attempt to reconstitute these social relations through a community of peers. "Latino gangs," observes William Finnegan, "tend to be less about making money than they are about identity."[60]

Some immigrant parents responded by temporarily sending youth back to Latin America, where the temptations were fewer and the discipline inside and outside the school sterner. Armando Hernández Bueno's son was doing poorly in school and becoming resentful of his parents after five years in the United States. Matters came to a head when Luis called the police after his father had struck him for refusing to carry groceries. Armando sent him to relatives in the Dominican Republic and enrolled him in a private school. Two years later, Luis's behavior was much improved, and Armando anticipated that he would be able to return to the United States in a few more years. The United States, concluded Armando, was "all twisted in knots as far as children are concerned." They had to send their son away "or lose him to the gangs." Sociologists Alejandro Portes and Rubén G. Rumbaut conclude that immigrant parents "are less worried about racial discrimination and lack of opportunities than about their young doing themselves in because of excessive freedom and lack of institutional restraints."[61] As Miguel, a thirty-year-old from Monterrey who has been roaming across the United States for ten years puts it, "America's this big place where you can fuck and work and get high."[62]

Mexican American families, the many challenges they face notwithstanding, still maintain relatively tight families. First- and second-generation students from Mexico have been more likely to express a sense of obligation to their families than white students, and *Mexicanos* have commonly exhibited a stronger orientation to family and to kin than have other ethnic groups. Hirsch reports that Mexican American women were both having fewer children and were continuing to insist that having children remained an essential part of being married, of adulthood itself, as it illustrated "that her body's power is employed in useful, socially approved ways rather than in purely selfish, even potentially destructive, ways."[63]

The Enríquez family illustrates how some Mexican American families have sought to incorporate the economic opportunities of the United States with the familial orientation of Mexico. Santiago and his four sons made a very good living at a Wisconsin meat-packing plant. They owned a four-bedroom home in Wisconsin, one of the most impressive homes in Cherán, and five gleaming pick-ups. But all four sons—and their little sister and four wives and five children—shared the Wisconsin home, where María, the family matriarch, cared for the children and kept house. Santiago planned to retire to Cherán within ten years.

Of course Cherán and the rest of Mexico changed while the Enríquez family was away, transformed by the money and the cultures that increasingly flowed across national and ethnic boundaries. Gang graffiti and violence proliferated in Mexican towns, and bonds of community and obligation became more tenuous. As in the United States, prosperity has been a powerful solvent of tradition.

The great enemy of traditional societies that have immigrated to the United States has always been time, and time has accelerated in the past few decades. The second generation stays in school much longer than it did even in the early twentieth century, and it is very difficult for even the most conservative ethnic communities to shield their children from our hyper-individualistic culture. That is why groups or cohorts that have arrived in the United States most recently tend to be the most conservative.

Countercultural subgroups can also be organized voluntarily, on the basis of shared beliefs rather than on the basis of ethnic identity. Since the 1960s, especially, a variety of radical groups formed sundry communes that attempted to qualify members' commitment to individualism. But the most successful countercultural groups, by far, have not required group living—at least not as it is commonly defined—and they style themselves as more conservative than radical: evangelical Christians and the Church of Latter Day Saints (Mormons).

To be sure, even conservative evangelicals were profoundly changed by modern expressive individualism, especially the cult of self-actualization. Most spoke of a very personal God who was more caring and forgiving than harsh and judgmental. Calvinist and other more traditional Christians worried that the evangelical megachurches presented a "me-centered" gospel in which the theology of self-fulfillment replaced the gospel of sin, suffering, and the cross.[64] A recent survey of unmarried conservative Protestants found that four out of five of them had engaged in sexual relations over the past year—albeit usually with the same partner. White, evangelical Christians appeared to be no more likely than their liberal counterparts to abstain from vaginal sex during adolescence, and teen pregnancy and sexually-transmitted diseases were high, in part because sexual intercourse tended to be more spontaneous (and, therefore, unprotected). Conservative Christians divorced and remarried at about the same rate as did the rest of the population, and remarriage was widely accepted among even fundamentalist leaders, which was a strong departure from the conservative Protestant tradition. Their celebrations of motherhood, notwithstanding, conservative Protestants have also joined the national trend toward dual-income families. A 1996 survey found that evangelical and fundamentalist wives were in fact more likely to work outside the home than their liberal Protestant counterparts. Though professed beliefs changed more slowly than behaviors, growing numbers of evangelical Christians did not object to premarital sex (particularly with the person one intended to marry), divorce and remarriage, working mothers, and even wives exercising more spiritual leadership in their churches and homes. "The rejection of the world—in the form of pleasure and fun—is no longer an essential aspect of conservative religiosity," concludes one scholar.[65]

But like traditional Mennonites, who send their daughters to public schools but insist that they wear head coverings, conservative Protestants have held the line firmly on selected aspects of culture change, particularly on abortion and same-sex relationships. They have also commonly embraced premillenialism—the belief that the world was bound to get worse and worse until God raptured (sent to heaven) true Christians before turning the earth and all its sinners over to Satan—and purport to accept the Bible as the inerrant voice of God.

Such ideas strike liberals as bizarre and inhumane and perform a crucial social function. Professing to believe in the Bible's inerrancy requires the jettisoning of modern science, not to mention sound biblical scholarship, but serves to posit an unchanging source of moral and spiritual authority in a bewildering postmodern world. So does reinforcing selected aspects of traditional religious observance. Scholars of sects, of religious groups with distinctive beliefs and practices, have long pointed out that such groups almost inevitably lose their peculiarities in the powerful solvent of modernity. One survival strategy is to acculturate selectively, to tolerate, or to even embrace some elements of individualism while placing more emphasis on the distinctive practices or beliefs that remain: boundary maintenance, in sociological terms. Premillenialism allows fundamentalist Christians to enjoy the fruits of consumer culture and self-actualization while reminding themselves that heaven is their ultimate destination and that the fleeting pleasures, accomplishments, and problems of this world are of little ultimate significance. The doctrine's global pessimism and "willfully mad rhetoric" help the believer to draw a sharp line between the saved and the damned, between the sect and the world.[66] Indeed, sexual abstinence pledges have tended to break down when they were commonplace. "Pledgers apparently gather strength from the sense that they are an embattled minority," observed Margaret Talbot.[67] Conservative beliefs about abortion and same-sex relations are very useful tools in ensuring boundary maintenance vis-à-vis secular culture, precisely because they are such hot-button, divisive issues. Taking a stand against abortion or same-sex marriage reminds the believer that she or he is part of a distinctive community of faith, which is inevitably at odds with "the world."

Opposing abortion also affords evangelicals a platform from which to criticize individualism. For most liberals, teen pregnancy is not so much a sin as a tragedy: it thrusts young women into the time-consuming role of mother before they can secure their educational and occupational security or their personal ambitions. Conservative women embrace pregnancy and motherhood as their ambition. Abortion is abhorrent, not simply because it takes a life, but also because it suggests a rejection of motherhood, of women who chose home over career. Pro-choice advocates are much more likely to be highly educated professional women, who are able to make a good living on their own. Pro-life advocates are much more apt to have selected motherhood as their primary focus at a young age. "For pro-life women the traditional division of life into separate male roles and female roles still works, but for pro-choice women it does not," Kristin Luker summarizes.[68]

But being a conservative Christian has not just been about having different beliefs. It is ultimately about living differently, and conservative Christians have in fact been remarkably successful at what countless of leftist communes have failed to do: creating a viable counterculture that is inhabited by millions of families. E. Bradford Wilcox's *Soft Patriarchs, New Men* details the ways in which churchgoing, evangelical husbands are substantially different from their liberal and secular counterparts. Such fathers are much more likely to spend time with their children and their wives; monitor their children's use of television; and have wives who feel that their husbands appreciate them. Indeed, conservative husbands tend to do more emotion work and less housework than their liberal counterparts, perhaps because liberal couples identify housework as such a key component of gender justice and certainly because conservative evangelical men were told over and over again how important it was for them to nurture and care for their wives and children. They heard this message, furthermore, in church services, in prayer groups, and in cell or small-group meetings that brought conservative evangelicals together several times a week, not just on Sunday mornings. Conservative Protestants created a strong sectarian framework that every couple of days reminded entire families that God's people must behave differently from the families they saw on TV, in their neighborhoods, or in their schools. "Conservative Protestant institutions," Wilcox concludes, "appear to be uniquely capable of fostering positive emotion work on the part of married men with children."[69] This is partly a case of ideology, of what one chooses to believe. Hence a conservative Christian counselor remarks that he tries "to encourage the development of interdependence," rather than the "autonomy and independence" favored by his secular or liberal counterparts.[70]

But qualifying one's devotion to one's self usually requires a strong institutional structure. Indeed, those who express conservative Protestant beliefs but who do not regularly attend church, who have conservative beliefs without an intense social framework, tend to have low levels of familial involvement. Such people resemble the conservative-minded youth, identified by Mark Regnerus and Jeremy Uecker, who indulge in "selective permissiveness": condemning abortion and homosexuality; attending church sporadically or not at all; and marrying, having children, and divorcing young. This explains why Republican-leaning states tend to have such high rates of divorce and Internet pornography. "Cultural conservatism," unaccompanied by the social structures offered by conservative churches, tends to devolve into (often unacknowledged) libertinism.[71]

Highly evangelical women expect their churches to insist that husbands maintain a high level of familial commitment. Men left to their own devices will, they believe, choose sin over virtue. As Barbara Ehrenreich pointed out in 1983, for conservative women "the crime of feminism lay not in hating men, but in trusting them too well."[72] A liberal attitude toward commitment served men's interests, not women's. Canadian philosophers Joseph Heath and Andrew Potter concurr: "If you were to ask a group of men to think up their ideal set of dating rules, they would probably choose something very much like the 'free love' arrangement that emerged out of the sexual revolution.[73] Conservative Christianity, by way of contrast, both puts men at the head of the family and insists that they act responsibly. It constitutes a sort of return to the qualified male dominance of the nineteenth century, a time in which men occupied positions of authority, but women's sensibilities in many ways dominated the broader culture. Hence Judith Stacey in 1990 characterized a woman's evangelical beliefs as her "strategy for achieving heterosexual intimacy," for it required "more profound changes in Al's [her husband's] prior ways of relating than in hers."[74]

Much the same could be said of dedicated Mormons, members of the Church of Latter-Day Saints. Mormons, in the words of their late president, Gordon B. Hinckley, "stand for something" and "expect things of our people."[75] These expectations are considerable: tithing 10 percent of one's income; spending two years on a church mission; abstaining from coffee, tea, and alcohol; and fasting one day in a month. Even more so than conservative evangelical Christians, Mormons continually remind one another that they are singular and chosen people. They certainly form distinctive families. Mormons tend to marry young and to have a lot of children—though those early marriages have contributed to a surprisingly high divorce rate. Mormon family structures are patently patriarchal. All men are priests, whereas no women can become priests. Women are simply mothers. But many Mormon mothers have thought that this a good bargain. For them, notes sociologist Lori Beaman, the male priesthood serves "as a mechanism for strengthening the inherently weak nature of men."[76]

* * *

An elderly Dinka woman warned John Bul Dau and others, who were about to emigrate in 2001 to the United States, that there "you don't know your brother, you don't know your cousin. You forget your family, and you will not send us money here." Sure enough, a Catholic relief worker soon advised the refugees, "Don't send money to Africa."[77]

But Dau, who had survived incredible hardships in fleeing Sudan, remembered the advice of his elders. He worked very hard at his jobs and in school and sent money to scores of Dinka who remained in refugee camps. He waited to marry until he found a Dinka woman whom he respected and then waited another year while his father investigated her family in Africa. Then he saved money to pay a dowry of cows to his future wife's family.

Dau soon realized that his life in the United States would be much different from his ancestors'. He learned to cook, for example, an activity that was reserved for Sudanese women. He sought a college education, lived in modern homes, and mixed with a wide variety of people. But the young man who left his refugee camp with fourteen cassette tapes of counsel from his Dinka elders remained determined to acculturate selectively. "America's greatest weakness," he believed, was to have "drifted far from the love of family." Hence his "mother will live with me in my house until she dies" and "will help raise my children to be good Dinka, while I will raise them to be good Americans."[78]

History suggests that Dau's children, and certainly grandchildren, may well disappoint him. Recent immigrants to the United States, now as before, often maintain much of their emphasis on familial obligations, particularly if they immigrate as families, enjoy a modicum of socioeconomic stability, and live in cohesive communities of like-minded kin. But schools, peers, intermarriage, and a pervasive culture that champions the pursuit of pleasure and freedom have drawn a wider and wider swath of the nation into its orbit, and even conservative ethnic groups tend to acculturate by the second generation's coming of age.

Slavery, poverty, and racism have long both undermined black families and have required black people to turn to one another for support. But poor black families have become more fragmented, even as mainstream, popular culture has made the alienated young black male the quintessential symbol of authenticity. This complex combination of racism, poverty, and hyperindividualism has undercut much of the community and the resilience that characterized black neighborhoods as recently as two generations ago, though much less so for mothers than for fathers.

Conservative religious groups have created what appears to be the most powerful alternative to the culture of self-actualization, as they both articulate a consistent alternative message and create social structures (worship services, frequent social gatherings, and often schools) that shelter their members from mainstream values and practices.

Most readers of this sentence, like its writer, cannot accept the conservatives' defense of male privilege, discrimination against gays and lesbians, and anti-intellectualism. But can liberals who share conservatives' wariness of a culture based on the endless pursuit of fun also create substantial oases of mutualism and obligation?

Conclusion

There has always been a tension between two deeply held American ideals: family and freedom. Many Europeans came to what would become the United States searching for the latter, as opportunities for wealth, comfort, and autonomy were rare at home. In the process, they fractured Native American and African families as well as their own. But patterns of obligation soon reasserted themselves and persisted across diverse populations, circumstances, and historical developments. Not until early in the twentieth century did the nation begin its decisive shift *From Obligation to Freedom*, and not until the 1960s did freedom clearly gain the upper hand.

Members of earlier families and communities resided in webs of demanding relationships. This was true of the Native Americans, the Europeans, and the West Africans of the sixteenth and seventeenth centuries, and it was true of the colonies that arose and developed in North America. Families and communities that were characterized by a strong sense of obligation survived political and industrial revolutions in the eighteenth and nineteenth centuries, respectively. They were often hierarchal and, at least by modern definitions, exploitative. But inequality did not preclude reciprocity or love.

Our long history of forming families and other relationships that are rooted in obligation has owed much to necessity. Indeed, the very invention of humanity was bound up in its ability to cooperate and collaborate, to nurture children, and to develop languages and tools. "Throughout our long prehistory there was less that hunter-gatherer bands could get away with, compared with modern man, without risking extinction," notes Andrew Oldenquist.[1] Most people who were living in the United States had little choice but to depend on one another through the nineteenth century. The hardships that dominated the lives of most black, white working-class, immigrant, and many rural families required the work of many hands—family, kin, and neighbors—for survival. Even the growing middle class embraced family life, for the family nurtured the habits of industry and thrift that individual and corporate success depended on. Capitalism encouraged and depended on strong families.

Then, in the twentieth century, capitalism changed. The sheer number and quality of consumer goods that became available to even working-class families soared. The foundation of the economy shifted from production to consumption, and cultural and social norms followed. Popular literature, music, and movies joined advertisers in emphasizing the importance of personal happiness and fulfillment. This surge of individualism encouraged oppressed minorities and white women to assert themselves, but it also contributed—by the second half of the twentieth century, especially—to a tremendous rise in familial and social fragmentation, to a growing incapacity to form durable relationships, particularly for men.

This interpretation in many ways meshes with those of conservative observers of the family. But I lay responsibility for familial fragmentation at the doorstep of two developments that conservatives usually celebrate: capitalism and freedom. Indeed, a central dilemma of modern life is that economic success and social solidarity require such contradictory impulses and skills. The logic of modern capitalism eschews the formation of any social or political commitment that might threaten the individual's resolute pursuit of wealth, autonomy, and pleasure. "We cannot," concludes C. B. Macpherson, "expect a valid theory of obligation [to be applied] to a liberal-democratic state in a possessive market economy."[2] Hence it has become political suicide to suggest increased taxes or regulation, notwithstanding the growing challenges of poverty, debt, and climate change.

The only large communities in which obligation routinely trumps freedom are conservative churches and communities that are peopled with recent immigrants, alternative universes in which spouses, parents, children, and kin are reminded regularly that they are surrounded by an alien and corrosive world that would have them forget that they are required to care for one another.

There is no putting the genie back in the bottle for the rest of us. We are essentially free to do as we wish. Neglecting our spouses, our parents, and our children seldom invites shame, let alone starvation. The relentless pursuit of highly personal goals may even yield riches and fame. Many liberal-minded people have succeeded in creating stable families with fluid gender roles and children who are secure, curious, and empathetic, and many voluntary communities function much like families. I think of the various nonsectarian groups that I have belonged to or observed over the years: the lodge memberships that my parents cherished during their last decades; the Radical Faerie House of Eugenia; the volunteers and the staff at food cooperatives, women's shelters, and Head Start centers; a lesbian cohousing complex; the parents whose children attend the same school or belong to the same sports teams; the women's book clubs and support groups; the liberal churches; the neighborhood associations (formal and informal); and even P.U.S. (Portland Unemployed Soccer) , an assortment of self-proclaimed slackers (spanning a half century and five continents) who got together to play a pick-up version of the world's game. Some of these endeavors are brittle or ephemeral. P.U.S. struggled with personality clashes even before Portland's aggressive kick-ball leagues appropriated its fields. But many of these little communities are surprisingly stubborn. An over-fifty soccer team I recently joined has members who have played and have drunk beer together for most of their lives—and have supported one another through divorces, children's mishaps, legal scrapes, illnesses, and deaths. Their style of play is not often sublime, in part, because of increasing age and declining skills, but also because of the team's anarchistic ethos. There is little tolerance for those who would impose order and authority at the expense of an individual's right to do stupid things on a soccer pitch.

That is the beauty of freedom. It allows us to commit ourselves to one another, not because we must—or believe that we must—but because we can. Liberal, freely chosen acts of obligation reject the coercion and exclusion that are practiced by conservative ethnic groups or by conservative churches. We are all free to spend more time with our families and our friends and to take their happiness seriously. Few modern forces encourage or prompt us to make such choices. But neither do they preclude these choices.

Choosing to create and sustain meaningful relationships is a radical act of nonconformity because it entails the acceptance of limits and the surrender of other possibilities. This is incompatible with our modern assumption that we owe it to ourselves to lunge at any compelling pleasure or any opportunity that presents itself. Being a good mother, father, daughter, son, sister, brother, grandmother, grandfather, aunt, uncle, niece, nephew, friend, or neighbor confronts us with the weight of other people's happiness and well-being, demands that must sometimes supersede our own.

I do not presume to know whether the formation of durable and loving families will require the overthrow of capitalism or entail some sort of massive state intervention. Certainly, many families would be immeasurably strengthened by access to medical care, good schools, and a decent income. But freedom from want hardly secures family stability. Indeed, economic opportunity has often served to make commitments to others optional. But it is increasingly clear that radical individualism is not sustainable. Our ecological, economic, political, and social futures depend on the recapturing of some elements of the mutualism and obligation that we have so assiduously been discarding over the past few generations. "Just because we no longer believe in the doctrines of the Great Chain of Being," notes philosopher Charles Taylor, does not mean that we cannot "see ourselves as part of a larger order that can make claims on us."[3]

Just about all of us realize this, if fitfully. Erica Jong's highly autobiographical *Fear of Flying* was interpreted as a clarion call to freedom when it appeared in 1973. "Even if you loved your husband," remarks protagonist Isadora Wing, "there came that inevitable year when fucking him turned as bland as Velveeta cheese: filling, fattening even, but no thrill to the taste buds, no bittersweet edge, no danger." Wing, in fact, leaves a serviceable husband for the possibilities of a "zipless fuck," an encounter of pure sensation and freedom untainted by any hint of obligation. But Jong's famous novel and her life turned out to be much more complicated. Wing ends up with a lover who is far from ideal, and she spends much of the novel agonizing over the choices she is presented with. When the opportunity for a truly zipless fuck appears, she recoils. "She punished herself with men," Jong later remarked. Jong was somewhat confounded by the oversimplified message that readers drew from her best seller, and she found that becoming a mother was "profoundly satisfying," even "at the expense of that swollen ego you thought so immutable." Jong was proud of having "raised a daughter who also recognizes no limits." But Molly Jong-Fast, like her mother, in fact came to welcome some limits. She resented her mother's highly independent lifestyle: "When you're twelve, there is nothing funny about your mother's fourth wedding." It was this stepfather's heart attack that jolted Jong-Fast out of a childhood of petulant self-indulgence and enabled her "to shed some of the selfishness that plagues me."[4]

Jong-Fast's childhood was far from typical. Most of us do not grow up with a celebrity mother who dates and marries frequently. But more and more of us are growing up with parents who are absent for large chunks of our lives, who are unsure about how to parent, who either leave us more or less on our own, or who encourage us to dream of colleges or careers that are likely to take us far away from them and the rest of our kin, dreams that are less and less likely to include the substance of family relationships.

Yet accruing obligations, feeling the weight of others press upon our hours and years, has always been at the center of what makes us human. These obligations should not preclude the pursuit of many of the other infinite possibilities that modern life has made available to so many of us. But a stubborn love and regard for others must also inform our lives.

Notes

Introduction

1. Micki McGee, *Self-Help, Inc.: Makeover Culture in American Life* (New York: Oxford University Press, 2005), 44.
2. Louis Dumont, *Homo Hierarchicus: An Essay on the Caste System,* trans. Mark Sainbury (Chicago: University of Chicago Press, 1970), 8.

1 Societies of Obligation

1. Thomas D. Dillehay, *The Settlement of the Americas: A New Prehistory* (New York: Basic Books, 2000), 266.
2. Michael S. Gazzaniga, *Human: The Science Behind What Makes Us Unique* (New York: HarperCollins, 2008), 83.
3. John T. Cacioppo and William Patrick, *Loneliness: Human Nature and the Need for Social Connection* (New York: W. W. Norton, 2008), 72, 143.
4. Raymond J. DeMallie, "Kinship and Biology in Sioux Culture," in *North American Indian Anthropology: Essays on Society and Culture*, ed. Raymond J. DeMallie and Alfonso Ortiz (Norman: University of Oklahoma Press, 1994), 126.
5. J. Gilbert McAllister, "Kiowa-Apache Social Organization," in *Social Anthropology of North American Tribes*, enlarged edition, ed. Fred Eggan (Chicago, IL: University of Chicago Press, 1955), 123.
6. Theda Perdue, *Cherokee Women: Gender and Culture Change, 1700–1835* (Lincoln: University of Nebraska Press, 1998), 49.
7. Perdue, *Cherokee Women*, 47.
8. Ella C. Deloria, *Speaking of Indians* (Vermillion, SD: Dakota Press, 1979), 17.
9. June McCormick Collins, *Valley of the Spirits: The Upper Skagit Indians of Western Washington* (Seattle: University of Washington Press, 1974), 120.
10. Nancy Shoemaker, *A Strange Likeness: Becoming Red and White in Eighteenth-Century North America* (New York: Oxford University Press, 2006), 118–19.
11. Allan Greer, *Mohawk Saint: Catherine Tekakwitha and the Jesuits* (New York: Oxford University Press, 2006), 26, 48.
12. Mary P. Ryan, *Mysteries of Sex: Tracing Women and Men through American History* (Chapel Hill: University of North Carolina Press, 2006), 35.
13. Perdue, *Cherokee Women*, 46.

14. Ramón Gutiérrez, *When Jesus Came, the Corn Mothers Went Away: Marriage, Sexuality, and Power in New Mexico, 1500–1846* (Stanford, CA: Stanford University Press, 1991), 17.
15. Jonathan Lear, *Radical Hope: Ethics in the Face of Cultural Devastation* (Cambridge, MA: Harvard University Press, 2006), 13, 23, emphasis in the original; Michael Stephen Kennedy, ed., *The Assiniboines* (Norman: Oklahoma University Press, 1961), 40, 47.
16. Lillian A. Ackerman, *A Necessary Balance: Gender and Power among Indians of the Columbia Plateau* (Norman: University of Oklahoma Press, 2003), 21.
17. Rebecca Morley, "Wife Beating and Modernization: The Case of Papua New Guinea," *Journal of Comparative Family Studies* 25 (Spring 1994): 42.
18. Eva Tulene Watt, assisted by Keith H. Basso, *Don't Let the Sun Step Over You: A White Mountain Apache Family Life (1860–1975)* (Tucson: University of Arizona Press, 2004), 42.
19. F. Kniffen, et al., "Walapai Ethnography," *Memoirs of the American Anthropological Association* 42 (1935): 139, quoted in Carol A. Markstrom, *Empowerment of North American Indian Girls: Ritual Expressions at Puberty* (Lincoln: University of Nebraska Press, 2008), 181.
20. Angel DeCora, "An Autobiography," *The Red Man*, March 1911, 279; Jarold Ramsey, comp. and ed., *Coyote Was Going There: Indian Literature of the Oregon Country* (Seattle: University of Washington Press, 1980), 58–60.
21. Verne F. Ray, *Primitive Pragmatists: The Modoc Indians of Northern California* (Seattle: University of Washington Press, 1963), 106.
22. Alice Schlegel, "The Adolescent Socialization of the Hopi Girl," *Ethnology* 12 (October 1973): 450–51.
23. Anthony F. C. Wallace, *The Death and Rebirth of the Seneca* (New York: Vintage, 1972), 61, 63–64.
24. Wallace, *Death and Rebirth*, 66–67.
25. John Iliffe, *Africans: The History of a Continent* (Cambridge: Cambridge University Press, 1995), 68.
26. Esther N. Goody, *Contexts of Kinship: An Essay in the Family Sociology of the Gonja of Northern Ghana* (Cambridge: Cambridge University Press, 1973), 50, 55.
27. Edna G. Bay, *Wives of the Leopard: Gender, Politics, and Culture in the Kingdom of Dahomey* (Charlottesville: University of Virginia Press, 1998), 17.
28. James H. Sweet, *Recreating Africa: Culture, Kinship, and Religion in the African-Portuguese World, 1441–1770* (Chapel Hill: University of North Carolina Press, 2003), 31–32.
29. Meyer Fortes, *The Web of Kinship among the Tallensi: The Second Part of an Analysis of the Social Structure of a Trans-Volta Tribe* (London: International African Institute by Oxford University Press, 1949), 18, 169.
30. Birgit Meyer, "'Delivered from the Powers of Darkness': Confessions of Satanic Riches in Christian Ghana," *Africa: Journal of the International African Institute* 65 (1995): 245–46.
31. Goody, *Contexts of Kinship*, 219.
32. Edna G. Bay, *Wives of the Leopard: Gender, Politics, and Culture in the Kingdom of Dahomey* (Charlottesville: University of Virginia Press, 1998), 13.
33. John S. Mbiti, *African Religions and Philosophy* (Garden City, NY: Anchor, 1970), 104–10.
34. Goody, *Contexts of Kinship*, 242.

35. G. K. Nukunya, *Kinship and Marriage among the Anlo Ewe* (London: Athlone Press and New York: Humanities Press, 1969), 153.
36. Kenneth Little, "The Mende in Sierra Leone," in *African Worlds: Studies in the Cosmological Ideas and Social Values of African Peoples*, ed. Daryll Forde (London: International African Institute and Oxford University Press, 1954), 122.
37. Nakunya, *Kinship and Marriage*, 155.
38. Nakunya, *Kinship and Marriage*, 158.
39. D. T. Niane, *Sundiata: An Epic of Old Mali* (Essex: Longman, 1965), 41, 81–82.
40. Igor Kopytoff and Suzanne Miers, "African 'Slavery' as an Institution of Marginality," in *Slavery in Africa: Historical and Anthropological Perspectives*, ed. Suzanne Miers and Igor Kopytoff (Madison: University of Wisconsin Press, 1977), 17.
41. T. C. McCaskie, *State and Society in Pre-Colonial Asante* (Cambridge: Cambridge University Press, 1995), 89.
42. Kwame Gyekye, *African Cultural Values: An Introduction* (Accra, Ghana: Sankofa Publishing, 2003), 45.
43. Claude Meillassoux, trans. Alide Dasnois, *The Anthropology of Slavery: The Womb of Iron and Gold* (Chicago, IL: University of Chicago Press, 1991), 128.
44. Dylan C. Penningroth, *The Claims of Kinfolk: African American Property and Community in the Nineteenth-Century South* (Chapel Hill: University of North Carolina Press, 2003), 22.
45. Randy L. Sparks, *The Two Princes of Calabar: An Eighteenth-Century Atlantic Odyssey* (Cambridge, MA: Harvard University Press, 2004), 38.
46. Mbiti, *African Religions and Philosophy*, 194, 136–37, 267, 272; Anthony Ephirim-Donkor, *African Spirituality: On Becoming Ancestors* (Trenton, NJ: Africa World Press, 1997), 144.
47. Gyekye, *African Cultural Values*, 37, 49, 50.
48. Gyekye, *Tradition and Modernity: Philosophical Reflections on the African Experience* (New York: Oxford University Press, 1997), 41.
49. Keith Wrightson, *English Society, 1580–1680* (New Brunswick, NJ: Rutgers University Press, 2000), 42.
50. Wrightson, *English Society*, 45.
51. E. M. W. Tillyard, *The Elizabethan World Picture* (Harmondsworth, Middlesex: Penguin, 1966), 39.
52. Stephen Foster, *Their Solitary Way: The Puritan Social Ethic in the First Century of Settlement in New England* (New Haven, CT: Yale University Press, 1971), 18.
53. Wrightson, *English Society*, 90.
54. Anthony Fletcher, *Gender, Sex and Subordination in England, 1500–1800* (New Haven, CT: Yale University Press, 1995), 71–72.
55. Fletcher, *Gender, Sex and Subordination*, 207.
56. Fletcher, *Gender, Sex and Subordination*, 112–13.
57. Ralph A. Houlbrooke, *The English Family, 1450–1700* (London: Longman, 1984), 105.
58. Linda A. Pollock, "Parent-Child Relations," in *Family Life in Early Modern Times, 1500–1789*, ed. David I. Kertzer and Marzio Barbagli (New Haven, CT: Yale University Press, 2001), 201.

59. Steven Ozment, *When Fathers Ruled: Family Life in Reformation Europe.* Cambridge, MA: Harvard University Press, 1983), 59.
60. Paul Riesman, *Freedom in Fulani Social Life: An Introspective Ethnography*, trans. Martha Fuller (Chicago, IL: University of Chicago Press, 1998), 153, 166–67, 173.

2 The Search for Order in North America

1. Jean O'Brien, "Divorced from the Land: Accommodation Strategies of Indian Women in Eighteenth-Century New England," in *Gender, Kinship, Power: A Comparative and Interdisciplinary History*, ed. Mary Jo Maynes, et al. (New York: Routledge, 1996), 326.
2. James F. Brooks, *Captives & Cousins: Slavery, Kinship, and Community in the Southwest Borderlands* (Williamsburg, VA: Omohundro Institute of Early American History and Culture and Chapel Hill: University of North Carolina Press, 2002), 365.
3. Matthew Dennis, *Cultivating a Landscape of Peace: Iroquois-European Encounters in Seventeenth-Century America* (Ithaca, NY: Cornell University Press, 1993), 168.
4. Ramón Gutiérrez, *When Jesus Came, the Corn Mothers Went Away: Marriage, Sexuality, and Power in New Mexico, 1500–1846* (Stanford, CA: Stanford University Press, 1991), 156, 206.
5. Steve J. Stern, *The Secret History of Gender: Women, Men, and Power in Late Colonial Mexico* (Chapel Hill: University of North Carolina Press, 1995), 87, 299.
6. James M. Japer, *Restless Nation: Starting Over in America* (Chicago, IL: University of Chicago Press, 2000), 227.
7. Darrett B. Rutman and Anita H. Rutman, "'Now-Wives and Sons-in-Law': Parental Death in a Seventeenth-Century Virginia County," in *The Chesapeake in the Seventeenth Century: Essays on Anglo-American Society*, ed. Thad W. Tate and David L. Ammerman (Chapel Hill: University of North Carolina Press, 1979), 158; Darrett B. Rutman and Anita B. Rutman, *A Place in Time: Middlesex County, Virginia, 1650–1750* (New York: W. W. Norton, 1984), 114.
8. James Horn, *Adapting to a New World: English Society in the Seventeenth-Century Chesapeake* (Williamsburg, VA: Omohundro Institute of Early American History and Culture and Chapel Hill: University of North Carolina Press, 1994), 244; Lorena S. Walsh, "Community Networks in the Early Chesapeake," in *Colonial Chesapeake Society*, ed. Lois Green Carr, Philip D. Morgan, and Jean B. Russo (Williamsburg, VA: Institute of Early American History and Culture and Chapel Hill: University of North Carolina Press, 1988), 225; Rutman and Rutman, *Place in Time*, 121.
9. Edmund S. Morgan, *The Puritan Family: Religion & Domestic Relations in Seventeenth-Century New England*, rev. ed. (New York: Harper & Row, 1966), 145, 149.
10. Helena M. Wall, *Fierce Communion: Family and Community in Early America* (Cambridge, MA: Harvard University Press, 1990), 83.
11. Morgan, *Puritan Family*, 19, 44.
12. Linda A Pollock, *Forgotten Children: Parent-Child Relations from 1500 to 1900* (Cambridge: Cambridge University Press, 1983), 114.

13. David D. Hall, ed., *Puritans in the New World: A Critical Anthology* (Princeton: Princeton University Press, 2004), 185–86.
14. "Governor John Winthrop Gives a Model of Christian Charity, 1630," in *Major Problems in American Colonial History*, 2nd ed., ed. Karen Ordahl Kupperman (Boston, MA: Houghton Mifflin, 2000), 92.
15. Melvin Yazawa, *From Colonies to Commonwealth: Familial Ideology and the Beginnings of the American Republic* (Baltimore, MD: Johns Hopkins University Press, 1985), 21.
16. Lisa Wilson, *Ye Heart of a Man: The Domestic Life of Men in Colonial New England* (New Haven, CT: Yale University Press, 1999), 3, 116.
17. Anne S. Lombard, *Making Manhood: Growing Up Male in Colonial New England* (Cambridge, MA: Harvard University Press, 2003), 170.
18. Margaret W. Masson, "The Typology of the Female as a Model for the Regenerate in Puritan Preaching, 1690–1730," *Signs* 2 (Winter 1976): 310.
19. James H. Sweet, *Recreating Africa: Culture, Kinship, and Religion in the African-Portuguese World, 1441–1770* (Chapel Hill: University of North Carolina Press, 2003), 32–33.
20. Stephanie E. Smallwood, *Saltwater Slavery: A Middle Passage from Africa to America Diaspora* (Cambridge, MA: Harvard University Press, 2007), 121, 189.
21. Allen Kulikoff, *Tobacco and Slaves: The Development of Southern Cultures in the Chesapeake, 1680–1800* (Williamsburg, VA: Omohundro Institute of Early American History and Culture and Chapel Hill: University of North Carolina Press, 1986), 72.
22. Philip D. Morgan, *Slave Counterpoint* (Williamsburg, VA: Omohundro Institute of Early American History and Culture and Chapel Hill: University of North Carolina Press, 1998), 529.
23. Alan Taylor, *American Colonies* (New York: Penguin, 2002), 58.

3 Revolution and Continuity

1. Thomas Bender, *Community and Social Change in America* (New Brunswick, NJ: Rutgers University Press, 1978), 69.
2. Richard L. Bushman, *The Refinement of America: Persons, Houses, Cities* (New York: Vintage, 1992), 184.
3. James A. Henretta and Gregory H. Nobles, *Evolution and Revolution: American Society, 1600–1820* (Lexington, MA: D. C. Heath, 1987), 72.
4. Rhys Isaac, *The Transformation of Virginia: 1740–1790* (Williamsburg, VA: Institute of Early American History and Culture and Chapel Hill: University of North Carolina Press, 1982), 111; T. H. Breen, *Tobacco Culture: The Mentality of the Great Tidewater Planters on the Eve of Revolution* (Princeton, NJ: Princeton University Press, 1985), 84–123.
5. Melvin Yazawa, *From Colonies to Commonwealth: Familial Ideology and the Beginnings of the American Republic* (Baltimore: The Johns Hopkins University Press, 1985), 61; Barry Alan Shain, *The Myth of American Individualism: The Protestant Origins of American Political Thought* (Princeton, NJ: Princeton University Press, 1994), 39.
6. Bushman, *Refinement of America*, 31, 39.
7. H. W. Brands, *The First American: The Life and Times of Benjamin Franklin* (New York: Anchor, 2000), 277.

8. Ian Watt, *Myths of Modern Individualism: Faust, Don Quixote, Don Juan, Robinson Crusoe* (Cambridge: Cambridge University Press, 1996), 174.
9. Bernard Bailyn, *The New England Merchants in the Seventeenth Century* (Cambridge, MA: Harvard University Press, 1979), 140.
10. Isaac, *Transformation of Virginia*, 168.
11. Gary B. Nash, *The Urban Crucible: Social Change, Political Consciousness, and the Origins of the American Revolution* (Cambridge, MA: Harvard University Press, 1979), 214–15.
12. Lisa Wilson, *Ye Heart of a Man: The Domestic Life of Men in Colonial New England* (New Haven, CT: Yale University Press, 1999), 88
13. Allan Kulikoff, *Tobacco and Slaves: The Development of Southern Cultures in the Chesapeake, 1680–1800* (Williamsburg, VA: Omohundro Institute of Early American History and Culture and Chapel Hill: University of North Carolina Press, 1986), 177.
14. Darrett B. Rutman and Anita H. Rutman, *A Place in Time: Middlesex County, Virginia, 1650–1750* (New York: W. W. Norton, 1984), 103.
15. Rhys Isaac, *Landon Carter's Uneasy Kingdom: Revolution and Rebellion on a Virginia Plantation* (Oxford: Oxford University Press, 2004), 179, 184.
16. Henretta and Nobles, *Evolution and Revolution*, 108.
17. "Thomas Hutchinson Criticizes the Declaration of Independence, 1776," in *Major Problems in the Era of the American Revolution, 1760–1791*, 2nd ed., ed. Richard D. Brown (Boston: Houghton Mifflin, 2000), 233.
18. Steven Mintz, *Huck's Raft: A History of American Childhood* (Cambridge, MA: Harvard University Press, 204), 56.
19. Mary Beth Norton, *Liberty's Daughters: The Revolutionary Experience of American Women, 1750–1800* (Ithaca, NY: Cornell University Press, 1996), 242.
20. Laurel Thatcher Ulrich, *A Midwife's Tale: The Life of Martha Ballard, Based on Her Diary, 1785–1812* (New York: Alfred A. Knopf, 1990), 230.
21. Shain, *Myth of American Individualism*, 190.
22. Jon Meacham, *American Gospel: God, the Founding Fathers, and the Making of a Nation* (New York: Random, 2006), 69.
23. Jack P. Greene, "The Concept of Virtue in Late Colonial British America," in *Virtue, Corruption, and Self-Interest: Political Values in the Eighteenth Century*, ed. Richard K. Matthews (Bethlehem, PA: Lehigh University Press, 1994), 35.
24. Daniel Walker Howe, *Making the American Self: Jonathan Edwards to Abraham Lincoln* (New York: Oxford University Press, 2009), 71.
25. Charles W. Akers, *Abigail Adams: A Revolutionary American Woman*, 3rd ed. (New York: Pearson, 2007), 40, 48, 57, 215.
26. Mary P. Ryan, *Mysteries of Sex: Tracing Women and Men through American History* (Chapel Hill: University of North Carolina Press, 2006), 77.

4 Containing the Bourgeois Family

1. David Thelen, *Paths of Resistance: Tradition and Dignity in Industrializing Missouri* (New York: Oxford University Press, 1986), 44–56.
2. Rodney Hessinger, *Seduced, Abandoned, and Reborn: Visions of Youth in Middle-Class America, 1780–1850* (Philadelphia: University of Pennsylvania Press, 2005), 128, 141.

3. Robert H. Wiebe, *Self-Rule: A Cultural History of American Democracy* (Chicago, IL: University of Chicago Press, 1995), 26.
4. W. J. Rorabaugh, *The Alcoholic Republic: An American Tradition* (New York: Oxford University Press, 1981).
5. Daniel Walker Howe, *Making the American Self: Jonathan Edwards to Abraham Lincoln* (New York: Oxford University Press, 2009), 109, emphasis in the original.
6. Lucy Larcom, *A New England Girlhood* (Gloucester, MA: Peter Smith, 1973), 74, 26, 27.
7. Joan Shelley Rubin, *The Making of Middlebrow Culture* (Chapel Hill: University of North Carolina Press, 1992), 18.
8. Joyce Appleby, *Inheriting the Revolution: The First Generation of Americans* (Cambridge, MA: Harvard University Press, 2000), 231.
9. Barbara Welter, *Dimity Convictions: The American Woman in the Nineteenth Century* (Athens: Ohio University Press, 1976), 76.
10. Minnie Jane Forster, *He Led Me through the Wilderness* (n.p.: n.p., 1947), 59.
11. Carroll Smith-Rosenberg, "The Female World of Love and Ritual: Relations between Women in Nineteenth-Century America," *Signs* 1 (Autumn 1975): 1–29.
12. Daniel Scott Smith, "Family Limitation, Sexual Control, and Domestic Feminism in Victorian America," in *Clio's Consciousness Raised: New Perspectives on the History of Women*, ed. Mary S. Hartmann and Lois Banner (New York: Harper and Row, 1974), 119–36.
13. E. Anthony Rotundo, *American Manhood: Transformations in Masculinity from the Revolution to the Modern Era* (New York: Basic Books, 1993), 30.
14. Ellen K. Rothman, *Hands and Hearts: A History of Courtship in America* (New York: Basic Books, 1984), 153.
15. Harriet Beecher Stowe, *Uncle Tom's Cabin, or Life among the Lowly* (Boston, MA: Houghton Mifflin, 1892), 48, 228.
16. Jane P. Tompkins, "Sentimental Power: *Uncle Tom's Cabin* and the Politics of Literary History," in *The New Feminist Criticism: Essays on Women, Literature, and Theory*, ed. Elaine Showalter (New York: Pantheon, 1985), 95, 98, 99.
17. Steven Mintz, *A Prison of Expectations: The Family in Victorian Culture* (New York: New York University Press, 1985), 129.
18. Ann Douglas, *The Feminization of American Culture* (New York: Alfred A. Knopf, 1977).
19. Blanche Glassman Hersh, *The Slavery of Sex* (Urbana: University of Illinois Press, 1978), 86, emphasis in the original.
20. Harriet Sigerman, "Laborers for Liberty, 1865–1890," in *No Small Courage: A History of Women in the United States*, ed. Nancy F. Cott (Oxford: Oxford University Press, 2000), 323; Michael Grossberg, *Governing the Hearth: Law and the Family in Nineteenth-Century America* (Chapel Hill: University of North Carolina Press, 1985).
21. Lee Virginia Chambers-Schiller, *Liberty, a Better Husband: Single Women in America: The Generations of 1780–1840* (New Haven, CT: Yale University Press, 1984), 213, emphasis in the original.
22. Jean H. Baker, *Sisters: The Lives of America's Suffragists* (New York: Hill and Wang, 2005), 52, 92.

23. Robyn Muncy, *Creating a Female Dominion in American Reform, 1890–1935* (New York: Oxford University Press, 1991), 5.
24. Mark Carnes, *Secret Ritual and Manhood in Victorian America* (New Haven, CT: Yale University Press, 1989), 100.
25. *The Journal of Henry D. Thoreau* (New York: Dover, 1962), Vol. I: 81.
26. Edgar Allan Poe, *The Black Cat and Other Tales* (Bogotá, Columbia: Panamericana, 2000), 23; Herman Melville, *Moby Dick, or, the Whale* (New York: Modern Library, 1950).
27. Rotundo, *American Manhood*, 35.
28. Howard P. Chudacoff, *The Age of the Bachelor: Creating an American Subculture* (Princeton, NJ: Princeton University Press, 1999), 36.
29. Richard D. Brown, *Modernization: The Transformation of American Life, 1600–1865* (New York: Hill and Wang, 1976), 144–45, 140.
30. Elizabeth Fox-Genovese, *Within the Plantation Household: Black and White Women of the Old South* (Chapel Hill: University of North Carolina Press, 1988), 100; Gavin Wright, *The Political Economy of the Cotton South: Households, Markets, and Wealth in the Nineteenth Century* (New York: W. W. Norton, 1978), 34–35.
31. Eugene Genovese, "'Our Family, White and Black': Family and Household in the Southern Slaveholders' World View," in *In Joy and in Sorrow: Women, Family, and Marriage in the Victorian South, 1830–1900*, ed. Carol Bleser (New York: Oxford University Press, 1991), 70, 71, emphasis in the original.
32. Stephanie McCurry, *Masters of Small Worlds: Yeoman Households, Gender Relations, and the Political Culture of the Antebellum South Carolina Low Country* (New York: Oxford University Press, 1995), 219, 223.
33. Peter W. Bardaglio, *Reconstructing the Household: Families, Sex and the Law in the Nineteenth-Century South* (Chapel Hill: University of North Carolina Press, 1995), 28.
34. Steven M. Stowe, *Intimacy and Power in the Old South: Ritual in the Lives of the Planters* (Baltimore: Johns Hopkins University Press, 1987), 191.
35. Joan E. Cashin, *A Family Venture: Men and Women on the Southern Frontier* (New York: Oxford University Press, 1991), 106.
36. Ted Ownby, *Subduing Satan: Religion, Recreation, and Manhood in the Rural South, 1865–1920* (Chapel Hill: University of North Carolina Press, 1990), 11.
37. Suzanne Lebsock, *The Free Women of Petersburg: Status and Culture in a Southern Town, 1784–1860* (New York: W. W. Norton, 1985), 32.
38. Elizabeth R. Varon, *We Mean to Be Counted: White Women and Politics in Antebellum Virginia* (Chapel Hill: University of North Carolina Press, 1998), 32.
39. Anne Firor Scott, *The Southern Lady: From Pedestal to Politics, 1830–1930* (Chicago, IL: University of Chicago Press, 1970), 19–20.
40. Ownby, *Subduing Satan*, 167–93.
41. Ruth Barnes Moynihan, *Rebel for Rights: Abigail Scott Duniway* (New Haven, CT: Yale University Press, 1983), 56.
42. David Peterson del Mar, *What Trouble I Have Seen: A History of Violence against Wives* (Cambridge, MA: Harvard University Press, 1996), 15.
43. Lillian Schlissel, *Women's Diaries of the Westward Journey* (New York: Schocken Books, 1982), 14.

44. John Mack Faragher, *Sugar Creek: Life on the Illinois Prairie* (New Haven, CT: Yale University Press, 1986), 205.
45. Peterson del Mar, *What Trouble I Have Seen*, 25.
46. David Peterson del Mar, *Beaten Down: A History of Interpersonal Violence in the West* (Seattle: University of Washington Press, 2002), 66, 84.
47. Clare V. McKanna, "Enclaves of Violence in Nineteenth-Century California," *Pacific Historical Review* 73 (August 2004): 399–400.
48. Andrew Delbanco, *Melville: His World and Work* (New York: Vintage, 2005), 184.
49. Delbanco, *Melville*, 12, 135–36.
50. Delbanco, *Melville*, 178.

5 Necessity and Tradition

1. Herbert G. Gutman, *The Black Family in Slavery and Freedom, 1750–1925* (New York: Vintage, 1977), 132.
2. Wilma King, *Stolen Childhood: Slave Youth in Nineteenth-Century America* (Bloomington: Indiana University Press, 1997), 10.
3. Brenda E. Stevenson, *Life in Black and White: Family and Community in the Slave South* (New York: Oxford University Press, 1997), 113, 249.
4. Marie Jenkins Schwartz, *Born in Bondage: Growing Up Enslaved in the Antebellum South* (Cambridge, MA: Harvard University Press, 2000), 100.
5. Catherine Clinton, "Southern Dishonor: Flesh, Blood, Race, and Bondage," in *In Joy and in Sorrow: Women, Family, and Marriage in the Victorian South, 1830–1900*, ed. Carol Bleser (New York: Oxford University Press, 1991), 64; Melton A. McLaurin, *Celia: A Slave* (Athens: University of Georgia Press, 1991), 20–30.
6. Mark F. Weiner, *Mistresses and Slaves: Plantation Women in South Carolina, 1830–80* (Urbana: University of Illinois Press, 1997), 140.
7. Brenda Stevenson, "Distress and Discord in Virginia Slave Families, 1830–1860," in Bleser, *In Joy and In Sorrow*, 120.
8. Ira Berlin, *Generations of Captivity: A History of African-American Slaves* (Cambridge, MA: Harvard University Press, 2003), 174, 219; Stevenson, "Distress and Discord," 108.
9. Walter Johnson, *Soul By Soul: Life inside the Antebellum Slave Market* (Cambridge, MA: Harvard University Press, 1999), 65.
10. Ann Patton Malone, *Sweet Chariot: Slave Family and Household Structure in Nineteenth-Century Louisiana* (Chapel Hill: University of North Carolina Press, 1992), 236.
11. Shane White and Graham White, *The Sounds of Slavery: Discovering African American History Through Songs, Sermons, and Speech* (Boston: Beacon, 2005), 30.
12. Schwartz, *Born in Bondage*, 101.
13. Emily West, *Chains of Love: Slave Couples in Antebellum South Carolina* (Urbana: University of Illinois Press, 2004), 35.
14. Anthony E. Kaye, *Joining Places: Slave Neighborhoods in the Old South* (Chapel Hill: University of North Carolina Press, 2007).
15. Schwartz, *Born in Bondage*, 171.
16. Deborah Gray White, *Ar'n't' I A Woman?: Female Slaves in the Plantation South* (New York: W. W. Norton, 1987), 153; Herbert G. Gutman, *The Black*

Family in Slavery and Freedom, 1750–1925 (New York: Vintage, 1977), 185–201.

17. Nell Irvin Painter, "Soul Murder and Slavery: Toward a Fully Loaded Cost Accounting," in *U.S. History as Women's History: New Feminist Essays*, ed. Linda K. Kerber, Alice Kessler-Harris, and Kathryn Kish Sklar (Chapel Hill: University of North Carolina Press, 1995), 134; Painter, *Sojourner Truth: A Life, a Symbol* (New York: W. W. Norton, 1997), 15.
18. Berlin, *Generations of Captivity*, 256.
19. C. Peter Ripley, "The Black Family in Transition: Louisiana, 1860–1865," *The Journal of Southern History* 41 (August 1975): 374.
20. Dylan C. Penningroth, *The Claims of Kinfolk: African American Property and Community in the Nineteenth-Century South* (Chapel Hill: University of North Carolina Press, 2003), 167.
21. King, *Stolen Childhoods*, 154.
22. Tera W. Hunter, *To 'Joy My Freedom: Southern Black Women's Lives and Labors after the Civil War* (Cambridge, MA: Harvard University Press, 1997), 37, emphasis in the original.
23. Gutman, *Black Family in Slavery and Freedom*, 141.
24. Stevenson, "Distress and Discord," 123, emphasis in the original.
25. Susan Eva O'Donovan, *Becoming Free in the Cotton South* (Cambridge, MA: Harvard University Press, 2007), 198.
26. Hunter, *To 'Joy My Freedom*, 40.
27. Chalmers Archer, Jr., *Growing Up Black in Rural Mississippi: Memories of a Family, Heritage of a Place* (New York: Walker, 1992), 20.
28. Eric Foner, *Reconstruction: America's Unfinished Revolution, 1863–1877* (New York: Harper & Row, 1988), 85.
29. Hunter, *To 'Joy My Freedom*, 51.
30. James Smallwood, "Emancipation and the Black Family: A Case Study in Texas," *Social Science Quarterly* 57 (March 1977): 849–57.
31. Penningroth, *Claims of Kinfolk*, 171.
32. Jane E. Dabel, *A Respectable Woman: The Public Roles of African American Women in 19th-Century New York* (New York: New York University Press, 2008), 4.
33. Leon Litwack, *North of Slavery: The Negro in the Free States, 1790–1860* (Chicago: University of Chicago Press, 1965), 175.
34. James Oliver Horton and Lois E. Horton, *Black Bostonians: Family Life and Community Struggle in the Antebellum North* (New York: Holmes & Meier, 1979), 24.
35. Donald Yacovone, "The Transformation of the Black Temperance Movement, 1827–1854: An Interpretation," *Journal of the Early Republic* 8 (Autumn 1988): 291.
36. Waldo E. Martin, Jr., *The Mind of Frederick Douglass* (Chapel Hill: University of North Carolina Press, 1984), 256–57.
37. Daniel Walker Howe, *Making the American Self: Jonathan Edwards to Abraham Lincoln* (New York: Oxford University Press, 2009), 150.
38. Robert J. Norrell, *Up from History: The Life of Booker T. Washington* (Cambridge, MA: Harvard University Press, 2009), 31–32.
39. William I. Thomas and Florian Znaniecki, *The Polish Peasant in Europe and America* (New York: Dover Publications, 1958), Vol. I: 804, 913.
40. Benson Tong, *Unsubmissive Women: Chinese Prostitutes in Nineteenth-Century San Francisco* (Norman: University of Oklahoma Press, 1994), 94–95;

Sucheng Chan, "Race, Ethnic Culture, and Gender in the Construction of Identities among Second-Generation Chinese Americans, 1880s–1930s," in *Claiming America: Constructing Chinese American Identities during the Exclusion Era*, ed. K. Scott Wong and Chan (Philadelphia, PA: Temple University Press, 1998),127.

41. Anonymous miner to wife, late nineteenth century, John Day, Oregon, in *Talking on Paper: An Anthology of Oregon Letters and Diaries*, ed. Shannon Applegate and Terence O'Donnell (Corvallis: Oregon State University Press, 1994), 215.
42. Michael Harris Bond and Kwang-kuo Hwang, "The Social Psychology of Chinese People," in *The Psychology of the Chinese People*, ed. Michael Harris Bond (Hong Kong: Oxford University Press, 1986), 213–14; Francis L. K. Hsu, *Americans and Chinese: Passage to Differences*, 3rd ed. (Honolulu: University Press of Hawaii, 1981), 88.
43. R. David Arkush and Leo O. Lee, ed. and trans., *Land Without Ghosts: Chinese Impressions of America from the Mid-Nineteenth Century to the Present* (Berkeley: University of California Press, 1989), 75.
44. Chan, "Race, Ethnic Culture, and Gender," 151.
45. John Bodnar, Roger Simon, and Michael P. Weber, *Lives of their Own: Blacks, Italians, and Poles in Pittsburgh, 1900–1960* (Urbana: University of Illinois Press, 1982), 93–94.
46. Stephen Lassonde, *Learning to Forget: Schooling and Family Life in New Haven's Working Class, 1870–1940* (New Haven, CT: Yale University Press, 2005), 84.
47. Elizabeth Ewen, *Immigrant Women in the Land of Dollars: Life and Culture on the Lower East Side, 1890–1925* (New York: Monthly Review Press, 1985), 98.
48. James R. Barrett, *Work and Community in the Jungle: Chicago's Packinghouse Workers, 1894–1922* (Urbana: University of Illinois Press, 1987), 99.
49. Bruce M. Stave and John F. Sutherland, with Aldo Salerno, *From the Old Country: An Oral History of European Migration to America* (New York: Twayne, 1994), 13.
50. Ewen, *Immigrant Women*, 32.
51. Pascal D'Angelo, *Son of Italy* (New York: Macmillan1924), 21.
52. Thomas and Znaniecki, *Polish Peasant.*
53. Miriam Cohen, *Workshop to Office: Two Generations of Italian Women in New York City, 1900–1950* (Ithaca, NY: Cornell University Press, 1992), 70.
54. Barrett, *Work and Community*, 75–76; David Peterson, "'From Bone Depth': German-American Communities in Rural Minnesota Before the Great War," *Journal of American Ethnic History* 11 (Winter 1992): 39; Tamara K. Hareven and John Modell, "Family Patterns," in *Harvard Encyclopedia of American Ethnic Groups*, ed. Stephan Thernstrom, Ann Orlov, and Oscar Handlin (Cambridge, MA: Harvard University Press, 1980), 351; Selma Cantor Berroll, *Growing Up American: Immigrant Children in America Then and Now* (New York: Twayne and London: Prentice Hall, 1995), 61.
55. Rose Pesotta, *Days of Our Lives* (Boston, MA: Excelsior Publishers, 1958), 8.
56. Sholom Aleichem, trans. Tamara Kahana, *The Great Fair: Scenes from my Childhood* (New York: Noonday Press, 1958), 45.
57. Steven Mintz, *Huck's Raft: A History of American Childhood* (Cambridge, MA: Harvard University Press, 2004), 209–10, emphasis in the original.
58. Robert L. Griswold, *Fatherhood in America: A History* (New York: BasicBooks, 1993), 72–73.

59. Sydney Stahl Weinberg, *The World of Our Mothers: The Lives of Jewish Immigrant Women* (New York: Schocken, 1990), 158; Hareven and Modell, "Family Patterns," 348.
60. James Axtell, *The European and the Indian: Essays in the Ethnohistory of Colonial North America* (Oxford: Oxford University Press, 1982), 99–100.
61. Robert A. Trennert, "Educating Indian Girls at Nonreservation Boarding Schools, 1878–1920," *Western Historical Quarterly* 13 (July 1982): 286.
62. David Wallace Adams, *Education for Extinction: American Indians and the Boarding School Experience, 1875–1928* (Lawrence: University Press of Kansas, 1995), 282.
63. Peter Iverson, *Carlos Montezuma and the Changing World of American Indians* (Albuquerque: University of New Mexico Press, 1982).
64. Nancy Shoemaker, "From Longhouse to Loghouse: Household Structure among the Senecas in 1900," *American Indian Quarterly* 15 (Summer 1991): 329–38; Bradley E. Ensor, "Kinship and Marriage among the Omaha, 1886–1902," *Ethnology* 42 (Winter 2003): 1–14; Frederick E. Hoxie, "Searching for Structure: Reconstructing Crow Family Life during the Reservation Era," *American Indian Quarterly* 15 (Summer 1991): 287–309.
65. Ann Marie Plane, *Colonial Intimacies: Indian Marriage in Early New England* (Ithaca, NY: Cornell University Press, 2000), 112: David Peterson del Mar, "Intermarriage and Agency: A Chinookan Case Study," *Ethnohistory* 42 (Winter 1995): 1–30.
66. Theda Perdue, *Cherokee Women: Gender and Culture Change* (Lincoln: University of Nebraska Press, 1998), 179.
67. Albert L. Hurtado, *Indian Survival on the California Frontier* (New Haven, CT: Yale University Press, 1988), 181.
68. *Testimionios: Early California through the Eyes of Women, 1815–1848*, trans. Rose Marie Beebe and Robert M. Senkewicz (Berkeley, CA: Heyday Books, 2006), 287, 191.
69. Richard Griswold del Castillo, *La Familia: Chicano Families in the Urban Southwest, 1848 to the Present* (Notre Dame, IN: University of Notre Dame Press, 1984), 81, 86–87.
70. Del Castillo, *La Familia*, 46, 62–63.
71. Christine Stansell, *City of Women: Sex and Class in New York, 1789–1860* (New York: Alfred A. Knopf, 1986), 199.
72. Michael Kaplan, "New York City Tavern Violence and the Creation of a Working-Class Male Identity," *Journal of the Early Republic* (Winter 1995): 592.
73. Gunther Peck, "Manly Gambles: The Politics of Risk on the Comstock Lode, 1860–1880," *Journal of Social History* 26 (Summer 1993): 714.
74. Paul Faler, "Cultural Aspects of the Industrial Revolution: Lynn, Massachusetts, Shoemakers and Industrial Morality, 1826–1860," *Labor History* 15 (Summer 1974): 379, 385.
75. Faler, "Cultural Aspects," 393, emphasis in the original.
76. Ruth M. Alexander, "'We Are Engaged as a Band of Sisters': Class and Domesticity in the Washingtonian Temperance Movement, 1840–1850," *Journal of American History* 75 (December 1988): 784–85.
77. Painter, *Sojourner Truth*, 167.
78. Painter, *Sojourner Truth*, 29, emphasis in the original.

6 The First Modern Family

1. Robert S. Lynd and Helen Merrell Lynd, *Middletown: A Study in Modern American Culture* (New York: Harcourt, Brace & World, 1956), 155.
2. David M. Katzman, *Seven Days a Week: Women and Domestic Service in Industrializing America* (Urbana: University of Illinois Press, 1981), 58.
3. Steven Mintz, *Huck's Raft: A History of American Childhood* (Cambridge, MA: Harvard University Press, 2005), 175.
4. Lynn Dumenil, *The Modern Temper: American Culture and Society in the 1920s* (New York: Hill and Wang, 1995), 31.
5. John Dos Passos, *Three Soldiers* (New York: Modern Library, 1932), 235.
6. Gerald F. Linderman, *The Mirror of War: American Society and the Spanish-American War* (Ann Arbor: University of Michigan Press, 1974), 113.
7. Jane Tompkins, *West of Everything: The Inner Life of Westerns* (New York: Oxford University Press, 1992), 144.
8. Ann Douglas, *Terrible Honesty: Mongrel Manhattan in the 1920s* (New York: Noonday Press, 1995), 221.
9. Joshua Zeitz, *Flapper: A Madcap Story of Sex, Style, Celebrity, and the Women Who Made America Modern* (New York: Three Rivers Press, 2005), 185.
10. Zeitz, *Flapper*, 67.
11. Daniel Bell, *The Cultural Contradictions of Capitalism* (New York: Basic Books, 1996), 21.
12. Lynd and Lynd, *Middletown*, 241–42.
13. Eva Illouz, *Consuming the Romantic Utopia: Love and the Cultural Contradictions of Capitalism* (Berkeley: University of California Press, 1997), 41.
14. Elaine Showalter, *A Jury of Her Peers: American Women Writers from Anne Bradstreet to Annie Proulx* (New York: Alfred A. Knopf, 2009), 330.
15. David M. Kennedy, *Birth Control in America: The Career of Margaret Sanger* (New Haven, CT: Yale University Press, 1971), 132.
16. Dumenil, *Modern Temper*, 153.
17. John C. Spurlock and Cynthia A. Magistro, *New and Improved: The Transformation of American Women's Emotional Culture* (New York: New York University Press, 1998), 14.
18. Illouz, *Consuming the Romantic Utopia*, 30, 40.
19. Warren I. Susman, *Culture as History: The Transformation of American Society in the Twentieth Century* (Washington: Smithsonian Institution Press, 2003), 277, 280.
20. Zeitz, *Flapper*, 260.
21. David Peterson del Mar, *What Trouble I Have Seen: A History of Violence against Wives* (Cambridge, MA: Harvard University Press, 1996), 100; Irene Taviss Thomson, "The Transformation of the Social Bond: Images of Individualism in the 1920s versus the 1970s," *Social Forces* 67 (June 1989): 859.
22. Andrew Delbanco, *The Death of Satan: How Americans Have Lost the Sense of Evil* (New York: Farrar, Straus and Giroux, 1995), 188.
23. F. Scott Fitzgerald, *The Great Gatsby* (New York: Scribner, 1995), 125.
24. Richard Ruland and Malcolm Bradbury, *From Puritanism to Postmodernism: A History of American Literature* (New York: Penguin, 1992), 300.
25. William Henry Chafe, *The American Woman: Her Changing Social, Economic, and Political Role, 1920–1970* (New York: Oxford University Press, 1972), 93.

26. Zeitz, *Flapper*, 69.
27. Mary P. Ryan, *Mysteries of Sex: Tracing Women and Men through American History* (Chapel Hill: University of North Carolina Press, 2006), 215.
28. Spurlock and Magistro, *New and Improved*, 40, 42–43.
29. Beth L. Bailey, *From Front Porch to Back Seat: Courtship in Twentieth-Century America* (Baltimore, MD: Johns Hopkins University Press, 1988).
30. Nathan Irvin Huggins, *Harlem Renaissance* (New York: Oxford University Press, 2007), 91–92.
31. Leon F. Litwack, *Trouble in Mind: Black Southerners in the Age of Jim Crow* (New York: Alfred A. Knopf, 1998), 437–78.
32. Evelyn Brooks Higginbotham, *Righteous Discontent: The Women's Movement in the Black Baptist Church, 1880–1920* (Cambridge, MA: Harvard University Press, 1993), 195.
33. Douglas, *Terrible Honesty*, 83.
34. Martin Summers, *Manliness and Its Discontents: The Black Middle Class and the Transformation of Masculinity, 1900–1930* (Chapel Hill: University of North Carolina Press, 2004), 237, 288.
35. Victoria W. Wolcott, *Remaking Respectability: African American Women in Interwar Detroit* (Chapel Hill: University of North Carolina Press, 2001), 128.
36. Audrey Olsen Faulkner, Marsel A. Heisel, Wendell Holbrook, and Shirley Geismar, *When I Was Comin' Up: An Oral History of Aged Blacks* (Hamden, CT: Archon Books, 1982), 24–45.
37. Richard Wright, *Black Boy: A Record of Childhood and Youth* (New York: Signet, 1963), 45.
38. Richard Wright, *Native Son* (New York: Harper & Row, 1966), 366.
39. Iceberg Slim, *Pimp* (Los Angeles: Holloway House, 2007), 27.
40. Robert Beck, *The Naked Soul of Iceberg Slim* (Los Angeles, CA: Holloway House, 1986), 43, 58.
41. Clarence Norris and Sybil D. Washington, *The Last of the Scottsboro Boys* (New York: G. P. Putnam's Sons, 1979), 28, 34.
42. Martin Luther King Sr., with Clayton Riley, *Daddy King: An Autobiography* (New York: William Morrow, 1980), 43.
43. Hortense Powdermaker, *After Freedom: A Cultural Study in the Deep South* (Madison: University of Wisconsin Press, 1993), 160, 200.
44. George J. Sánchez, *Becoming Mexican American: Ethnicity, Culture, and Identity in Chicano Los Angeles, 1900–1945* (New York: Oxford University Press, 1993), 90.
45. Sánchez, *Becoming Mexican American*, 143–44, 186.
46. Vicki L. Ruiz, "'Star Struck': Acculturation, Adolescence, and Mexican American Women, 1920–1950," in *Small Worlds: Children & Adolescents in America, 1850–1950*, ed. Elliott West and Paula Petrik (Lawrence: University Press of Kansas, 1992), 74.
47. Vicki L. Ruiz, *From Out of the Shadows: Mexican Women in Twentieth-Century America* (New York: Oxford, 1998), 64.
48. Mary Paik Lee, "From *Quiet Odyssey*," in *The Norton Book of American Autobiography*, ed. Jay Parini (New York: W. W. Norton, 1999), 373.
49. Joseph Lopreato, *Italian Americans* (New York: Random House, 1970), 63.
50. Kathy Peiss, *Cheap Amusements: Working Women and Leisure in Turn-of-the-Century New York* (Philadelphia, PA: Temple University Press, 1986).

51. Lynd and Lynd, *Middletown*, 144, 146, 151.
52. Robert L. Griswold, *Fatherhood in America: A History* (New York: Basic Books, 1993), 101.
53. Lynd and Lynd, *Middletown*, 151.
54. Peterson del Mar, *What Trouble I Have Seen*, 101–02.
55. Susan Porter Benson, "Living on the Margin: Working-Class Marriages and Family Survival Strategies in the United States, 1919–1941," in *The Sex of Things: Gender and Consumption in Historical Perspective*, ed. Victoria de Grazia, with Ellen Furlough (Berkeley: University of California Press, 1996), 235.
56. Lynd and Lynd, *Middletown*, 127.
57. Peterson del Mar, *What Trouble I Have Seen*, 101–02, emphasis in the original.
58. Spurlock and Magistro, *New and Improved*, 77–78.
59. Benson, "Living on the Margin," 236.
60. Peterson del Mar, *What Trouble I've Seen*, 123–24.
61. David Peterson del Mar, *Beaten Down: A History of Interpersonal Violence in the West* (Seattle: University of Washington Press, 2002), 123.
62. Peterson del Mar, *Beaten Down*, 125.
63. Roger Lane, *Murder in America: A History* (Columbus: Ohio State University Press, 1997), 233.
64. Peterson del Mar, *Beaten Down*, 120.
65. David Stenn, *Clara Bow: Runnin' Wild* (New York: Cooper Square Press, 2000), 18.
66. Stenn, *Clara Bow*, 21, 87.
67. Stenn, *Clara Bow*, 198, 102.
68. Jacquelyn Dowd Hall, et al., *Like a Family: The Making of a Southern Cotton Mill World* (Chapel Hill: University of North Carolina Press, 1987), 145.

7 The Family in Crisis and After

1. Steven Mintz and Susan Kellogg, *Domestic Revolutions: A Social History of American Family Life* (New York: Free Press, 1989), 138, 134; David M. Kennedy, *Freedom from Fear: The American People in Depression and War, 1929–1945* (New York: Oxford University Press, 1999), 163.
2. Lizabeth Cohen, *Making a New Deal: Industrial Workers in Chicago, 1919–1939* (Cambridge: Cambridge University Press, 1990), 248.
3. Caroline Bird, *The Invisible Scar* (New York: David McKay, 1966), 26; Mintz and Kellogg, *Domestic Revolutions*, 133.
4. Rick Bragg, *Ava's Man* (New York: Vintage, 2002), 112.
5. Mary P. Ryan, *Mysteries of Sex: Tracing Women and Men through American History* (Chapel Hill: University of North Carolina Press, 2006), 223; Steven Mintz, *Huck's Raft: A History of American Childhood* (Cambridge, MA: Harvard University Press, 2004), 237.
6. Mintz and Kellogg, *Domestic Revolutions*, 147.
7. Elaine Tyler May, *Homeward Bound: American Families in the Cold War Era* (New York: Basic Books, 1988), 49–50; Becky M. Nicolaides, *My Blue Heaven: Life and Politics in the Working-Class Suburbs of Los Angeles, 1920–1965* (Chicago: University of Chicago Press, 2002), 116.
8. Winona L. Morgan, *The Family Meets the Depression: A Study of a Group of Highly Selected Families* (Minneapolis: University of Minnesota Press, 1939).

9. Mintz, *Huck's Raft*, 237; Julia Kirk Blackwelder, *Now Hiring: The Feminization of Work in the United States, 1900–1995* (College Station: Texas A & M University Press, 1997), 229.
10. Robert S. McElvaine, ed., *Down and Out in the Great Depression: Letters from the "Forgotten Man"* (Chapel Hill: University of North Carolina Press, 1983), 83.
11. Ossie Guffy, as told to Caryl Ledner, *Ossie: The Autobiography of a Black Woman* (New York: W. W. Norton, 1971), 18–19; Maya Angelou, *I Know Why the Caged Bird Sings* (New York: Bantam, 1983).
12. Camille Guerin-Gonzalez, *Mexican Workers and American Dreams: Immigration, Repatriation, and California Farm Labor, 1900–1939* (New Brunswick, NJ: Rutgers University Press, 1994), 107.
13. Frances Esquibel Tywoniak and Mario T. García, *Migrant Daughter: Coming of Age as a Mexican American Woman* (Berkeley: University of California Press, 2000), 8–9.
14. Mirra Komarovsky, *The Unemployed Man and his Family: The Effect of Unemployment Upon the Status of the Man in Fifty-Nine Families* (New York: Octagon Books, 1971), 55.
15. Bill Osgerby, "A Pedigree of the Consuming Male: Masculinity, Consumption and the American 'Leisure Class,'" in *Masculinity and Men's Lifestyle Magazines*, ed. Bethan Benwell (Oxford: Blackwell and Malden, MA: The Sociological Review, 2003), 74, 67; Clair Brown, *American Standards of Living, 1918–1988* (Oxford: Blackwell), 103–14.
16. George A. Lundberg, Mirra Komarovsky, and Mary Alice McInerny, *Leisure: A Suburban Study* (New York: Columbia University Press, 1934) 183.
17. Charles F. McGovern, *Consumption and Citizenship, 1890–1945* (Chapel Hill: University of North Carolina Press, 2006), 339.
18. Mintz, *Huck's Raft*, 258–59.
19. Mark Jonathan Harris, Franklin D. Mitchell, and Steven J. Schechter, *The Homefront: America during World War II* (New York: G. P. Putnam's Sons, 1984), 171–72, 182–83 180; Mintz and Kellogg, *Domestic Revolutions*, 153.
20. William M. Tuttle, Jr., *"Daddy's Gone to War": The Second World War in the Lives of America's Children* (New York: Oxford University Press, 1993), 47–48.
21. Robert L. Griswold, *Fatherhood in America: A History* (New York: BasicBooks, 1993), 178–79; Tuttle, *"Daddy's Gone to War,"* 220.
22. Harris, Mitchell, and Schechter, *Homefront*, 230–31.
23. Harris, Mitchell, and Schechter, *Homefront*, 172.
24. Shidzué Ishimoto, *Facing Two Ways: The Story of My Life* (Stanford, CA: Stanford University Press, 1984), 11.
25. Jeanne Wakatsuki Houston and James D. Houston, *Farewell to Manzanar* (Boston, MA: Houghton Mifflin, 1973), 60.
26. Richard Griswold del Castillo, *La Familia: Chicano Families in the Urban Southwest, 1848 to the Present* (Notre Dame, IN: University of Notre Dame Press, 1984), 105.
27. George J. Sánchez, *Becoming Mexican American: Ethnicity, Culture, and Identity in Chicano Los Angeles, 1900–1945* (New York: Oxford, 1993), 268.
28. Esquibel and García, *Migrant Daughter*, 43, 79, 121.
29. May, *Homeward Bound*, 169.

30. Stephanie Coontz, *Marriage, a History: From Obedience to Intimacy, or How Love Conquered Marriage* (New York: Viking, 2005), 240.
31. Lynn Spigel, *Make Room for TV: Television and the Family Ideal in Postwar America* (Chicago, IL: University of Chicago Press, 1992), 38; Brown, *American Standards of Living*, 217.
32. Alan Petigny, *The Permissive Society: America, 1941–1965* (Cambridge: Cambridge University Press, 2009), 244, 29.
33. Art Gallaher, Jr., *Plainville Fifteen Years Later* (New York: Columbia University Press, 1961), 124.
34. Gary Cross, *Kid's Stuff: Toys and the Changing World of American Childhood* (Cambridge, MA: Harvard University Press, 1997), 153.
35. Martha Wolfenstein, "Fun Morality," in *Culture and Commitment, 1929–1945*, ed. Warren Susman (New York: George Barziller, 1973), 87, 84, 90.
36. May, *Homeward Bound*, 24.
37. Ryan, *Mysteries of Sex*, 232.
38. Mirra Komarovsky, *Blue-Collar Marriage* (New York: Vintage, 1967), 241.
39. David Peterson del Mar, *Through the Eyes of a Child: The First 120 Years of the Boys and Girls Aid Society of Oregon* (Portland, OR: Boys and Girls Aid Society, 2005), 130; May, *Homeward Bound*, 20; Ryan, *Mysteries of Sex*, 229; E. Wayne Carp, *Family Matters: Secrecy and Disclosure in the History of Adoption* (Cambridge, MA: Harvard University Press, 1998), 29.
40. May, *Homeward Bound*, 28–29.
41. Jessica Weiss, *To Have and to Hold: Marriage, the Baby Boom, and Social Change* (Chicago. IL: University of Chicago Press, 2000), 32–33.
42. Mintz, *Huck's Raft*, 282.
43. Brett Harvey, *The Fifties: A Women's Oral History* (New York: HarperCollins, 1993), 97.
44. Ryan, *Mysteries of Sex*, 236.
45. Betty Friedan, *The Feminine Mystique* (New York: Dell, 1989); May, *Homeward Bound*, 193.
46. May, *Homeward Bound*, 194–95, 199.
47. Benita Eisler, *Private Lives: Men and Women of the Fifties* (New York: Franklin Watts, 1986), 334.
48. Barbara Ehrenreich, *The Hearts of Men: American Dreams and the Flight from Commitment* (New York: Anchor Press, 1983), 44, 47, 51.
49. Wini Breines, *Young, White, and Miserable: Growing Up Female in the Fifties* (Boston, MA: Beacon Press, 1992), 145.
50. Beth Bailey, "From Panty Raids to Revolution: Youth and Authority, 1950–1970," in *Generations of Youth: Youth Cultures and History in Twentieth-Century America*, ed. Joe Austin and Michael Nevin Willard (New York: New York University Press, 1998), 188.
51. Peter Guralnick, *Last Train to Memphis: The Rise of Elvis Presley* (London: Abacus, 1995), 63, 188.
52. Alan Ehrenhalt, *The Lost City: The Forgotten Virtues of Community in America* (New York: Basic Books, 1995), 243–44; Mark Regnerus and Jeremy Uecker, *Premarital Sex in America: How Young Americans Meet, Mate, and Think about Marrying* (Oxford: Oxford University Press, 2011), 229.
53. Carson McCullers, *The Heart is a Lonely Hunter* (New York: Bantam, 1967), 169.

54. Saul Bellow, *Dangling Man* (New York: Penguin, 1971), 154, 88.
55. Sylvia Plath, *The Bell Jar* (New York: Bantam, 1975), 62–63.
56. John Updike, *Rabbit, Run* (New York: Fawcett, 1996), 94, 128.
57. Morris Dickstein, *Leopards in the Temple: The Transformation of American Fiction, 1945–1970* (Cambridge, MA: Harvard University Press, 2002), 103.
58. Petigny, *Permissive Society*, 54.
59. Ehrenhalt, *Lost City*, 140, 152, 236, 32.
60. Gail Levin, *Edward Hopper: An Intimate Biography*, updated and expanded (New York: Rizzoli, 2007), 351, 491.
61. Levin, *Edward Hopper*, 460.

8 Freedom's Florescence

1. Robert B. Putnam, *Bowling Alone: The Collapse and Revival of American Community* (New York: Touchstone, 2001), 222; Clair Brown, *American Standards of Living, 1918–1988* (Cambridge, MA: Blackwell, 1994), 271–72; 312–54; Michael B. Katz, *In the Shadow of the Poorhouse: A Social History of Welfare in America*, rev. ed. (New York: BasicBooks, 1996), 274.
2. Barry Schwartz, *The Paradox of Choice: Why Less Is More* (New York: HarperCollins, 2004).
3. Daniel Bell, *The Cultural Contradictions of Capitalism* (New York: Basic Books, 1996), 84.
4. David Frum, *How We Got Here, the 70's: The Decade that Brought you Modern Life (For Better or Worse)* (New York: Basic Books, 2000), 71.
5. Robert N. Bellah et al., *Habits of the Heart: Individualism and Commitment in American Life* (New York: Harper & Row, 1986), 66.
6. Jefferson Cowie, *Stayin' Alive: The 1970s and the Last Days of the Working Class* (New York: Free Press, 2010), 310.
7. Thomas Frank, *The Conquest of Cool: Business Culture, Counterculture, and the Rise of Hip Consumerism* (Chicago, IL: University of Chicago Press, 1997), 121–22.
8. Ann Swindler, *Talk of Love: How Culture Matters* (Chicago, IL: University of Chicago Press, 2001), 150.
9. Sara Evans, *Personal Politics: The Roots of Women's Liberation in the Civil Rights Movement and the New Left* (New York: Vintage, 1980), 170, 179.
10. Ruth Rosen, *The World Split Open: How the Modern Women's Movement Changed America* (New York: Penguin, 2000), 199.
11. Deborah Siegel, *Sisterhood, Interrupted: From Radical Women to Grlls Gone Wild* (New York: Palgrave Macmillan, 2007), 148.
12. Susan Faludi, "American Electra: Feminism's Ritual Matricide," *Harper's Magazine*, October 2010, 42.
13. Sarah M. Evans, *Tidal Wave: How Women Changed America at Century's End* (New York: Free Press, 2004), 59.
14. Mark Lilla, "The Tea Party Jacobins," *The New York Review*, 27 May 2010, 56.
15. Pierre Bourdieu, *Distinction: A Social Critique of the Judgement of Taste*, trans. Richard Nice (Cambridge, MA: Harvard University Press, 1984), 367.
16. Joseph Heath and Andrew Potter, *Nation of Rebels: Why Counterculture Became Consumer Culture* (New York: HarperBusiness, 2004), 229–30.

17. Charles L. Ponce de Leon, "The New Historiography of the 1980s," *Reviews in American History* 36 (2008): 313.
18. Cowie, *Stayin' Alive*, 16.
19. Daniel T. Rodgers, *Age of Fracture* (Cambridge, MA: Harvard University Press, 2011), 29–30, 33.
20. Irene Taviss Thomson, "The Transformation of the Social Bond: Images of Individualism in the 1920s versus the 1970s," *Social Forces* 67 (June 1989): 862–63.
21. Martin E. P. Seligman, "Why Is There So Much Depression Today? The Waxing of the Individual and the Waning of the Commons," in *Contemporary Psychological Approaches to Depression: Theory, Research, and Treatment*, ed. Rick E. Ingram (New York: Plenum Press, 1990), 7.
22. Frum, *How We Got Here*, 102–03; Irene Taviss Thomson, "From Other-Direction to the Me Decade: The Development of Fluid Identities and Personal Role Definitions," *Sociological Inquiry* 55 (July 1985): 284.
23. Frank, *Conquest of Cool*, 227–28.
24. Heath and Potter, *Nation of Rebels*, 55.
25. Peter Clecak, *America's Quest for the Ideal Self: Dissent and Fulfillment in the 60s and 70s* (New York: Oxford University Press, 1983).
26. Claude S. Fischer and Michael Hout, *Century of Difference: How America Changed in the Last One Hundred Years* (New York: Russell Sage Foundation, 2006), 78–79; Larry L. Bumpass, "What's Happening to the Family? Interactions between Demographic and Institutional Change," *Demography* 27 (November 1990): 492; Putnam, *Bowling Alone*; Paul R. Amato et al., *Alone Together: How Marriage in America is Changing* (Cambridge, MA: Harvard University Press, 2007), 178–83.
27. Yasushi Watanabe, *The American Family: Across the Class Divide* (London: Pluto Press, 2004), 129, 155, 151.
28. Watanabe, *American Family*, 189.
29. Alane Salierno Mason, "Respect," in *The Norton Book of American Autobiography*, ed. Jay Parini (New York: W. W. Norton, 1999), 685.
30. Ron Powers, *Tom and Huck Don't Live Here Anymore: Childhood and Murder in the Heart of America* (New York: St. Martin's, 2001).
31. Andrew Oldenquist, *The Non-Suicidal Society* (Bloomington: Indiana University Press, 1986), 7; Avner Offer, *The Challenge of Affluence: Self-Control and Well-Being in the United States and Britain since 1950* (Oxford: Oxford University Press, 2006), 347–51; Roger Lane, *Murder in America: A History* (Columbus: Ohio University Press, 2006), 308; Jean Stockard and Robert M. O'Brien, "Cohort Effects on Suicide Rates: International Variations," *American Sociological Review* (December 2002): 862; Schwartz, *Paradox of Choice*.
32. Anthony Giddens, *Modernity and Self-Identity in the Late Modern Age* (Stanford, CA: Stanford University Press, 1991), 6.
33. Milton C. Regan, Jr., *Family Law and the Pursuit of Intimacy* (New York: New York University Press, 1993), 53.
34. Zygmunt Bauman, *Liquid Love: On the Frailty of Human Bonds* (Cambridge: Polity, 2003), 47.
35. Elaine Tyler May, *Barren in the Promised Land: Childless Americans and the Pursuit of Happiness* (New York: BasicBooks, 1995), 198, 189; Daphne Spain and Suzanne M. Bianchi, *Balancing Act: Motherhood, Marriage, and*

Employment among American Women (New York: Russell Sage Foundation, 1996), 26, 30, 201–02.

36. Maggie Gallagher, *The Abolition of Marriage: How We Destroy Lasting Love* (Washington, D.C.: Regnery, 1996), 208, 215.
37. Barbara Dafoe Whitehead, *The Divorce Culture: Rethinking Our Commitments to Marriage and Family* (New York: Vintage, 1998), 71, 76.
38. Regan, *Family Law* 65.
39. Ann Hulbert, *Raising America: Experts, Parents, and a Century of Advice About Children* (New York: Alfred A. Knopf, 2003), 258–59.
40. Gary Cross, *The Cute and the Cool: Wondrous Innocence and Modern American Children's Culture* (Oxford: Oxford University Press, 2004), 41.
41. Benjamin R. Barber, *Consumed: How Markets Corrupt Children, Infantilize Adults, and Swallow Citizens Whole* (New York: W. W. Norton, 2007), 81, 21–22.
42. Joel Best, *Threatened Children: Rhetoric and Concern about Child-Victims* (Chicago: University of Chicago Press, 1990), 141, 175.
43. Paula S. Fass, *Kidnapped: Child Abduction in America* (New York: Oxford University Press, 1997), 255; LeRoy Ashby, *Endangered Children: Dependency, Neglect, and Abuse in American History* (New York: Twayne, 1997), 136, 151.
44. Adrie Kusserow, *American Individualisms: Child Rearing and Social Class in Three Neighborhoods* (New York: Palgrave Macmillan, 2004), 82; Annette Lareau, *Unequal Childhoods: Class, Race, and Family Life* (Berkeley: University of California Press, 2003).
45. Raffi Khatchadourian, "Neptune's Navy: Paul Watson's Wild Crusade to Save the Oceans," *The New Yorker*, 5 November 2007, 67; Andrew Hacker, "Gore Family Values," *New York Review*, December 5, 2002, 22; William Watts, "America's Hopes and Fears: The Future Can Fend for Itself," *Psychology Today*, September 1981, 40; Bumpass, "What's Happening to the Family?" 486.
46. Donna Gaines, *Teenage Wasteland: Suburbia's Dead End Kids* (Chicago: University of Chicago Press, 1998), 139.
47. Powers, *Tom and Huck*, 106–13.
48. Heath and Potter, *Nation of Rebels*, 66; Bernard Lefkowitz, *Our Guys: The Glen Ridge Rape and the Secret Life of the Perfect Suburb* (New York: Vintage, 1998); Alexandra Robbins, *Pledged: The Secret Life of Sororities* (New York: Hyperion, 2004).
49. Elizabeth Wurtzel, "Parental Guidance Suggested," in *Norton Book of American Biography*, 696.
50. Donald Spoto, *Marilyn Monroe: The Biography* (New York: HarperCollins, 1993), 292.
51. Norval D. Glenn, "The Recent Trend in Marital Success in the United States," *Journal of Marriage and the Family* 53 (May 1991): 268, emphasis in the original; Andrew J. Cherlin, *The Marriage-Go-Round: The State of Marriage and the Family in America Today* (New York: Vintage, 2010), 3.
52. Avner Offer, *The Challenge of Affluence: Self-Control and Well-Being in the United States and Britain since 1950* (Oxford: Oxford University Press, 2007), 345.
53. Cherlin, *Marriage-Go-Round*, 196.
54. Mary P. Ryan, *Mysteries of Sex: Tracing Women and Men through American History* (Chapel Hill: University of North Carolina Press, 2006), 277.

55. Lillian B. Rubin, *Families on the Fault Line: America's Working Class Speaks about the Family, the Economy, Race, and Ethnicity* (New York: HarperCollins, 1994), 90.
56. Miriam M. Johnson, *Strong Mothers, Weak Wives: The Search for Gender Equality* (Berkeley: University of California Press, 1988), 126.
57. Andrew Hacker, *Mismatch: The Growing Gulf between Women and Men* (New York: Scribner, 2003), 197, emphasis in the original.
58. Larry Colton, *Goat Brothers* (New York: Doubleday, 1993), 348.
59. John Updike, *Rabbit is Rich* (New York: Fawcett, 1996), 36.
60. Nicholas W. Townsend, *The Package Deal: Marriage, Work, and Fatherhood in Men's Lives* (Philadelphia, PA: Temple University Press, 2002).
61. David G. Myers, *The American Paradox: Spiritual Hunger in an Age of Plenty* (New Haven, CT: Yale University Press, 2000), 17; Sharon Thompson, *Going All the Way: Teenage Girls' Tales of Sex, Romance, and Pregnancy* (New York: Hill and Wang, 1995).
62. Michael Kimmel, *Guyland: The Perilous World Where Boys Become Men* (New York: HarperCollins, 2008), 260.
63. Susan Maushart, *Wifework: What Marriage Really Means for Women* (New York: Bloomsbury 2001), 215.
64. Arlie Russell Hochschild, with Anne Machung, *The Second Shift* (New York: Penguin, 2003), 47.
65. Ralph LaRossa, "Fatherhood and Social Change," *Family Relations* 37 (October 1988): 454.
66. Timothy J. Biblarz and Judith Stacey, "How Does the Gender of Parents Matter?" *Journal of Marriage and the Family* 72 (February 2010): 17.
67. Elizabeth Lapovsky Kennedy and Madeline D. Davis, *Boots of Leather, Slippers of Gold: The History of a Lesbian Community* (New York: Penguin, 1994), 284, 234.
68. Lillian Faderman, *Odd Girls and Twilight Lovers: A History of Lesbian Life in Twentieth-Century America* (New York: Penguin, 1992), 234.
69. Philip Blumstein and Pepper Schwartz, *American Couples: Money, Work, Sex* (New York: Pocket Books, 1985), 272.
70. Charles Kaiser, *The Gay Metropolis, 1940–1996* (Boston, MA: Houghton Mifflin, 1997), 291; Brian Powell et al., *Counted Out: Same-Sex Relations and America's Definitions of Family* (New York: Russell Sage Foundation, 2010), 29.
71. Faderman, *Odd Girls and Twilight Lovers*, 291, emphasis in the original.
72. Kaiser, *Gay Metropolis*, 346.
73. Ariel Levy, *Female Chauvinist Pigs: Women and the Rise of Raunch Culture* (New York: Free Press, 2005), 119, emphasis in the original.
74. Kath Weston, *Families We Choose: Lesbians, Gays, Kinship* (New York: Columbia University Press, 1991). This argument is repeated and supported throughout the book, but especially in 77–136.
75. Peter M. Nardi, *Gay Men's Friendships: Invincible Communities* (Chicago: University of Chicago Press, 1999), 123.
76. Maria P. P. Root, *Love's Revolution: Interracial Marriage* (Philadelphia, PA: Temple University Press, 2001), 184.
77. David G. Myers, *The American Paradox: Spiritual Hunger in an Age of Hunger* (New Haven, CT: Yale University Press, 2001), 75.
78. Charles R. Cross, *Heavier than Heaven: A Biography of Kurt Cobain* (New York: Hyperion, 2001), 22.

79. Ryan Moore, "'...And Tomorrow Is Just Another Crazy Scam': Postmodernity, Youth, and the Downward Mobility of the Middle Class," in *Generations of Youth: Youth Cultures and History in Twentieth-Century America*, ed. Joe Austin and Michael Nevin Willard (New York: New York University Press, 1998), 254.

9 Countercultures?

1. Angela J. Hattery and Early Smith, *African American Families* (Los Angeles: Sage, 2007), 289.
2. Bart Landry, *The New Black Middle Class* (Berkeley: University of California Press, 1987), 207–09; Beth Anne Shelton and Daphne John, "Ethncity, Race, and Difference: A Comparison of White, Black, and Hispanic Men's Household Labor Time," in *Men, Work, and Family*, ed. Jane C. Hood (Newbury Park, CA: Sage, 1993), 38–41; Leonor Boulin Johnson and Robert Staples, *Black Families at the Crossroads: Challenges and Prospects*, rev. ed. (San Francisco, CA: Jossey-Bass, 2005), 85, 205.
3. Mary E. Pattillo, "Sweet Mothers and Gangbangers: Managing Crime in a Black Middle-Class Neighborhood," in *Social Forces* 76 (March 1998): 763; Johnson and Staples, *Black Families at the Crossroads*, 78–79.
4. Hattery and Smith, *African American Families*, 71, 198, 209–10, 251, 266, 289; Orlando Patterson, *Rituals of Blood: Consequences of Slavery in Two American Centuries* (New York: Basic Civitas, 1998), 61; Bruce Western, *Punishment and Inequality in America* (New York: Russell Sage Foundation, 2006), 131–67.
5. Hattery and Smith, *African American Families*, 210.
6. Jonathan Kozol, *The Shame of the Nation: The Restoration of Apartheid Schooling in America* (New York: Three Rivers Press, 2005), 179–80, 9, 45, emphasis in original.
7. Geoffrey Canada, *Fist Stick Knife Gun: A Personal History of Violence in America* (Boston, MA: Beacon Press, 1995), 149–51.
8. Nathan McCall, *Makes Me Wanna Holler: A Young Black Man in America* (New York: Random House, 1994), 100–01.
9. Orlando Patterson, "A Poverty of the Mind," *New York Times*, March 26, 2006, 13.
10. David Marriott, *On Black Men* (New York: Columbia University Press, 2000), x; Jennifer L. Hochschild, *Facing up to the American Dream: Race, Class, and the Soul of the Nation* (Princeton, NJ: Princeton University Press, 1995), 202.
11. Elliott Liebow, *Tally's Corner: A Study of Negro Streetcorner Men* (Boston, MA: Little, Brown, and Company, 1967), 70, 135–36, 215.
12. Lee Rainwater, *Behind Ghetto Walls: Black Families in a Federal Slum* (Chicago, IL: Aldine, 1970), 163, 285–86, 229.
13. Elijah Anderson, *Code of the Street: Decency, Violence, and the Moral Life of the Inner City* (New York: W. W. Norton, 1999), 150–52.
14. William Finnegan, *Cold New World: Growing Up in a Harder Country* (New York: Random House, 1998), 64.
15. David J. Pate, Jr., "The Life Circumstances of African American Fathers with Children on W-2: An Ethnographic Inquiry," *Focus* 22 (Summer 2002): 25–30.

16. Katherine Boo, "The Marriage Cure," *New Yorker*, August 18 and 25, 2003, 111.
17. Carol B. Stack, *All Our Kin: Strategies for Survival in a Black Community* (New York: Harper, 1975), 32.
18. Katherine S. Newman, *No Shame in My Game: The Working Poor in the Inner City* (New York: Vintage and New York: Russell Sage Foundation, 1999), 197.
19. Sharon Hays, *Flat Broke with Children: Women in the Age of Welfare Reform* (New York: Oxford University Press, 2003), 209.
20. Kathryn Edin and Maria Kefalas, *Promises I Can Keep: Why Poor Women Put Motherhood before Marriage* (Berkeley: University of California Press, 2005), 173, emphasis in the original.
21. Adrie Kusserow, *American Individualisms: Child Rearing and Social Class in Three Neighborhoods* (New York: Palgrave Macmillan, 2004), 55.
22. Newman, *No Shame in My Game*, 211.
23. Rubin, *Families on the Fault Line*, 88.
24. Paul R. Amato, Alan Booth, David R. Johnson, and Stacy J. Rogers, *Alone Together: How Marriage in America is Changing* (Cambridge, MA: Harvard University Press, 2007), 229, 123–24, 139; 172–73.
25. Jeffeson Cowie, *Stayin' Alive: The 1970s and the Last Days of the Working Class* (New York: Free Press, 2010), 209.
26. Andrew J. Cherlin, *The Marriage Go-Round: The State of Marriage and the Family in America Today* (New York: Vintage, 2010), 168.
27. Arnold Dashefsky and Irving M. Levine,"The Jewish Family: Continuity and Change," in *Families and Religions: Conflict and Change in Modern Society*, ed. William V. D'Antonio and Joan Aldous (Beverly Hills, CA: Sage, 1983), 181, emphasis in the original.
28. Lynne Davidman, *Tradition in a Rootless World: Women Turn to Orthodox Judaism* (Berkeley: University of California Press, 1991), 95.
29. R. David Arkush and Leo O. Lee. eds. and trans., *Land Without Ghosts: Chinese Impressions of America from the Mid-Nineteenth Century to the Present* (Berkeley: University of California Press, 1989), 229.
30. Ruth K. Chao, "Beyond Parental Control and Authoritarian Parenting Style: Understanding Chinese Parenting through the Cultural Notion of Training," *Child Development* 65 (August 1994): 111–19.
31. Min Zhou and Carl L. Bankston, III, *Growing Up American: How Vietnamese Children Adapt to Life in the United States* (New York: Russell Sage Foundation, 1998), 166.
32. Alejandro Portes and Rubén G. Rumbaut, *Legacies: The Story of the Immigrant Second Generation* (Berkeley: University of California Press and New York: Russell Sage Foundation, 2001), 71.
33. Ying Ying Yu, "A Duty to Family, Heritage and Country," National Public Radio, *Morning Edition*, July 17, 2006.
34. Nancy J. Smith-Hefner, *Khmer American: Identity and Moral Education in a Diasporic Community* (Berkeley: University of California Press, 1999), 87, 95, 139.
35. James M. Freeman, *Hearts of Sorrow: Vietnamese-American Lives* (Stanford, CA: Stanford University Press, 1989), 368.
36. Margaret A. Gibson, *Accommodation without Assimilation: Sikh Immigrants in an American High School* (Ithaca, NY: Cornell University Press, 1988), 128.
37. Zhou and Bankston, *Growing Up American*, 87

38. Nazli Kibria, *Family Tightrope: The Changing Lives of Vietnamese Americans* (Princeton, NJ: Princeton University Press, 1993), 109, 133, 131.
39. Zhou and Bankston, *Growing Up American*, 106.
40. Kibria, *Family Tightrope*, 165.
41. Ronet Bachman, *Death and Violence on the Reservation: Homicide, Family Violence, and Suicide in American Indian Populations* (New York: Auburn House, 1992), 7; Evelyn Lance Blanchard and Steven Unger, "Destruction of American Indian Families," *Social Casework* 58 (May 1977): 312.
42. Sherman Alexie, *The Lone Ranger and Tonto Fistfight in Heaven* (New York: Atlantic Monthly Press, 1993), 2.
43. Jennifer S. Hirsch, *A Courtship after Marriage: Sexuality and Love in Mexican Transnational Families* (Berkeley: University of California Press, 2003), 233.
44. Gabriel Thompson, *There's No José Here: Following the Hidden Lives of Mexican Immigrants* (New York: Nation Books, 2007), 33, emphasis in original.
45. Ruben Martinez, *Crossing Over: A Mexican Family on the Migrant Trail* (New York: Picador, 2001), 149.
46. Hirsch, *Courtship after Marriage*, 89, 1.
47. Robert Courtney Smith, *Mexican New York: Transnational Lives of New Immigrants* (Berkeley: University of California Press, 2006), 97–98, emphasis in the original.
48. Hirsch, *Courtship after Marriage*, 105, 115–17.
49. Hirsch, *Courtship after Marriage*, 163, 282.
50. Hirsch, *Courtship after Marriage*, 147, 153.
51. Smith, *Mexican New York*, 109–10.
52. Sonia Nazario, *Enrique's Journey* (New York: Random House, 2007), 198–99.
53. Luis J. Rodriguez, *Always Running: La Vida Loca: Gang Days in L.A.* (Willimantic, CT: Curbstone Press, 1993), 45.
54. Alejandro Portes, "Children of Immigrants: Segmented Assimilation and its Determinants," in *The Economic Sociology of Immigration: Essays on Networks, Ethnicity, and Entrepreneurship*, ed. Portes (New York: Russell Sage Foundation, 1995), 255.
55. John Phillip Santos, *Places Left Unfinished at the Time of Creation* (New York: Penguin, 1999), 264.
56. Martinez, *Crossing Over*, 235.
57. Esmeralda Santiago, *When I Was Puerto Rican* (New York: Vintage, 1993), 254.
58. Smith, *Mexican New York*, 143.
59. James Diego Vigil, "Gangs, Social Control, and Ethnicity: Ways to Redirect," in *Identity and Inner-City Youth: Beyond Ethnicity and Gender*, ed. Shirley Brice Heath and Milbrey W. McLoughlin (New York: Teachers College Press, 1993), 107.
60. Finnegan, *Cold New World*, 233.
61. Portes and Rumbaut, *Legacies*, 98.
62. Martinez, *Crossing Over*, 270.
63. Hirsch, *Courtship after Marriage*, 241.
64. Frances Fitgeralds, "Come One, Come All: Building a Megachurch in New England," *New Yorker*, December 3, 2007, 55.

65. Joseph B. Tamney, *The Resilience of Conservative Religion: The Case of Popular, Conservative Protestant Congregations* (Cambridge: Cambridge University Press, 2002), 230; Andrew Greeley and Michael Hout, *The Truth about Conservative Christians: What They Think and What They Believe* (Chicago, IL: University of Chicago Press, 2006), 130–31; Mark D. Regnerus, *Forbidden Fruit: Sex and Religion in the Lives of American Teenagers* (New York: Oxford University Press, 2007), 98–101, 137–38; Sally K. Gallagher, *Evangelical Identity and Gendered Family Life* (New Brunswick, NJ: Rutgers University Press, 2003), 134.
66. Susan Friend Harding, *The Book of Jerry Falwell: Fundamentalist Language and Politics* (Princeton, NJ: Princeton University Press, 2000), 238.
67. Margaret Talbot, "Red Sex, Blue Sex," *The New Yorker*, November 3, 2008, 65.
68. Kristin Luker, *Abortion and the Politics of Motherhood* (Berkeley: University of California Press, 1984), 200.
69. W. Bradford Wilcox, *Soft Patriarchs, New Men: How Christianity Shapes Fathers and Husbands* (Chicago, IL: University of Chicago Press, 2004), 186.
70. Tamney, *Resilience of Conservative Religion*, 242.
71. Mark Regnerus and Jeremy Uecker, *Premarital Sex in America: How Young Americans Meet, Mate, and Think about Marrying* (Oxford: Oxford University Press, 2011), 224.
72. Barbara Ehrenreich, *The Hearts of Men: American Dreams and the Flight from Commitment* (New York: Anchor, 1983), 152.
73. Joseph Heath and Andrew Potter, *Nation of Rebels: Why Counterculture Became Consumer Culture* (New York: HarperBusiness, 2004), 67.
74. Judith Stacey, *Brave New Families: Stories of Domestic Upheaval in Late Twentieth Century America* (New York: BasicBooks, 1990), 59.
75. Claudia L. Bushman, *Contemporary Mormonism: Latter-Day Saints in Modern America* (Westport, CT: Praeger, 2006), 35.
76. Lori G. Beaman, "Molly Mormons, Mormon Feminists and Moderates: Religious Diversity and the Latter Day Saints Church," *Sociology of Religion* 62 (Spring 2001): 80; Armand L. Mauss, *The Angel and the Beehive: The Mormon Struggle with Assimilation* (Urbana: University of Illinois Press, 1994),132–36.
77. John Bul Dau, *God Grew Tired of Us* (Washington, D.C.: National Geographic, 2007), 168, 176.
78. Dau, *God Grew Tired of Us*, 279–80.

Conclusion

1. Andrew Oldenquist, *The Non-Suicidal Society* (Bloomington: Indiana University Press, 1986), 169.
2. E. B. Macpherson, *The Political Theory of Possessive Individualism: Hobbes to Locke* (Oxford: Oxford University Press, 1962), 275.
3. Charles Taylor, *The Ethics of Authenticity* (Cambridge, MA: Harvard University Press, 1991), 89.
4. Erica Jong, *Fear of Flying* (New York: Signet, 1973), 8; Erica Jong, *Fear of Fifty: A Midlife Memoir* (New York: HarperCollins, 1994), 32, 36, 34–35; Molly Jong-Fast, *Girl (Maladjusted)* (New York: Villard, 2006), 113, 120.

Additional Reading

Alba, Richard D. *Italian Americans: Into the Twilight of Ethnicity*. Englewood, NJ: Prentice-Hall, 1985.

Albert, Patricia C. "Symbiosis, Merger, and War: Contrasting Forms of IntertribalRelationship among Historic Plains Indians." In *The Political Economy of NorthAmerican Indians*, edited by John H. Moore, 94–132. Norman: University ofOklahoma Press, 1993.

Altman, Dennis. *The Homosexualization of America, the Americanization of the Homosexual*. New York: St. Martin's Press, 1982.

Amato, Paul R. "The Consequences of Divorce for Adults and Children." *Journal of Marriage and the Family* 62 (November 2000): 1269–87.

Amato, Paul R., and Alan Booth. *A Generation at Risk: Growing Up in an Era of Family Upheaval*. Cambridge, MA: Harvard University Press, 1997.

Amato, Paul R., et al. "Continuity and Change in Marital Quality between 1980 and 2000." *Journal of Marriage and the Family* 65 (February 2003): 1–22.

Amussen, Susan Dwyer. *An Ordered Society: Gender and Class in Early Modern England*. Oxford: Basil Blackwell, 1988.

Anderson, Virginia De John. "Religion, the Common Thread." *New England Quarterly* 59 (September 1985): 418–24.

Atherton, Lewis. *Main Street on the Middle Border*. New York: Quadrangle, [1966].

Ayers, Edward L. *Vengeance and Justice: Crime and Punishment in the Nineteenth-Century American South*. New York: Oxford University Press, 1984.

Bailey, Anne C. *African Voices of the Atlantic Slave Trade: Beyond the Silence and the Shame*. Boston, MA: Beacon Press, 2005.

Baker, Paula. "The Domestication of Politics: Women and American Political Society, 1780–1920." *American Historical Review* 89 (June 1984): 620–47.

Barr, Juliana. "Beyond their Control: Spaniards in Native Texas." In *Choice, Persuasion, and Coercion: Social Control on Spain's North American Frontiers*, edited by Jesús F. de la Teja and Ross Frank, 149–77. Albuquerque: University of New Mexico Press, 2005.

———. *Peace Came in the Form of a Woman: Indians and Spaniards in the Texas Borderlands*. Chapel Hill: University of North Carolina Press, 2007.

Barron, Hal S. *Mixed Harvest: The Second Great Transformation in the Rural North, 1870–1930*. Chapel Hill: University of North Carolina Press, 1997.

Bartels, F. L. "Akan Indigenous Education." In *Conflict and Harmony in Education in Tropical Africa*, edited by Godfrey N. Brown and Mervyn Hiskett, 39–64. London: George Allen & Unwin, 1975.

Bartkowski, John P. *Remaking the Godly Marriage: Gender Negotiation in Evangelical Families.* New Brunswick, NJ: Rutgers University Press, 2001.

Bederman, Gail. *Manliness and Civilization: A Cultural History of Gender and Race in the United States, 1880–1917.* Chicago: University of Chicago Press, 1995.

———. "'The Women Have Had Charge of the Church Work Long Enough': The Men and Religion Forward Movement of 1911–1912 and the Masculinization of Middle-Class Protestantism." *American Quarterly* 41 (September 1989): 432–65.

Berger, Iris, and E. Frances White. *Women in Sub-Saharan Africa: Restoring Women to History.* Bloomington: Indiana University Press, 1999.

Berlin, Ira. *Many Thousands Gone: The First Centuries of Slavery in North America.* Cambridge, MA: Harvard University Press, 1998.

Berry, Daina Ramey. *"Swing the Sickle for the Harvest is Ripe": Gender and Slavery in Antebellum Georgia.* Urbana: University of Illinois Press, 2007.

Bianchi, Suzanne M., et al. "Is Anyone Doing the Housework? Trends in the Gender Division of Household Labor." *Social Forces* 79 (September 2000): 191–228.

Bielby, W. T., and D. D. Bielby. "I Will Follow Him: Family Ties, Gender-Role Beliefs, and Reluctance to Relocate for a Better Job." *American Journal of Sociology* 97 (1992): 1241–67.

Billingsly, Andrew. *Climbing Jacob's Ladder: The Enduring Legacy of African-American Families.* New York: Touchstone, 1992.

Binnema, Theodore. *Common and Contested Ground: A Human and Environmental History of the Northwestern Plains.* Norman: University of Oklahoma, 2001.

Blair, Karen J. *The Clubwoman as Feminist: True Womanhood Redefined, 1868–1914.* New York: Holmes & Meier, 1980.

Blair, Sampson Lee, and Daniel T. Lichter. "Measuring the Division of Household Labor: Gender Segregation of Housework among American Couples." *Journal of Family Issues* 12 (March 1991): 91–113.

Bodnar, John. *The Transplanted: A History of Immigrants in Urban America.* Bloomington: Indiana University Press, 1987.

Bonomi, Patricia U. *Under the Cope of Heaven: Religions, Society, and Politics in Colonial America*, updated edition. Oxford: Oxford University Press, 2003.

Bordin, Ruth. *Women and Temperance: The Quest for Power and Liberty, 1873–1900.* Philadelphia, PA: Temple University Press, 1981.

Boyd, Todd. *Am I Black Enough for You? Popular Culture from the 'Hood and Beyond.* Bloomington: Indiana University Press, 1997.

Boyer, Paul, and Stephen Nissenbaum, *Salem Possessed: The Social Origins of Witchcraft.* Cambridge, MA: Harvard University Press, 1974.

Boylan, Anne M. "Women and Politics in the Era before Seneca Falls." *Journal of the Early Republic* 10 (Fall 1990): 363–82.

Braund, Kathryn Holland. "Guardians of Tradition and Handmaidens to Change: Women's Roles in Creek Economic and Social Life during the Eighteenth Century." *American Indian Quarterly* 14 (Summer 1990): 239–58.

Breen, T. H. *"Myne Owne Ground": Race and Freedom on Virginia's Eastern Shore, 1640–1676.* New York: Oxford University Press, 1980.

Brick, Howard. *Age of Contradiction: American Thought and Culture in the 1960s.* Ithaca, NY: Cornell University Press, 2001.

Brown, Kathleen M. *Good Wives, Nasty Wenches, and Anxious Patriarchs: Gender, Race, and Power in Colonial Virginia.* Williamsburg, VA: Omohundro Institute of Early American History and Culture and Chapel Hill: University of North Carolina Press, 1996.

Bucholz, Robert, and Newton Key. *Early Modern England, 1485–1714: A Narrative History.* Malden, MA: Blackwell, 2004.

Bukowczyk, John J. *And My Children Did Not Know Me: A History of Polish-Americans.* Bloomington: Indiana University Press, 1987.

Burton, Orville Vernon. *In My Father's House Are Many Mansions: Family and Community in Edgefield, South Carolina.* Chapel Hill: University of North Carolina Press, 1985.

Bushman, Richard L. *From Puritan to Yankee: Character and the Social Order in Connecticut, 1690–1765.* New York: W. W. Norton, 1970.

Butler, Anne M. *Daughters of Joy, Sisters of Misery: Prostitutes in the American West.* Urbana: University of Illinois Press, 1985.

Bynum, Victoria E. "Reshaping the Bonds of Womanhood: Divorce in Reconstruction North Carolina." In *Divided Houses: Gender and the Civil War,* edited by Catherine Clinton and Nina Silber, 320–33. New York: Oxford University Press, 1992.

———. *Unruly Women: The Politics of Social and Sexual Control in the Old South.* Chapel Hill: University of North Carolina Press, 1992.

Camarillo, Albert. *Chicanos in a Changing Society: From Mexican Pueblos to American Barrios in Santa Barbara and Southern California, 1848—1930.* Cambridge, MA: Harvard University Press, 1979.

Carlson, Paul H. *The Plains Indians.* College Station: Texas A & M University Press, 1998.

Carr, Lois Green, and Lorena S. Walsh. "The Planter's Wife: The Experience of White Woman in Seventeenth-Century Maryland." *William and Mary Quarterly* 34 (1977): 542–71.

Carr, Lois Green, and Russell R. Menard, and Lorena S. Walsh. *Robert Cole's World: Agriculture and Society in Early Maryland.* Williamsburg: Institute of Early American History and Culture and Chapel Hill: University of North Carolina Press, 1991.

Carroll, Mark M. *Homesteads Ungovernable: Families, Sex, Race, and the Law in Frontier Texas, 1823–1860.* Austin: University of Texas Press, 2001.

Carter, Christine Jacobson. *Southern Single Blessedness: Unmarried Women in the Urban South, 1800–1865.* Urbana: University of Illinois Press, 2006.

Cawelti, John G. *The Six-Gun Mystique*, 2nd ed. Bowling Green, OH: Bowling Green State University Popular Press, 1984.

Chafe, William H. *Women and Equality: Changing Patterns in American Culture.* Oxford: Oxford University Press, 1977.

Chafetz, Janet Saltzman. "Chicken or Egg? A Theory of the Relationship between Feminist Movements and Family Change." In *Gender and Family Change in Industrialized Countries*, edited by Karen Oppenheim Mason and An-Magritt Jensen, 63–81. Oxford: Oxford University Press, 2003.

Chan, Anthony B. *Gold Mountain: The Chinese in the New World.* Vancouver: New Star Books, 1983.

Chan, Sucheng. *This Bittersweet Soil: The Chinese in California Agriculture, 1860–1910.* Berkeley: University of California Press, 1986.

Chudacoff, Howard P. *How Old Are You? Age Consciousness in American Culture.* Princeton, NJ: Princeton University Press, 1989.

Cinel, Dino. *From Italy to San Francisco: The Immigrant Experience.* Stanford, CA: Stanford University Press, 1982.

———. "The Seasonal Emigrations of Italians in the Nineteenth Century: From Internal to International Destinations." *Journal of Ethnic Studies* 10 (Spring 1982): 43–68.

Clay, C. G. A. *Economic Expansion and Social Change: England, 1500–1700*, 2 vols. Cambridge: Cambridge University Press, 1984.

Coale, Ansley J., and Norfleet W. Rives, Jr. "A Statistical Reconstruction of the Black Population of the United States, 1880—1970: Estimates of True Numbers by Age and Sex, Birth Rates, and Total Fertility." *Population Index* 39 (January 1973): 3–36.

Cohen, Jeffrey H. *The Culture of Migration in Southern Mexico*. Austin: University of Texas Press, 2004.

Cohen, Miriam. *Workshop to Office: Two Generations of Italian Women in New York City, 1900–1950*. Ithaca, NY: Cornell University Press, 1992.

Cohen, Patricia Cline. "Unregulated Youth: Masculinity and Murder in the 1830s City." *Radical History Review* 52 (Winter 1992): 33–52.

Collins, Gail. *When Everything Changed: The Amazing Journey of American Women from 1960 to the Present*. New York: Little, Brown, and Company, 2009.

Coltrane, Scott. *Family Man: Fatherhood, Housework, and Gender Equity*. New York: Oxford University Press, 1996.

Coontz, Stephanie. *The Social Origins of Private Life: A History of American Families, 1600–1900*. London: Verso, 1988.

Cornwall, Mariel, Tim B. Heaton, and Lawrence A. Young, eds. *Contemporary Mormonism: Social Science Perspectives*. Urbana: University of Illinois Press, 1994.

Cose, Ellis. *The Envy of the World: On Being a Black Man in America*. New York: Washington Square Press, 2002.

Costin, Lela B., Howard Jacob Karger, and David Stoesz. *The Politics of Child Abuse in America*. New York: Oxford University Press, 1996.

Cott, Nancy F. *The Bonds of Motherhood: "Woman's Sphere" in New England, 1780–1835* New Haven, CT: Yale University Press, 1977.

———. "Divorce and the Changing Status of Women in Eighteenth Century Massachusetts." *William and Mary Quarterly* 33 (October, 1976): 586–614.

———. "Passionless: An Interpretation of Victorian Sexual Ideology, 1790–1850." *Signs* 4 (Winter 1978): 219–36.

Courtwright, David T. *Violent Land: Single Men and Social Disorder from the Frontier to the Inner City*. Cambridge, MA: Harvard University Press, 1996.

Cowan, Ruth Schwartz. *More Work for Mother: The Ironies of Household Technology from the Open Hearth to the Microwave*. New York: Basic Books, 1983.

———. *A Social History of American Technology*. New York: Oxford University Press, 1997.

Coward, Barry. *Social Change and Continuity: England, 1550–1750*, rev. ed. London: Longman, 1997.

Cross, Gary. *The Cute and the Cool: Wondrous Innocence and Modern American Children's Culture*. New York: Oxford University Press, 2004.

———. *Men to Boys: The Making of Modern Immaturity*. New York: Columbia University Press, 2008.

Crow Dog, Mary, and Richard Erdoes. *Lakota Woman*. New York: Harper, 1991.

Crown, Patricia L. ed. *Women and Men in the Prehistoric Southwest: Labor, Power, and Prestige*. Santa Fe, NM: School of American Research Press, 2000.

Dannenbaum, Jed. *Drink and Disorder: Temperance Reform in Cincinnati from the Washingtonian Revival to the WCTU*. Urbana: University of Illinois Press, 1984.

Danzger, M. Herbert. *Returning to Tradition: The Contemporary Revival of Orthodox Judaism*. New Haven, CT: Yale University Press, 1989.

Dawley, Alan. *Class and Community: The Industrial Revolution in Lynn*. Cambridge, MA: Harvard University Press, 1976.

Deal, J. Douglas. *Race and Class in Colonial Virginia: Indians, Englishmen, and Africans on the Eastern Shore during the Seventeenth Century*. New York: Garland, 1993.

Degler, Carl. *At Odds: Women and the Family in America from the Revolution to the Present*. New York: Oxford University Press, 1980.

De la Teja, Jesús F. *San Antonio de Bėxar: A Community on New Spain's Northern Frontier*. Albuquerque: University of New Mexico Press, 1995.

D'Emilio, John. "Capitalism and Gay Identity." In *Powers of Desire: The Politics of Sexuality*, edited by Ann Snitow, Christine Stansell, and Sharon Thompson, 100–13. New York: Monthly Review Press, 1983.

Demos, John. "Images of the American Family, Then and Now." In *Changing Images of the Family*, edited by Virginia Tufte and Barbara Myerhoff, 43–60. New Haven, CT: Yale University Press, 1979.

———. *A Little Commonwealth: Family Life in Plymouth Colony*. London: Oxford University Press, 1970.

———. "Old Age in Early New England," in *Turning Points: Historical and Sociological Essays on the Family*, edited by Demos and Sarane Spence Boocock, 248–87. Chicago: University of Illinois Press, 1978.

DeParle, Jason. *American Dream: Three Women, Ten Kids, and a Nation's Drive to End Welfare*. New York: Penguin Books, 2005.

Deutsch, Sarah. *No Separate Refuge: Culture, Class, and Gender on an Anglo-Hispanic Frontier in the American Southwest, 1880–1940*. New York: Oxford University Press, 1987.

———. Women and the City: Gender, Space, and Power in Boston, 1870–1940. Oxford: Oxford University Press, 2000.

Di Leonardo, Micaelao. "The Female World of Cards and Holidays: Women, Families, and the Work of Kinship." *Signs* 12 (Spring 1987): 440–53.

Dollard, John. *Caste and Class in a Southern Town*. New Haven, CT: Yale University Press, 1937.

Dorsey, Bruce. *Reforming Men and Women: Gender in the Antebellum City*. Ithaca, NY: Cornell University Press, 2002.

Douvan, Elizabeth. "The Age of Narcissism, 1963–1982." In *American Childhood: A Research Guide and Historical Handbook*, edited by Joseph M. Hawes and N. Ray Hiner, 587–617. Westport, CT: Greenwood Press, 1985.

Dublin, Thomas. *Women at Work: The Transformation of Work and Community in Lowell, Massachusetts, 1826–1860*. New York: Columbia University Press, 1979.

DuBois, Ellen Carol, and Linda Gordon. "Seeking Ecstasy on the Battlefield: Danger and Pleasure in Nineteenth-Century Feminist Sexual Thought." *In Pleasure and Danger: Exploring Female Sexuality*, edited by Carole S. Vance, 31–49. Boston, MA: Routledge & Kegan Paul, 1984.

Dudley, David L. *My Father's Shadow: Intergenerational Conflict in African American Men's Autobiography*. Philadelphia: University of Pennsylvania Press, 1991.

Easterlin, Richard A., and Eileen M. Crimmins. "Recent Social Trends: Changes in Personal Aspirations of American Youth." *Sociology and Social Research* 72 (July 1988): 217–23.

Echols, Alice. "The Demise of Female Intimacy in the Twentieth Century." *Michigan Occasional Paper* No. 6, Fall 1978. [Ann Arbor: Women's Studies Program, University of Michigan.]

Echols, Alice. *Scars of Sweet Paradise: The Life and Times of Janis Joplin.* New York: Henry Hold, 2000.

Eckholm, Erik. "Plight Deepens for Black Men, Studies Warn." New York Times, March 20, 2006.

Edsforth, Ronald. *Class Conflict and Cultural Consensus: The Making of a Mass Consumer Society in Flint, Michigan.* New Brunswick, NJ: Rutgers University Press, 1987.

Edwards, Laura F. *Gendered Strife and Confusion: The Political Culture of Reconstruction.* Urbana: University of Illinois Press, 1997.

Ekberg, Carl J. *Stealing Indian Women: Native Slavery in the Illinois Country.* Urbana: University of Illinois Press, 2007.

Elder, Glen H., Jr. *Children of the Great Depression: Social Change in Life Experience.* Chicago, IL: University of Chicago Press, 1974.

England, Paula. "The Gender Revolution: Uneven and Stalled." *Gender & Society* 24 (April 2010): 149–66.

Epstein, Barbara Leslie. *The Politics of Domesticity: Women, Evangelism, and Temperance in Nineteenth-Century America.* Middletown, CT: Wesleyan University Press, 1981.

Epstein, Jonathan S., ed. *Adolescents and their Music: If It's Too Loud, You're Too Old.* New York: Garland, 1995.

Erenberg, Lewis A. *Steppin' Out: New York Nightlife and the Transformation of American Culture, 1890–1930.* Westport, CT: Greenwood Press, 1981.

Ethridge, Robbie. *Creek Country: The Creek Indians and their World.* Chapel Hill: University of North Carolina Press, 2003.

Fage, J. D. "Slavery and Society in Western Africa, c. 1445-c. 1700." *Journal of African History* 21 (1980): 289–310.

Faludi, Susan. *Stiffed: The Betrayal of the American Man.* New York: William Morrow, 1994.

Faragher, John Mack. *Women and Men on the Overland Trail.* New Haven, CT: Yale University Press, 1979.

Fass, Paula S. *The Damned and the Beautiful: American Youth in the 1920s.* Oxford: Oxford University Press, 1977.

Faust, Drew Gilpin. *Mothers of Invention: Women of the Slaveholding South in the American Civil War.* Chapel Hill: University of North Carolina Press, 1996.

Finkelstein, Barbara. "Casting Networks of Good Influence: The Reconstruction of Childhood in the United States, 1790–1870." *In American Childhood: A Research Guide and Historical Handbook,* edited by Joseph M. Hawes and N. Ray Hiner. Westport, CT: Greenwood Press, 1985.

Fischer, Claude S. "Ever-More Rooted Americans." In *City & Community* 1 (June 2002): 177–98.

Fischer, Claude S., and Michael Hout. *Century of Difference: How America Changed in the Last One Hundred Years.* New York: Russell Sage Foundation, 2006.

Fischer, David Hackett. *Albion's Seed: Four British Folkways in America.* New York: Oxford University Press, 1989.

———. *Growing Old in America,* expanded ed. Oxford: Oxford University Press, 1978.

Fishbein, Leslie. "The Demise of the Cult of True Womanhood in Early American Film, 1900–1930." *Journal of Popular Film and Television* 12 (Summer 1984): 66–72.

Fliegelman, Jay. *Prodigals and Pilgrims: The American Revolution against Patriarchal Authority, 1750–1800.* Cambridge: Cambridge University Press, 1982.

Fong-Torres, Ben. *The Rice Room: Growing Up Chinese American, from Number Two Son to Rock'n'Roll.* New York: Plume, 1995.

Forham, Signithia. *Blacked Out: Dilemmas of Race, Identity, and Success at Capital High.* Chicago, IL: University Press, 1996.

Forret, Jeff. "Conflict and the 'Slave Community': Violence among Slaves in Upcountry South Carolina."*Journal of Southern History* 74 (August 2008): 551–88.

Foster, Frances Smith.*'Til Death or Distance Do Us Part': Love and Marriage in African America.* New York: Oxford University Press, 2010.

Foster, Stephen. *Their Solitary Way: The Puritan Social Ethic in the First Century of Settlement in New England.* New Haven, CT: Yale University Press, 1971.

Fowler-Salamini, Heather, and Mary Kay Vaughan, eds. *Women of the Mexican Countryside, 1850–1990: Creating Spaces, Shaping Transitions.* Tucson: University of Arizona Press, 1994.

Frank, Stephen M. *Life with Father: Parenthood and Masculinity in the Nineteenth-Century American North.* Baltimore, MD: Johns Hopkins University Press, 1998.

Franklin, Donna L. *Ensuring Inequality: The Structural Transformation of the African-American Family.* New York: Oxford University Press, 1997.

Freedman, Estelle. "Separatism as Strategy: Female Institution Building and American Feminism, 1870–1930." *Feminist Studies* 5 (Fall 1979): 512–29.

Fuligni, Andrew J., Vivian Tseng, and Mary Lam. "Attitudes toward Family Obligations among American Adolescents with Asian, Latin American, and European Backgrounds." *Child Development* 70 (July/August 1999): 1030–44.

Gabaccia, Donna R. *From the Other Side: Women, Gender, and Immigrant Life in the U.S., 1820–1990.* Bloomington: Indiana University Press, 1994.

Galbraith, John Kenneth. *The Culture of Contentment.* Boston, MA: Houghton Mifflin, 1992.

Gallagher, Maggie, and David Blankenhorn. "Family Feud." *American Prospect* 33 (July-August 1997): 12–16.

Gans, Herbert J. *The Levittowners: Ways of Life and Politics in a New SuburbanCommunity.* New York: Vintage, 1967.

———. "Second Generation Decline: Scenarios for the Economic and Ethnic Futures of the Post–1965 American Immigrants." *Ethnic and Racial Studies* 15 (April 1992): 173–92.

———. *The Urban Villagers: Group and Class in the Life of Italian-Americans,* updated and expanded. New York: The Free Press, 1982.

Garceau, Dee. *The Important Things of Life: Women, Work, and Family in Sweetwater County, Wyoming, 1880–1929.* Lincoln: University of Nebraska Press, 1997.

Genovese, Eugene D. *Roll, Jordan, Roll: The World the Slaves Made.* New York: Vintage, 1976.

George, Nelson. *Hip Hop America.* New York: Viking, 1998.

Geronimus, Arline T., and Sanders Korenman. "The Socioeconomic Consequences of Teen Childbearing Reconsidered." *The Quarterly Journal of Economics* 107 (November 1992): 1187–1214.

Geronimus, Arline T., Sanders Korenman, and Marianne M. Hillemeier. "Does Young Maternal Age Adversely Affect Child Development? Evidence from Cousin Comparisons in the United States." *Population and Development Review* 20 (September 1994): 585–609.

Gerson, Kathleen. *No Man's Land: Men's Changing Commitments to Family and Work*. New York: BasicBooks, 1993.

Gessain, Monique. "Coniagui Women." In *Women of Tropical Africa*, edited by Denise Paulme, trans. H. M. Wright, 17–46. Berkeley: University of California Press, 1963.

Gilbert, James. *A Cycle of Outrage: America's Reaction to the Juvenile Delinquent in the 1950s*. New York: Oxford University Press, 1986.

Gillespie, D. L. "Who Has the Power? The Marital Struggle." *Journal of Marriage and the Family* 33 (1971): 445–58.

Ginsburg, Faye D. *Contested Lives: The Abortion Debate in an American Community*. Berkeley: University of California Press, 1989.

Glover, Lorri. *All Our Relations: Blood Ties and Emotional Bonds among the Early South Carolina Gentry*. Baltimore: Johns Hopkins University Press, 2000.

Glymph, Thavolia. *Out of the House of Bondage: The Transformation of the Plantation Household*. New York: Cambridge University Press, 2008.

Godbeer, Richard. *Sexual Revolution in Early America*. Baltimore: The Johns Hopkins University Press, 2002.

Goldman, Marion S. *Gold Diggers and Silver Miners: Prostitution and Social Life on the Comstock Lode*. Ann Arbor: University of Michigan Press, 1981.

Gonzalez, Gilbert G., and Raul A. Fernandez. *A Century of Chicano History: Empire, Nations, and Migration*. New York: Routledge, 2003.

Gonzales, Manuel G. *Mexicanos: A History of Mexicans in the United States*. Bloomington: Indiana University Press, 1999.

Goode, Erich, and Nachman Ben-Yehuda. *Moral Panics: The Social Construction of Deviance*. Oxford: Blackwell, 2009.

Goody, Jack. *Comparative Studies in Kinship*. London: Routledge & Kegan Paul, 1969.

Gordon, Linda. *Heroes of their Own Lives: The Politics and History of Family Violence, Boston, 1880–1960*. New York: Viking, 1988.

———. "Why Nineteenth-Century Feminists Did Not Support 'Birth Control' and Twentieth-Century Feminists Do: Feminism, Reproduction, and the Family." In *Rethinking the Family*, edited by Barrie Thorne, with Marilyn Yalom, 40–53. New York: Longman, 1982.

Gorn, Elliott J. "'Good-Bye Boys, I Die a True American': Homicide, Nativism, and Working-Class Culture in Antebellum New York City."*Journal of American History* 74 (September 1987): 388–410.

———. *The Manly Art: Bare-Knuckle Prize Fighting in America*. Ithaca, NY: Cornell University Press, 1986.

Graham, Michael. "Meetinghouse and Chapel: Religion and Community in Seventeenth- Century Maryland." In *Colonial Chesapeake Society*, edited by Lois Green Carr, Philip D. Morgan, and Jean B. Russo, 242–74. Williamsburg: Institute of Early American History and Chapel Hill: University of North Carolina Press, 1988.

Grant, Julia. *Raising Baby by the Book: The Education of American Mothers*. New Haven, CT: Yale University Press, 1998.

Grasmuck, Sherri, and Patricia R. Pessar. *Between Two Islands: Dominican InternationalMigration*. Berkeley: University of California Press, 1991.

Greenberg, Kenneth S. *Honor and Slavery: Lies, Duels, Noses, Masks, Dressing as a Woman, Gifts, Strangers, Humanitarianism, Death, Slave Rebellions, the Pro-Slavery Argument, Baseball, Hunting, and Gambling in the Old South*. Princeton, NJ: Princeton University Press, 1996.

Greene, Jack P. *Pursuits of Happiness: The Social Development of Early Modern British Colonies and the Formation of American Culture.* Chapel Hill: University of North Carolina Press, 1988.

Greenfield, Robert. *Timothy Leary: A Biography.* Orlando, FL: Harvest, 2007.

Greenstein, Theodore N. "Husbands' Participation in Domestic Labor: Interactive Effects of Wives' and Husbands' Gender Ideologies." *Journal of Marriage and the Family* 58 (August 1996): 585–95.

Greven, Philip J., Jr. *Four Generations: Population, Land, and Family in Colonial Andover, Massachusetts.* Ithaca, NY: Cornell University Press, 1970.

Grinev, Andrei Val'terovich. *The Tlingit Indians in Russian America, 1741–1867.* Translated by Richard L. Bland and Katerina G. Solovjova. Lincoln: University of Nebraska Press, 2005.

Griswold del Castillo, Richard. *La Familia: Chicano Families in the Urban Southwest, 1848 to the Present.* Notre Dame, IN: University of Notre Dame Press, 1984.

Griswold, Robert L. *Family and Divorce in California, 1850–1890: Victorian Illusions and Everyday Realities.* Albany: State University of New York Press, 1982.

Gross, Robert A. *The Minutemen and their World.* New York: Hill and Wang, 1976.

Guilbault, Rose Castillo. *Farmworker's Daughter: Growing up Mexican in America.* Berkeley, CA: Heydey Books, 2006.

Gundersen, John R. *To Be Useful to the World: Women in Revolutionary America, 1740– 1790.* New York: Twayne and London: Prentice Hall International, 1996.

Haag, Pamela. "The 'Ill Use of a Wife': Patterns of Working-Class Violence in Domestic and Public New York City, 1860–1880." *Journal of Social History* 25 (Spring 1992): 447–77.

———. "In Search of 'The Real Thing': Ideologies of Love, Modern Romance, and Women's Sexual Subjectivity in the United States, 1920–40." *Journal of the History of Sexuality* 2 (April 1992): 547–77.

Hackett, David G. *The Rude Hand of Innovation: Religion and Social Order in Albany, New York, 1652–1836.* New York: Oxford University Press, 1991.

Hackstaff, Karla B. *Marriage in a Culture of Divorce.* Philadelphia, PA: Temple University Press, 1999.

Hall, Gwendolyn Midlo. *Africans in Colonial Louisiana: The Development of Afro-Creole Culture in the Eighteenth Century.* Baton Rouge: Louisiana State University Press, 1992.

Hansen, Karen V. A Very Social Time: Crafting Community in Antebellum New England. Berkeley: University of California Press, 1994.

Hareven, Tamara K. *Family Time and Industrial Time: The Relationship between the Family and Work in a New England Industrial Community.* Cambridge: Cambridge University Press, 1982.

Hareven, Tamara K., and Maris A. Vinovskis. "Marital Fertility, Ethnicity, and Occupation in Urban Families: An Analysis of South Boston and the South End in 1880." *Journal of Social History* 3 (Spring 1975): 69–93.

Harris, William. "Work and the Family in Black Atlanta, 1880." *Journal of Social History* 9 (Spring 1976): 319–30.

Hart, Dianne Walta. *Undocumented in L.A.: An Immigrant's Story.* Wilmington, DE: SR Books, 1997.

Hartog, Hendrik. *Man and Wife in America: A History.* Cambridge, MA: Harvard University Press, 2000.

Haslett, Adam. "Love Supreme: Gay Nuptials and the Making of Modern Marriage." *New Yorker,* May 31, 2004.

Hays, Sharon.*The Cultural Contradictions of Motherhood*. New Haven, CT: Yale University Press, 1996.

Heinze, Andrew R. *Adapting to Abundance: Jewish Immigrants, Mass Consumption, and the Search for the American Identity*. New York: Columbia University Press, 1990.

Herman, Ellen. *Kinship by Design: A History of Adoption in the Modern United States*. Chicago: University of Chicago Press, 2008.

Hertzberg, Arthur. *The Jews in America, Four Centuries of an Uneasy Encounter: A History*. New York: Simon and Schuster, 1989.

Hetherington, E. Mavis, and W. Glenn Clingempeel. "Coping with Marital Transitions: A Family Systems Perspective." *Monographs of the Society for Research in Child Development* 57 (1992): 1–242.

Hewlett, Sylvia Ann, and Cornel West. *The War against Parents: What We Can Do for America's Beleaguered Moms and Dads*. Boston, MA: Houghton Mifflin, 1998.

Heywood, Linda M., and John K. Thornton. *Central Africans, Atlantic Creoles, and the Foundation of the Americas, 1585–1660*. Cambridge: Cambridge University Press, 2007.

Higham, John. "The Reorientation of American Culture in the 1890s." In *The Origins of Modern Consciousness*, edited by John Weiss, 25–48. Detroit, MI: Wayne State University Press, 1965.

Hill, Robert B. *The Strengths of African American Families: Twenty-Five Years Later*. Lanham, MD: University Press of America, 1999.

Hine, Darlene C. "Female Slave Resistance: The Economics of Sex." *Western Journal of Black Studies* 3 (Summer 1979): 123–27.

Hirsch, Susan E. *Roots of the American Working Class: The Industrialization of Crafts in Newark, 1800—1860*. [Philadelphia]: University of Pennsylvania Press, 1978.

Holzer, Harry J, and Paul Offner. "Trends in Employment Outcomes of Young Black Men, 1979–2000." Institute for Research on Poverty, Discussion Paper no. 1247- 02, February 2002.

Hondagneu-Sotelo, Pierrette. *Gendered Transitions: Mexican Experiences of Immigration*. Berkeley: University of California Press, 1994.

Horn, James. "Servant Emigration to the Chesapeake in the Seventeenth Century." In *The Chesapeake in the Seventeenth Century: Essays on Anglo-American Society*, edited by Thad W. Tate and David L. Ammerman, 51–95. Williamsburg, VA: Institute of Early American History and Culture and Chapel Hill: University of North Carolina Press, 1979.

Howe, Daniel Walker. *What Hath God Wrought: The Transformation of America, 1815–1848*. Oxford: Oxford University Press, 2007.

Hudson, Larry E., Jr. *To Have and to Hold: Slave Work and the Family Life in Antebellum South Carolina*. Athens: University of Georgia Press, 1997.

Hunter, Jane H. *How Young Ladies Became Girls: The Victorian Origins of American Girlhood*. New Haven, CT: Yale University Press, 2002.

Hurtado, Albert. *Indian Survival on the California Frontier*. New Haven, CT: Yale University Press, 1990.

———. *Intimate Frontiers: Sex, Gender, and Culture in Old California*. Albuquerque: University of New Mexico Press, 1999.

Iannaccone, Laurence R., and Carrie A. Miles. "Dealing with Social Change: The Mormon Church's Response to Change in Women's Roles." *Social Forces* 68 (June 1990): 1231–50.

Inness, Sherrie A., ed.. *Delinquents and Debutantes: Twentieth-Century American Girls' Cultures.* New York: New York University Press, 1998.

Jabour, Anya. "Marriage and Family in the Nineteenth-Century South." *In Major Problems in the History of American Families and Children: Documents and Essays,* edited by Anya Jabour, 121–30. Boston, MA: Houghton Mifflin, 2005.

Jackson, Kenneth T. *Crabgrass Frontier: The Suburbanization of the United States.* New York: Oxford University Press, 1985.

Jeffrey, Julie Roy. *Frontier Women: The Trans-Mississippi West, 1840–1880.* New York: Hill & Wang, 1979.

Jenkins, Philip. *Moral Panic: Changing Concepts of the Child Molester in Modern America.* New Haven, CT: Yale University Press, 1998.

Jensen, Joan M. *Loosening the Bonds: Mid-Atlantic Farm Women, 1750–1850.* New Haven, CT: Yale University Press, 1986.

Johansen, Shawn. *Family Men: Middle-Class Fatherhood in Early Industrializing America.* New York: Routledge, 2001.

Jones, Jacqueline. *Labor of Love, Labor of Sorrow: Black Women, Work, and the Family from Slavery to the Present.* New York: Vintage, 1985.

Jones, Joy. "'Marriage Is for White People.'" Washington Post, March 26, 2006, B1.

Jordan, Winthrop D. "Familial Politics: Thomas Paine and the Killing of the King, 1776." *Journal of American History* 60 (September 1973): 294–308.

Kaestle, Carl F. *Pillars of the Republic: Common Schools and American Society, 1780–1860* New York: Hill and Wang, 1983.

Kantner, John. *Ancient Puebloan Southwest.* Cambridge: Cambridge University Press, 2004.

Karlsen, Carol F. *The Devil in the Shape of a Woman: Witchcraft in Colonial New England.* New York: Norton, 1987.

Kay, Marvin L. Michael, and Lorin Lee Cary. *Slavery in North Carolina, 1748–1775.* Chapel Hill: University of North Carolina Press, 1995.

Kelly, Catherine E. *In the New England Fashion: Reshaping Women's Lives in the Nineteenth Century.* Ithaca, NY: Cornell University Press, 1999.

Kerber, Linda K. "Can a Woman Be an Individual? The Discourse of Self-Reliance." In *American Chameleon: Individualism in Trans-National Context,* edited by Richard. O. Curry and Lawrence B. Goodheart, 151–66. Kent, OH: Kent State University Press, 1991.

———. *Women of the Republic: Intellect and Ideology in Revolutionary America.* New York: W. W. Norton, 1986.

Kessler-Harris, Alice. *Out to Work: A History of Wage-Earning Women in the United States.* Oxford: Oxford University Press, 1982.

Kessner, Thomas. *The Golden Door: Italian and Jewish Immigrant Mobility in New York City, 1880–1915.* New York: Oxford University Press, 1977.

King, Wilma. *African American Childhoods: Historical Perspectives from Slavery to Civil Rights.* New York: Palgrave Macmillan, 2005.

Kirschner, Don S. *The Paradox of Professionalism: Reform and Public Service in Urban America, 1900–1940.* New York: Greenwood Press, 1986.

Kitwana, Bakari. *The Hip Hop Generation: Young Blacks and the Crisis in African American Culture.* New York: Basic Books, 2002.

Klein, Martin, and Paul E. Lovejoy. "Slavery in West Africa." In *The Uncommon Market: Essays in the Economic History of the Atlantic Slave Trade,* edited by Henry A. Gemery and Jan S. Hogendorn, 181–212. New York: Academic Press, 1979.

Klepp, Susan E. *Revolutionary Conceptions: Women, Fertility, and Family Limitation in America, 1760–1820*. Chapel Hill: University of North Carolina Press, 2009.

Knapp, Keith Nathaniel. *Selfless Offspring: Filial Children and Social Order in Medieval China*. Honolulu: University of Hawai'i Press, 2005.

Kolchin, Peter. *American Slavery, 1619–1877.* New York: Hill and Wang, 1993.

———. "Reevaluating the Antebellum Slave Community: A Comparative Perspective." *Journal of American History* 70 (December 1983): 579–601.

Komter, Aafke. "Hidden Power in Marriage." *Gender and Society* 3 (June 1989): 187–216.

Kulikoff, Allan. *The Agrarian Origins of American Capitalism*. Charlottesville: University Press of Virginia, 1992.

Kutsche, Paul. "Household and Family in Hispanic Northern New Mexico." *Journal of Comparative Family Studies* 14 (Summer 1983): 151–65.

Landers, Jane. *Black Society in Spanish Florida*. Urbana: University of Illinois Press, 1999.

Lane, Robert E. *The Loss of Happiness in Market Democracies*. New Haven, CT: Yale University Press, 2000.

Lane, Roger. *Violent Death in the City: Suicide, Accident, and Murder in Nineteenth-Century Philadelphia*. Cambridge, MA: Harvard University Press, 1979.

Lansing, Michael. "Plains Indian Women and Interracial Marriage in the Upper Missouri Trade, 1804–1869." *Western Historical Quarterly* 31 (Winter 2000): 413–33.

Laslett, Barbara. "The Family as a Public and Private Institution: An Historical Perspective." *Journal of Marriage and the Family* 35 (August 1973): 480–92.

———. "Family Membership, Past and Present." *Social Problems* 25 (June 1978): 476–90.

Laurie, Bruce. *Artisans into Workers: Labor in Nineteenth-Century America*. New York: Hill and Wang, 1989.

Leach, William. *Land of Desire: Merchants, Power, and the Rise of a New American Culture*. New York: Pantheon, 1993.

———. "Transformations in a Culture of Consumption: Women and Department Stores, 1890–1925." *Journal of American History* 71 (September 1984): 319–42.

Lears, T. J. Jackson. *No Place of Grace: Antimodernism and the Transformation of American Culture, 1880–1920*. New York: Pantheon Books, 1981.

Lecompte, Janet. "The Independent Women of Hispanic New Mexico, 1821–1846." *Western Historical Quarterly* 12 (January 1981): 17–35.

Lemon, James T. *The Best Poor Man's Country: A Geographical Study of Early Southeastern Pennsylvania*. Baltimore, MD: Johns Hopkins University Press, 1972.

Levine, Lawrence W. *Black Culture and Black Consciousness: Afro-American Folk Thought from Slavery to Freedom*. New York: Oxford University Press, 1977.

Levitt, Peggy. *The Transnational Villagers*. Berkeley: University of California Press, 2001.

Levy, Ariel. "Lesbian Nation." *The New Yorker*, March 2, 2009.

Levy, Barry. *Quakers and the American Family: British Settlement in the Delaware Valley*. New York: Oxford University Press, 1988.

Lewis, Hylan. *Blackways of Kent*. Chapel Hill: University of North Carolina Press, 1955.

Lewis, Jan. "Mother's Love: The Construction of an Emotion in Nineteenth-Century America." *In Social History and Issues in Human Consciousness: Some Interdisciplinary Connections*, edited by Andrew E. Barnes and Peter N. Stearns, New York: New York University Press, 1989.

Linderman, Gerald F. *Embattled Courage: The Experience of Combat in the American Civil War*. New York: Free Press, 1987.

Lindsey, Brink. *The Age of Abundance: How Prosperity Transformed America's Politics and Culture*. New York: Collins, 2008.

Litwack, Leon F. *Been in the Storm So Long: The Aftermath of Slavery*. New York: Alfred A. Knopf, 1979.

Lurie, Nancy Oestreich, ed. *Mountain Wolf Woman, Sister of Crashing Thunder: The Autobiography of a Winnebago Indian*. Ann Arbor: University of Michigan Press, 1961.

Lynd, Robert S., and Helen Merrell Lynd. *Middletown in Transition: A Study in Cultural Conflicts*. New York: Harcourt, Brace, 1937.

Lyons, Gene. "The Apocalypse Will Be Televised: Armageddon in an Age of Entertainment." *Harper's Magazine*, November 2004, 85–90.

Lystra, Karen. *Searching the Heart: Women, Men, and Romantic Love in Nineteenth-Century America*. New York: Oxford University Press, 1989.

Mackey, Richard A., Bernard A. O'Brien, and Eileen F. Mackey. *Gay and Lesbian Couples: Voices from Lasting Relationships*. Westport, CT: Praeger, 1997.

MacLeod, Anne Scott. *American Childhood: Essays on Children's Literature of the Nineteenth and Twentieth Centuries*. Athens: University of Georgia Press, 1994.

Macleod, David I. *The Age of the Child: Children in America, 1890–1920*. New York: Twayne and London: Prentice Hall International, 1998.

Majors, Richard, and Janet Mancini Billson. *Cool Pose: The Dilemmas of Black Manhood in America*. New York: Lexington, 1992.

Malmsheimer, Lonna M. "Daughters of Zion: New England Roots of American Feminism." *New England Quarterly* 50 (September, 1977): 484–504.

Mandell, Daniel R. "The Saga of Sarah Muckamugg: Indian and African American Intermarriage in Colonial New England." In *Sex, Love, Race: Crossing Boundaries in North American History*, edited by Martha Hodes, 72–90. New York: New York University Press, 1999.

———. "Shifting Boundaries of Race and Ethnicity: Indian-Black Intermarriage in Southern New England, 1760–1880." *Journal of American History* 85 (September 1998): 466–501.

Mansfield, Harvey C. *Manliness*. New Haven, CT: Yale University Press, 2006.

Markstrom, Carol A. *Empowerment of North American Indian Girls: Ritual Expressions At Puberty*. Lincoln: University of Nebraska Press, 2008.

Marten, James. *The Children's Civil War*. Chapel Hill: University of North Carolina Press, 1998.

Matsumoto, Valerie. "Japanese American Women during World War II." *Frontiers: A Journal of Women Studies* 8 (1984): 6–14.

May, Elaine Tyler. *Great Expectations: Marriage and Divorce in Post-Victorian America*. Chicago, IL: University of Chicago Press, 1980.

May, Lary. *Screening Out the Past: The Birth of Mass Culture and the Motion Picture Industry*. Chicago, IL: University of Chicago Press, 1983.

McCusker, John J., and Russell R. Menard. *The Economy of British America, 1607–1789*. Chapel Hill: University of North Carolina Press, 1985.

McKanna, Clare V. *Homicide, Race, and Justice in the American West, 1880–1920*. Tucson: University of Arizona Press, 1997.

McLaurin, Melton A. *Celia: A Slave*. Athens: University of Georgia Press, 1991.

McMahon, Darrin M. *Happiness: A History*. New York: Grove, 2006.

McMillen, Sally G. *Motherhood in the Old South: Pregnancy, Childbirth, and Infant Rearing*. Baton Rouge: Louisiana State University Press, 1990.

McPherson, Miller, Lynn Smith-Lovin, and Matthew E. Brashears. "Social Isolation in America: Changes in Core Discussion Networks over Two Decades." *American Sociological Review* 71 (June 2006): 353–75.

Meeker, Edward. "Freedom, Economic Opportunity, and Fertility: Black Americans, 1860–1910." *Economic Inquiry* 15 (July 1977): 397–412.

Menard, Louis. "Cat People: What Dr. Seuss Really Taught Us." *The New Yorker*, December 23, 2002.

Menard, Russell R. "British Migration to the Chesapeake Colonies in the Seventeenth Century." In *Colonial Chesapeake Society*, edited by Lois Green Carr, Philip D. Morgan, and Jean B. Russo, 99–132. Williamsburg, VA: Institute of Early American History and Culture and Chapel Hill: University of North Carolina Press, 1988.

———. "From Servant to Freeholder: Status Mobility and Property Accumulation in Seventeenth-Century Maryland." *William and Mary Quarterly* 30 (1973): 37–64.

Menkiti, Ifeanyi A. "Person and Community in African Traditional Thought." In *African Philosophy: An Introduction*, 3rd ed., edited by Richard A. Wright. Lanham, MD: University Press of America, 1984.

Merrill, Francis E. *Social Problems on the Home Front: A Study of War-time Influences*. New York: Harper & Brothers, 1948.

Meyrowitz, Joshua. "The Adultlike Child and the Childlike Adult: Socialization in an Electronic Age." *Daedalus* 113 (Summer 1984): 19–48.

Michel, Sonya. *Children's Interests/Mothers' Rights: The Shaping of America's Child Care Policy*. New Haven, CT: Yale University Press, 1999.

Mihesuah, Devon A. *Cultivating the Rosebuds: The Education of Women at the Cherokee Female Seminary, 1851–1909*. Urbana: University of Illinois Press, 1993.

Miller, Douglas T., and Marion Nowak. *The Fifties: The Way We Really Were*. Garden City, NY: Doubleday, 1977.

Miller, Jody. *Getting Played: African American Girls, Urban Inequality, and Gendered Violence*. New York: New York University Press, 2008.

Milner, Christina, and Richard Milner. *Black Players: The Secret World of Black Pimps*. Boston, MA: Little, Brown, 1972.

Mintz, Sidney W., and Richard Price. *The Birth of an African-American Culture: An Anthropological Perspective*. Boston, MA: Beacon, 1992.

Mintz, Steven. *Huck's Raft: A History of American Childhood*. Cambridge, MA: Harvard University Press, 2004.

Mirandé, Alfredo. "The Chicano Family: A Reanalysis of Conflicting Views." *Journal of Marriage and the Family* 39 (November 1977): 747–56.

Mitchell, Lee Clark. *Westerns: Making the Man in Fiction and Film*. Chicago, IL: The University of Chicago Press, 1996.

Mitchell, Michelel. *Righteous Propagation: African Americans and the Politics of Racial Destiny after Reconstruction*. Chapel Hill: University of North Carolina Press, 2004.

Mitchell, Pablo. "Accomplished Ladies and Coyotes: Marriage, Power, and Straying from the Flock in Territorial New Mexico, 1880–1920." In *Sex, Love, Race: Crossing Boundaries in North American History*, edited by Martha Hodes, 331–51. New York: New York University Press, 1999.

Mitchell, Reid. *The Vacant Chair: The Northern Soldier Leaves Home*. New York: Oxford University Press, 1993.

Moch, Leslie Page. "The European Perspective: Changing Conditions and Multiple Migrations, 1750–1914." In *European Migrants: Global and Local Perspectives*, edited by Dirk Hoerder and Moch, 115–40. Boston: Northeastern University Press, 1996.

Modell, John. *Into One's Own: From Youth to Adulthood in the United States, 1920–* Berkeley: University of California Press, 1989.

Monroy, Douglas. *Thrown Among Strangers: The Making of Mexican Culture in Frontier California*. Berkeley: University of California Press, 1990.

Morris, Christopher. "Within the Slave Cabin: Violence in Mississippi Slave Families." In *Over the Threshold: Intimate Violence in Early America*, edited by Christine Daniels and Michael V. Kennedy, 265–85. New York: Routledge, 1999.

Moskowitz, Eva. "'It's Good to Blow Your Top': Women's Magazines and a Discourse of Discontent, 1945–1965." *Journal of Women's History* 8 (Fall 1996): 66–98.

Moskowitz, Eva S. *In Therapy We Trust: America's Obsession with Self-Fulfillment*. Baltimore: The Johns Hopkins University Press, 2001.

Motz, Marilyn Ferris. *True Sisterhood: Michigan Women and their Kin, 1820–1920*. Albany: State University of New York Press, 1983.

Muckley, Peter A. "Iceberg Slim: Robert Beck—A True Essay at a BioCriticism of an Ex-Outlaw Artist." *The Black Scholar* 26 (Winter/Spring 1996): 18–25.

Murphy, Mary. "'...And All That Jazz': Changing Manners and Morals in Butte after World War I." *Montana: The Magazine of Western History* 46 (Winter 1996): 50–63.

Nadeshiko, Amerika. "Japanese Immigrant Women in the United States, 1900–1914." *Pacific Historical Review* 49 (May 1980): 339–57.

Nightingale, Carl Husemaker. *On the Edge: A History of Poor Black Children and their American Dreams*. New York: BasicBooks, 1993.

Norton, Mary Beth. *Founding Mothers & Fathers: Gendered Power and the Forming of American Society*. New York: Vintage, 1997.

O'Connell, J. F., K. Hawkes, and N. G. Blurton Jones. "Grandmothering and the Evolution of *Homo Erectus*." *Journal of Human Evolution* 36 (May 1999): 461– 85.

Odem, Mary E. "Teenage Girls, Sexuality, and Working-Class Parents in Early Twentieth-Century California." In *Generations of Youth: Youth Cultures and History in Twentieth-Century America*, edited by Joe Austin and Michael Nevin Willard, 50–64. New York: New York University Press, 1998.

Ono, Hiram. "Historical Time and U.S. Marital Dissolution." *Social Forces* 77 (March 1999): 969–99.

Osterud, Nancy *Grey. Bonds of Community: The Lives of Farm Women in Nineteenth-Century New York*. Ithaca, NY: Cornell University Press, 1991.

Ozorak, Elizabeth Weiss. "The Power, but Not the Glory: How Women Empower Themselves through Religion." *Journal for the Scientific Study of Religion* 35 (March, 1996): 17–29.

Pagan, John Ruston. *Anne Orthwood's Bastard: Sex and Law in Early Virginia*. Oxford: Oxford University Press, 2003.

Pargas, Damian Alan. "Work and Slave Family Life in Antebellum Northern Virginia." *Journal of Family History* 31 (October 2006): 335–57.

Pascoe, Peggy. *Relations of Rescue: The Search for Female Moral Authority in the American West, 1874–1939*. New York: Oxford University Press, 1990.

Patterson, Orlando. R*ituals of Blood: Consequences of Slavery in Two American Centuries*. New York: Basic Civitas, 1998.

Patterson, Orlando. *Slavery and Social Death: A Comparative Study.* Cambridge, MA: Harvard University Press, 1982.

Pattillo-McCoy, Mary. *Black Picket Fences: Privilege and Peril among the Black Middle Class.* Chicago, IL: University of Chicago Press, 1999.

Pattison, Robert. *The Triumph of Vulgarity: Rock Music in the Mirror of Romanticism.* New York: Oxford University Press, 1987.

Peña, Manuel. "Class, Gender, and Machismo: The 'Treacherous-Woman' Folklore of Mexican Male Workers." *Gender & Society* 5 (March 1991): 30–46.

Pendergast, Tom. *Creating the Modern Man: American Magazines and Consumer Culture, 1900–1950.* Columbia: University of Missouri Press, 2000.

Penningroth, Dylan C. "The Claims of Slaves and Ex-Slaves to Family and Property: A Transatlantic Comparison."*American Historical Review* 112 (October 2007): 1039–69.

Perbi, Akosua Adoma. *A History of Indigenous Slavery in Ghana: From the 15*th *to the 19*th *Centuries.* Accra, Ghana: Sub-Saharan Publishers, 2004.

Pérez, Lisandro. "Cuban Miami." *In Miami Now! Immigration, Ethnicity, and Social Change,* edited by Guillermo J. Grenier and Alex Stepick, III. Gainseville: University Press of Florida, 1992.

Perlmann, Joel. *Ethnic Differences: Schooling and Social Structure among the Irish, Italians, Jews, and Blacks in an American City, 1880–1935.* Cambridge: Cambridge University Press, 1988.

Perry, James R. *The Formation of a Society on Virginia's Eastern Shore, 1615–1655* Williamsburg, VA: Institute of Early American History and Culture and Chapel Hill: University of North Carolina Press, 1990.

Pesantubbee, Michelene E. *Choctaw Women in a Chaotic World: The Clash of Cultures in the Colonial Southeast.* Albuquerque: University of New Mexico Press, 2005.

Pessar, Patricia R. "The Dominicans: Women in the Household and the Garment Industry." In *New Immigrants in New York*, edited by Nancy Foner, 103–29. New York: Columbia University Press, 1987.

Pleck, Elizabeth. *Domestic Tyranny: The Making of Social Policy against Family Violence from Colonial Times to the Present.* New York: Oxford University Press, 1987.

Pugh, David G. *Sons of Liberty: The Masculine Mind in Nineteenth-Century America.* Westport, CT: Greenwood Press, 1983.

Reis, Elizabeth. *Damned Women: Sinners and Witches in Puritan New England.* Ithaca, NY: Cornell University Press, 1997.

Root, Maria P. P., ed. *Racially Mixed People in America.* Newbury Park, CA: Sage, 1992.

Rorabaugh, W. J. *The Alcoholic Republic: An American Tradition.* New York: Oxford University Press, 1979.

Rosenzweig, Roy. *Eight Hours for What We Will: Workers and Leisure in an Industrial City, 1870–1920.* Cambridge: Cambridge University Press, 1983.

Rothman, Gerald C. *Philanthropists, Therapists, and Activists: A Century of Ideological Conflict in Social Work.* Cambridge, MA: Schenkman, 1985.

Rothman, Joshua D. *Notorious in the Neighborhood: Sex and Families across the Color Line in Virginia, 1787–1861.* Chapel Hill, North Carolina: University of North Carolina Press, 2007.

Rothman, Sheila M. *Woman's Proper Place: A History of Changing Ideals and Practices, 1870 to the Present.* New York: Basic Books, 1978.

Rothstein, Frances Abrahamer. *Globalization in Rural Mexico: Three Decades of Change*. Austin: University of Texas Press, 2007.

Rotundo, E. Anthony. *American Manhood: Transformations in Masculinity from the Revolution to the Modern Era*. New York: Basic, 1993.

Rubin, Lillian B. *Families on the Fault Line: America's Working Class Speaks about the Family, the Economy, Race, and Ethnicity*. New York: HarperCollins, 1994.

Ruggles, Steven. "The Transformation of American Family Structure." *American Historical Review* 99 (February 1994): 103–28.

Ruiz, Vicki L. *Cannery Women, Cannery Lives: Mexican Women, Unionization, and the California Food Processing Industry, 1930–1950*. Albuquerque: University of New Mexico Press, 1987.

Ryan, Mary P. *Cradle of the Middle Class: The Family in Oneida County, New York, 1790–1865*. Cambridge: Cambridge University Press, 1981.

Salamon, Sonya. *Prairie Patrimony: Family, Farming, and Community in the Midwest*. Chapel Hill: University of North Carolina Press, 1992.

Saum, Lewis O. *The Popular Mood of Pre-Civil War America*. Westport, CT: Greenwood Press, 1980.

Schwalm, Leslie A. *A Hard Fight for We: Women's Transition from Slavery to Freedom in South Carolina*. Urbana: University of Illinois Press, 1997.

Schwartz Cowan, Ruth. *More Work for Mother: The Ironies of Household Technology from the Open Hearth to the Microwave*. New York: Basic Books, 1983.

Seed, Patricia. *To Love, Honor, and Obey in Colonial Mexico: Conflicts over Marriage Choice, 1574–1821*. Stanford, CA: Stanford University Press, 1988.

Seidman, Steven. *Romantic Longings: Love in America, 1830–1980*. New York: Routledge, 1991.

Self, Robert O. *American Babylon: Race and the Struggle for Postwar Oakland*. Princeton, NJ: Princeton University Press, 2003.

Shakur, Sanyika. *Monster: The Autobiography of an L.A. Gang Member*. New York: Atlantic Monthly Press, 1993.

Sharpe, Tanya Telfair. *Behind the Eight Ball: Sex for Crack Cocaine Exchange and Poor Black Women*. New York: Haworth Press, 2005.

Shifflett, Crandall A. "The Household Composition of Rural Black Families: Louisa County, Virginia, 1880." *Journal of Interdisciplinary History* 6 (Fall 1975): 235–60.

Shoemaker, Nancy. "The Rise or Fall of Iroquois Women." *Journal of Women's History* 2 (Winter 1991): 39–57.

Shoemaker, Nancy, ed. *Negotiators of Change: Historical Perspectives on Native American Women*. London: Routledge, 1995.

Siegel, Bernard J. "Defensive Structuring and Environmental Stress."*American Journal of Sociology* 76 (1970): 11–32.

Simons, Ronald L., ed. *Understanding Differences between Divorced and Intact Families: Stress, Interaction, and Child Outcome*. Thousand Oaks, CA: Sage Publications, 1996.

Simpson, Colton, with Ann Pearlman. *Inside the Crips: Life Inside L.A.'s Most Notorious Gang*. New York: St. Martin's Press, 2005.

Simpson, Jeffrey A., Bruce Campbell, and Ellen Berscheid. "The Association Between Romantic Love and Marriage: Kephart (1967) Twice Revisited." *Personality and Social Psychology Bulletin* 12 (September 1986): 363–72.

Sklar, Kathryn Kish. *Catharine Beecher: A Study in American Domesticity*. New Haven, CT: Yale University Press, 1973.

Skolnick, Arlene. *Embattled Paradise: The American Family in an Age of Uncertainty.* New York City: Basic Books, 1991.

Slater, Peter Gregg. *Children in the New England Mind: In Death and in Life.* Hamden, CT: Archon, 1977.

Sleeper-Smith, Susan. *Indian Women and French Men: Rethinking Cultural Encounters in the Western Great Lakes.* Amherst: University of Massachusetts Press, 2001.

Smith, Billy G. *The "Lower Sort": Philadelphia's Laboring People, 1750–1800.* Ithaca, NY: Cornell University Press, 1990.

Smith, Daniel Blake. *Inside the Great House: Planter Family Life in Eighteenth-Century Chesapeake Society.* Ithaca, NY: Cornell University Press, 1980.

Smith, Daniel Scott. "Parental Power and Marriage Patterns: An Analysis of Historical Trends in Hingham, Massachusetts." *Journal of Marriage and the Family* 35 (August 1973): 419–28.

Smith, Daniel Scott, and Michael S. Hindus. "Premarital Pregnancy in America, 1640–1971: An Overview and Interpretation." *Journal of Interdisciplinary History* 4 (Spring 1975): 537–70.

Smith-Hefner, Nancy J. *Khmer American: Identity and Moral Education in a Diasporic Community.* Berkeley: University of California Press, 1999.

Smith, Judith E. *Family Connections: A History of Italian and Jewish Immigrant Lives in Providence, Rhode Island, 1900–1940.* Albany: State University of New York Press, 1985.

Snyder, Terri L. " 'As If There Was Not Master or Woman in the Land': Gender, Dependency, and Household Violence in Virginia, 1646–1720." In *Over the Threshold: Intimate Violence in Early America*, edited by Christine Daniels and Michael V. Kennedy, 219–36. New York: Routledge, 1999.

Spear, Jennifer. "Colonial Intimacies: Legislating Sex in French Louisiana." *William and Mary Quarterly* 60 (January 2003): 75–98.

———. " 'They Need Wives': Métissage and the Regulation of Sexuality in French Louisiana, 1699–1730." In *Sex, Love, Race: Crossing Boundaries in North American History*, edited by Martha Hodes, 35–59. New York: New York University Press, 1999.

Spitze, Glenna, and John R. Logan. "Helping as a Component of Parent-Child Relations." *Research on Aging* 14 (September 1992): 291–312.

Stearns, Peter N. *Be a Man! Males in Modern Society*, 2nd ed. New York: Holmes & Meier, 1990.

Steckel, Richard H. "Slave Marriage and the Family." *Journal of Family History* 5 (Winter 1980): 406–21.

Stein, Judith. *Pivotal Decade: How the United States Traded Factories for Finance in The Seventies.* New Haven, CT: Yale University Press, 2010.

Stier, Haya, and Marta Tienda. "Are Men Marginal to the Family: Insights from Chicago's Inner City.In *Men, Work, and Family*, edited by Jane C. Hood, 23–44. Newbury Park, CA: Sage, 1993.

Stock, Catherine McNicol. *Main Street in Crisis: The Great Depression and the Old Middle Class on the Northern Plains.* Chapel Hill: University of North Carolina Press, 1992.

Stott, Richard B. *Workers in the Metropolis: Class, Ethnicity, and Youth in Antebellum New York City.* Ithaca, NY: Cornell University Press, 1990.

Stremlau, Rose. " 'To Domesticate and Civilize Wild Indians': Allotment and the Campaign to Reform Indian Families, 1875–1887." *Journal of Family History* 30 (July 2005): 265–86.

Strickland, Charles E., and Andrew M. Ambrose. "The Baby Boom, Prosperity, and the Changing Worlds of Children, 1945–1963." In *American Childhood: A Research Guide and Historical Handbook*, edited by Joseph M. Hawes and N. Ray Hiner, 533–85. Westport, CT: Greenwood Press, 1985.

Suárez-Orozco, Carola, and Marcelo M. Suárez-Orozco. *Children of Immigration*. Cambridge, MA: Harvard University Press, 2001.

———. *Transformations: Immigration, Family Life, and Achievement Motivation among Latino Adolescents*. Stanford, CA: Stanford University Press, 1995.

Suárez-Orozco, Marcelo M., and Carola E. Suárez-Orozco. "The Cultural Patterning of Achievement Motivation: A Comparison of Mexican, Mexican Immigrant, Mexican-American, and Non-Latino White American Students." In *California's Immigrant Children: Theory, Research, and Implications for Educational Policy*, edited by Rubén G. Rumbaut and Wayne A. Cornelius, 161–90. San Diego: Center for U.S.-Mexican Studies, University of California, San Diego, 1995.

Swadesh, Frances Leon. "Structure of Hispanic-Indian Relations in New Mexico." In *The Survival of Spanish American Villages*, edited by Paul Kutsche, 53–61. Colorado Springs: Colorado College, 1979.

Szasz, Margaret Connell. "Native American Children." In *American Childhood: A Research Guide and Historical Handbook*, edited by Joseph Hawes and N. Ray Hiner, 311–32. Westport, CT: Greenwood Press, 1985.

Tentler, Leslie Woodcock. *Wage-Earning Women: Industrial Work and Family Life in the United States, 1900–1930*. New York: Oxford University Press, 1979.

Testi, Arnaldo. "The Gender of Reform Politics: Theodore Roosevelt and the Culture of Masculinity." *Journal of American History* 81 (March 1995): 1509–33.

Thompson, Roger. *Sex in Middlesex: Popular Mores in a Massachusetts County, 1649–1699*. Amherst: University of Massachusetts Press, 1986.

Thornton, Arland, and Linda Young DeMarco. "Four Decades of Trends in Attitudes toward Family Issues in the United States: The 1960s through the 1990s." *Journal of Marriage and the Family* 63 (November 2001): 1009–37. Vandewater, Elizabeth A., and Jennifer E. Lansford. "Influences of Family Structure and Parental Conflict on Children's Well-Being." *Family Relations* 47 (October 1998): 323–30.

Thornton, Thomas F. *Being and Place among the Tlingit*. Seattle: University of Washington Press, 2008.

Townsend, Camilla. *Pocahontas and the Powhatan Dilemma*. New York: Hill and Wang, 2004.

Townsend, Kim. "Francis Parkman and the Male Tradition." *American Quarterly* 38 (Spring 1986): 97–113.

Tracy, Patricia J. *Jonathan Edwards, Pastor: Religion and Society in Eighteenth-Century Northhamption*. New York: Hill and Wang, 1980.

Trattner, Walter I. *From Poor Law to Welfare State: A History of Social Welfare in America*, 6th ed. New York: Free Press, 1999.

Turner, Steve. *The Man Called Cash: The Life, Love, and Faith of an American Legend*. Nashville, TN: W Publishing Group, 2004.

Uchida, Yoshiko. *Desert Exile: The Uprooting of a Japanese American Family*. Seattle: University of Washington Press, 1982.

Ulrich, Laurel Thatcher. *Good Wives: Image and Reality in the Lives of Women in Northern New England, 1650–1750*. New York: Oxford University Press, 1983.

———. "Vertuous Women Found: New England Ministerial Literature, 1668–1735." *American Quarterly* 28 (Spring 1976): 20–40.

Umansky, Lauri. *Motherhood Reconceived: Feminism and the Legacies of the Sixties.* New York: New York University Press, 1996.

Usner, Daniel H., Jr. *Indians, Settlers, and Slaves in a Frontier Exchange Economy: The Lower Mississippi Valley before 1783.* Williamsburg, VA: Institute of Early American History and Culture and Chapel Hill: University of North Carolina Press, 1992.

Valle, Isabel. *Fields of Toil: A Migrant Family's Journey.* Pullman: Washington State University Press, 1994.

Vega, William A. "Hispanic Families in the 1980s: A Decade of Research." *Journal of Marriage and the Family* 52 (November 1990): 1015–24.

Veroff, Joseph, Elizabeth Douvan, and Richard A. Kulka. *The Inner American: A Self-Portrait from 1957 to 1976.* New York: Basic Books, 1981.

Vigil, James Diego. *Barrio Gangs: Street Life and Identity in Southern California.* Austin: University of Texas Press, 1988.

———. *The Projects: Gang and Non-Gang Families in East Los Angeles.* Austin: University of Texas Press, 2007.

Wacquant, Loïc J. D., and William Julius Wilson. "The Cost of Racial and Class Exclusion in the Inner City." *Annals of the American Academy of Political and Social Science* 501 (January 1989): 8–25.

Walker, J. "Couples Watching Television: Gender, Power, and the Remote Control." *Journal of Marriage and the Family* 58 (1996): 813–23.

Wandersee, Winifred D. *Women's Work and Family Values, 1920–1940.* Cambridge, MA: Harvard University Press, 1982.

Washington, Margaret. *Sojourner Truth's America.* Urbana: University of Illinois Press, 2009.

Webber, Thomas L. *Deep like the Rivers: Education in the Slave Quarter Community,* New York: W. W. Norton, 1978.

Wei, William. "Among American Youth: American Dream, American Nightmare." In *Generations of Youth: Youth Cultures and History in Twentieth-Century America,* edited by Joe Austin and Michael Nevin Willard, 311–325. New York: New York University Press, 1998.

Westbrook, Robert B. " 'I Want a Girl, Just Like the Girl That Married Harry James': American Women and the Problem of Political Obligation in World War II." *American Quarterly* 42 (December 1990): 587–614.

West, Cornel. *Race Matters.* New York: Vintage, 1994.

West, Elliott, *Growing Up with the Country: Childhood on the Far Western Frontier.* Albuquerque: University of New Mexico Press, 1989.

West, Emily. "Tensions, Tempers, and Temptations: Marital Discord among Slaves in Antebellum South Carolina." *American Nineteenth Century History* 5 (Summer 2004): 1–18.

West, James. *Plainville, U.S.A.* New York: Columbia University Press, 1966.

Whitehead, Barbara Dafoe. "The Decline of Marriage as the Social Basis of Childrearing ." In *Promises to Keep: Decline and Renewal of Marriage in America,* edited by David Popenoe, Jean Bethke Elshtain, and David Blankenhorn, 3–14. Lanham, MD: Rowman and Littlefield, 1996.

White, Deborah Gray. "Female Slaves: Sex Roles and Status in the Antebellum Plantation South." *Journal of Family History* 8 (Fall 1983): 248–61.

———. *Too Heavy a Load: Black Women in Defense of Themselves, 1894–1994* New York: W. W. Norton, 1999.

White, Kevin. *The First Sexual Revolution: The Emergence of Male Heterosexuality in Modern America.* New York: New York University Press, 1993.

White, Lynn K., and Alan Booth. "The Quality and Stability of Remarriages: The Role of Stepchildren." *American Sociological Review* 50 (October 1985): 689–98.

White, Richard. *The Middle Ground: Indians, Empires, and Republics in the Great Lakes Region, 1650–1815*. Cambridge: Cambridge University Press, 1991.

Wilcox, W. Bradford, and Steven L. Nock. "What's Love Got To Do With It? Equality, Equity, Commitment and Women's Marital Quality." *Social Forces* 84 (March 2006): 1321–45.

Wilentz, Sean. *Chants Democratic: New York City and the Rise of the American Working Class, 1788–1850*. New York: Oxford University Press, 1984.

Wilson, James Q. *The Marriage Problem: How Our Culture Has Weakened Families*. New York: HarperCollins, 2002.

Wilson, Monica. *Rituals of Kinship among the Nyakyusa*. London: International African Institute, 1970.

Wolf, Diane L. "Family Secrets: Transnational Struggles among Children of Filipino Immigrants." *Sociological Perspectives* 40 (1977): 454–82.

Wolf, Stephanie Grauman. *As Various as their Land: The Everyday Lives of Eighteenth-Century Americans*. New York: Harper Perennial, 1993.

Woo, Deborah. "Social Patterns in Intimacy and Support: European Americans and Chinese Americans." In *With This Ring: Divorce, Intimacy, and Cohabitation from a Multicultural Perspective*, edited by R. Robin Miller and Sandra Lee Browning. Stamford, CT: JAI Press, 2000.

Wood, Gordon S. *The Creation of the American Republic, 1776–1787*. New York: W. W. Norton, 1972.

Wrightson, Keith. *Earthly Necessities: Economic Lives in Early Modern Britain*. New Haven, CT: Yale University Press, 2000.

Wyatt-Brown, *Bertram. Southern Honor: Ethics and Behavior in the Old South*. New York: Oxford University Press, 1982.

Wyllie, Irvin G. *The Self-Made Man in America: The Myth of Rags to Riches*. New York: Free Press and London: Collier-Macmillan, 1966.

Yans-McLaughlin, Virginia. *Family and Community: Italian Immigrants in Buffalo*, Urbana: University of Illinois Press, 1982.

Zalewski, Daniel. "The Defiant Ones." *New Yorker*, October 19, 2009.

Zelizer, Viviana A. *Pricing the Priceless Child: The Changing Social Value of Children*. New York: Basic Books, 1985.

Zhou, Min. "Growing Up American: The Challenge Confronting Immigrant Children and Children of Immigrants." *Annual Review of Sociology* 23 (1997): 63–95.

Zuckerman, Michael. "The Fabrication of Identity in Early America." *William and Mary Quarterly* 34 (April 1977): 183–214.

———. "The Nursery Tales of Horatio Alger." *American Quarterly* 24 (May 1972): 191–209.

Zunz, Oliver. *The Changing Face of Inequality: Urbanization, Industrial Development, and Immigrants in Detroit, 1880–1920*. Chicago: University of Chicago Press, 1982.

Index